Peoples and Empires
of West Africa

Peoples and Empires of West Africa

West Africa in History 1000–1800

G. T. Stride, B.A. & Caroline Ifeka, Ph. D.
with advice from Professor J. F. Ade Ajayi

Africana Publishing Corporation · New York

Published
in the United States of America 1971
by Africana Publishing Corporation
101 Fifth Avenue
New York, N.Y. 10003

Library of Congress catalog card no. 72-143111
ISBN 0 8419 0069 8

1-19-73

Photoset and printed in Malta
by St Paul's Press Ltd

Contents

Acknowledgements

The authors and publishers are very grateful to the following for permission to use photographs and illustrations owned by them for reproduction in this book:

Edward Arnold Ltd for *The city of Benin in the seventeenth century.*
The British Museum for *An ivory mask from Benin* and *An Asante stool.*
J. Allan Cash for *Women and children in a Fulani Village* and *Gates into the old city of Kano.*
The Mary Evans Picture Library for *A Kanuri warrior on horseback, Three Kanuri warriors* and *Masters and slaves on a plantation in the Southern USA.*
The Mansell Collection for *Bronze works of art discovered in the River Niger area, A desert caravan, Prince Henry, 'The Navigator', A band of captives driven into slavery, A view of Elmina* and *A war canoe on the River Niger.*
The Radio Times Hulton Picture Library for *A Portuguese caravel of the fifteenth century.*
Cliché Ifan for *Kumbi-Saleh: niche of a house (twelfth-thirteenth century) in the capital of ancient Ghana*

List of Maps

List of Illustrations

Introduction

When this book was first conceived a few years ago, it was intended to meet a new challenge. The West African Examinations Council rightly decided that it had to take the initiative in seeing that the intelligent youth of West Africa should cease meaningless study of the history of cultures of which they had no experience and should instead explore the past of their own and kindred peoples. This change of attitude was long overdue and the ground had been prepared for it by diligent research at university level that had proved West Africa had a dynamic and purposeful past of its own which was dependent neither on European influence nor on European personnel. Unfortunately, at that time, all school text-books were heavily over-loaded with accounts of European activities in West Africa and the sections devoted to purely West African activities were too slim and generalized to provide sufficient material to meet the detailed requirements of the West African Examination Council's question papers. It was therefore decided to produce a book that would serve two purposes. In the first place, it would make available at school level the more accurate evaluation of West Africa's history pieced together by the objective research of a new and more far-seeing school of historians, both African and non-African. Secondly, it would present this material in a form specifically related to the needs of the West African Examination Council's School Certificate examination in West Africa.

Although the book has taken longer to prepare than anticipated and other books have been produced to meet these demands, the original objectives have been scrupulously adhered to. We claim to be up-to-date in assessment of West African history and not to have evaded stating controversy where historical guide-lines cannot be clearly distinguished. Above all we have kept in mind the needs of examination students. Those areas of study which are most suitable for examination, both from the point of view of available knowledge and of the youth of the majority of candidates, are the areas which we have given fullest treatment. Where the past has had its climactic moments, we have set out to be both imaginative and analytical in the belief that the appeal of history to the young is its romance, its value the process of weighing evidence and evaluating it. If the accounts that we have given have differed radically from those that the student may find in other books pitched at a comparable public, we have usually stated the two views or the two systems of dating. There are two reasons for this. In the first place, scientific study of West African history is still in its infancy and in many spheres works within a framework of scholastic doubt. Consequently, although we feel that the concepts of scholastic doubt appropriate to the academician are an unsuitable basis for youthful study, we have tried to avoid the dogmatic approach of consistent over-simplification. Secondly, we have borne in mind the fact that the good young student will read a variety of books on his subject. He will find different accounts, say on the traditions relating to Sunni Ali, which without clarification will provide him with contradictory facts among which he has no means of discriminating. We have tried to show him that what he reads in one book does not necessarily destroy the utility of another tied to a different version of events.

For a history book, this volume contains a great deal of folk traditions. This has been deliberate. It underlines the material on which present and future historians will have to work analytically and indicates the value and limitations of such material for historical study. Above all, oral traditions are a living part of any West African's history, and there is no doubt in our mind that one of the vital facets of historical study is to relate the individual to his cultural heritage.

In preparing this book for examination candidates, we have made a detailed analysis of the major problems of the history of our period. We have also indicated where relevant how they relate to developments of the nineteenth century. As these major problems are ones most appropriate to examinations, we would claim that a thorough and thoughtful study of this volume will fully meet all the examination needs of candidates studying this period in West African history.

G. T. Stride
Caroline Ifeka
Ibadan 1969

1

Life zones of West Africa

THE INFLUENCE OF GEOGRAPHY UPON HISTORY

Even today, the way in which people live is affected by the area into which they are born. For example, a Kalahari Bushman is not likely to travel to the moon in our lifetime, whereas more and more young Americans will be flying farther and farther into space. Americans have developed an advanced technology based on human ingenuity and endeavour; but it is unlikely that they could ever have embarked on space research had they not had a land of abundant foodstuffs and large mineral resources. On the other hand an American dropped into the Kalahari desert without a compass, food supplies and other equipment would be as fatally lost as a Bushman placed before the instrument panel of a space ship heading towards the moon.

It is also necessary to recognize that man himself and time are very important factors affecting historical change. Consider the oil sheikdoms of the Persian Gulf. Until recently they were poverty-stricken areas of desert, even though vast reservoirs of oil lay hidden underground. Now that these resources have been exploited the sheiks and some of their people live in ease and luxury. How to assemble a drilling rig is now far more important than knowing how to cure a sick camel. Although the oil had always been there, it did not affect the lives of the people until its uses had been discovered and world demand for it had grown, so that international companies were prepared to invest fortunes in prospecting and drilling.

One of the best examples of the inter-relationship between man and geography is furnished by the history of Egypt. From earliest times its climate, security from attack and the bounty of the Nile provided abundant food and leisure, enabling its ingenious people to develop one of the greatest civilizations the

1

world has ever known. Later on, internal strife, invasions and the re-orientation of trade routes destroyed its greatness and prosperity. By the beginning of the nineteenth century it was a backward outpost of the Ottoman empire and had little significance in international politics until the 1870s, when the Suez canal was cut. Had the isthmus of Suez not been so narrow and had the geological structure made canal-building impossible, the modern history of Egypt would have been very different from what it has been. Even the Egyptian decision to nationalize the canal was not unconnected with the need to control the waters of the Nile through a high dam at Aswan.

In the remote past the effect of geographical environment on history was greater than it is today. Peoples dwelling in open plains tended to be warlike in order to defend themselves from invaders. Others living in remote, inaccessible areas often had little need to be aggressive; also they were not very likely to learn about outside developments in agriculture, industry or politics. Thus their rate of technical advance was extremely slow. This can be seen from the fact that quite recently stone age societies have been discovered in remote upland valleys in New Guinea.

During prehistoric times, man's knowledge was inadequate to enable him markedly to alter, adapt or control his environment except over a very long period. Those who lived in areas where food was abundant and soils were fertile and easy to cultivate soon found they had leisure. They had time to develop crafts such as weaving and pottery and to practise the art of decorating their utensils, houses and bodies. They had a surplus of food and manufactured goods for trade and enough time and wealth to be able to devote themselves to politics and war.

So it came about that states emerged with increasingly complex administrative and social systems. If the area provided good, strong building materials these processes were likely to be accelerated. This was even more true if deposits of metals such as copper, tin, zinc and especially iron were available and if the people could either discover for themselves or learn from neighbours how to process them. As metal tools replaced stone ones, agriculture and manufacture could develop at a faster rate. Iron weapons gave their possessors such military superiority over stone

Map I   The Principal Peoples and Languages of West Africa

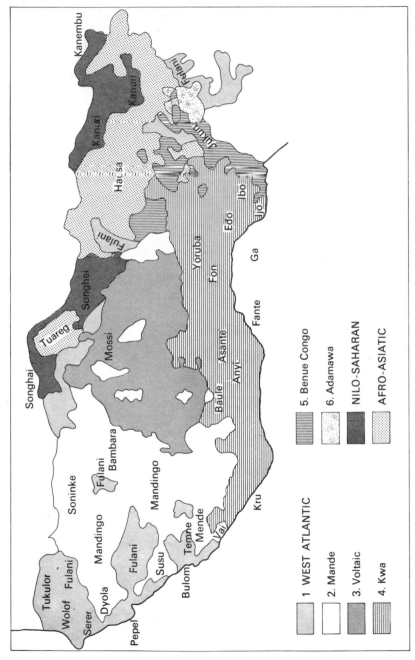

Kanembu
Fulani
Kanuri
Kanuri
Hausa
Fulani
Nupe
Ibo
Edo
Ijo
Songhai
Tuareg
Yoruba
Fon
Ga
Mossi
Asante
Fante
Baule
Anyi
Songhai
Kru
Fulani
Bambara
Mandingo
Soninke
Mandingo
Fulani
Susu
Temne
Mende
Vai
Bulom
Tukulor
Wolof   Fulani
Serer
Dyola
Pepel

1 WEST ATLANTIC

2. Mande

3. Voltaic

4. Kwa

5. Benue Congo

6. Adamawa

NILO-SAHARAN

AFRO-ASIATIC

3

age peoples that they were able to create large empires.

The advantages of people living in geographically favoured areas are too numerous to mention in detail. However, geography is not the only factor to shape the history of a people. Human ingenuity and persistence, even chance, also play extremely important parts, sometimes even more important than geographical factors. Bearing this in mind, the concept of life zones is a valuable aid to understanding the evolution of early societies.

THE CONCEPT OF LIFE ZONES

The concept of life zones, developed by human geographers, is founded on the principle that the way in which societies have evolved has been conditioned by their geographical environment. A life zone is a region with its own distinctive terrain, climate and natural vegetation. But it is much more than that. It is also an area in which peoples obtain their livelihoods in similar ways; their social customs are all broadly alike; their forms of political institutions follow the same patterns; and their religions have much in common. Even the development of languages has been affected by geographical factors.

Geography can explain differences as well as similarities between peoples within a life zone. For example, if a group of people formed settlements spread out over a vast plain with easy communications they would probably keep in touch with each other; and centuries later, in spite of the growth of local dialects, they would all understand each other's language. If, on the other hand, a group spread through dense forest, each settlement would develop in isolation and major linguistic differences would arise. The chances are that the settlements on the plain would eventually be united into an empire; while those in the forest would more likely remain small, isolated units, possibly not even needing formal rulers. Such small forest states would be much freer from outside influence and new ideas than the states of the open country, where easy communications could lead to outside influences introducing different languages, customs and religions.

Applying the concept of life zones to West Africa, we have three major zones: the coastal strip, the forest, and the Sudan savanna. Within these major divisions there are a number of smaller but

4

still distinctive zones. In studying these units we shall see how geography has affected patterns of life; we shall also see how at critical points in history West Africans have used or modified their environments.

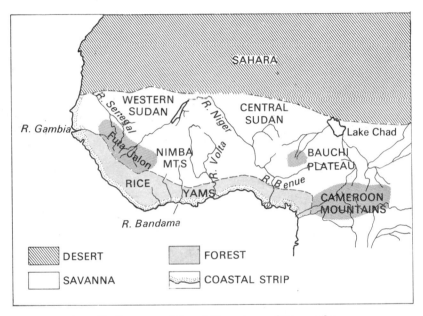

Map II The Life Zones and Food Frontiers of West Africa

THE COASTAL ZONE

Geographical factors
The coastal zone extends inland for between twenty and eighty miles. It is a low-lying land of plains in Senegambia, of mangrove swamps in Portuguese Guinea, Sierra Leone and the Niger delta, and of lagoons and creeks from the Ivory Coast to the Niger delta. There are considerable differences in rainfall within this zone. For instance, rain can fall throughout most of the year in the Niger delta, whereas on the Ghanaian coast it only rains between May and October. In spite of these climatic variations, all coastal peoples appear to have lived in a similar way by the eleventh century.

5

Peoples

Who the original peoples of the coastal areas were we do not know. Some of the oldest inhabitants of the Atlantic coast are, however, the Jola, Pepel and Serer of Senegambia, and the Sherbro and Bulom of Sierra Leone. All these people speak West Atlantic languages. Along the Guinea coast the lagoon folk of the Ivory Coast, the Guan of southern Ghana and the Ijo of the Niger delta must be included among the most ancient of coastal dwellers. These peoples were probably established in their coastal homes by the beginning of our period and all speak languages of the Kwa group.

The coastal peoples of the Guinea coast and Sierra Leone were more isolated and self-contained than peoples on the coast of Senegambia. Perhaps the outstanding example of a closed community are the Kru people of Liberia, who alone among West African peoples do not have 'sickle-cells' in their blood. Sickle-cells are nature's way of protecting West Africans against malaria. Malarial parasites multiply in the red blood cells, feeding on haemoglobin which carries oxygen to all parts of the body. Whereas ordinary red blood cells are disc-shaped, cells containing sickle-cell haemoglobin tend to be pointed, like a crescent.

Economy

Except in the area of the Senegambia plains, where conditions were similar to those in the savanna zones, coastal peoples lived in hamlets or villages situated on dry ground. Originally, they had probably led fairly nomadic lives and occupied themselves with fishing, hunting and gathering wild berries and vegetables. By the beginning of our period, however, knowledge of settled cultivation had probably reached the coast from the interior with a beneficial result on food resources. A 'food frontier' arose along the line of the river Bandama: to the west, the staple crop was rice introduced by Mande migrants from the Niger valley, while to the east yams were the basic food. Knowledge of yams was brought from the forest belt and it is thought that the Guan of modern Ghana were already growing them by A.D. 1000. Other additions to the coast's food supplies had been the introduction of domestic animals including small, humpless cattle, pigs, goats and fowls.

That knowledge of the farming techniques of the interior had

6

reached the coast suggests that trade links had already been forged. The coastal peoples had learnt the arts of fish-curing and of refining salt from sea-water and thus they had two valuable exports to the interior. In turn, they were ready to buy meat, fruit, vegetables, cloth and possibly metal goods from the interior. Some areas had their own speciality products such as the oyster industry off the Senegal coast near St Louis. Archaeologists think this industry may have been flourishing as early as the fourth century A.D.

Political organization
The effect of isolation on political organization is clearly visible among the peoples of the coastal zone. In the area around St Louis in Senegal, the fertile land is flat and it is reasonably easy to move quickly across it. Communication with the interior did not present insuperable difficulties. Consequently, among the Jola and Pepel, villages were in easy contact and were united in chiefdoms, possibly mainly to co-ordinate defence against marauding Mandingos. The chief, however, was really more of a religious figure whose political authority may only have existed in time of war. On the whole, lineage elders played the dominant part in public affairs, at least in peace-time.

Archaeologists have found evidence that, by the eleventh century, the people of St Louis had a sophisticated iron age culture. They polished stone axes, beat bark into cloth, and possibly bought other cloth from the interior. They built solid houses and fortified their settlements, and in their graves have been found fragments of pottery and rings of both copper and iron. At Rao, near the mouth of the Senegal, there may well have been a centralized state.

Elsewhere in the coastal zone, however, remoteness and difficult communications were the usual pattern. Along the coast of Sierra Leone and Liberia, small communities were hemmed in by mountains, thick forest or unnavigable rivers. Villages were generally self-sufficient and apart from occasional trading contacts were not in regular association with other villages. However, sometimes villages recognized a common chief or co-operated with each other through secret societies in which lineage and village elders played important roles in government.

On the Gulf of Guinea the influence of ecological and climatic

7

factors is even more obvious. Settlements in both the Ivory Coast and Niger delta were of necessity small as the amount of dry land suitable for housebuilding was very limited in any one place. Government of these small communities was in the hands of village elders, and there were no chiefs with political authority.

Religion and art
Coastal peoples believed that supernatural beings and forces were at work both in their natural environment in the form of sudden storms or catastrophic epidemics, and in their social relationships. In the event of a sudden natural disaster, or an increase in the number of deaths, villagers would seek an explanation in the wrath of supernatural beings or ancestors. Thus religious beliefs provided an explanation of unpleasant events and buttressed the authority of the elders, who could invoke the supernatural when villagers were disobedient.

People used materials at hand to express their beliefs. Representational work like statues tells us how they thought of the gods and spirits. The ivory carvings, statues, bracelets and soapstone carvings of the Bulom of Sierra Leone were much admired by early Portuguese. The Ga of southern Ghana had goldsmiths who modelled beautiful jewellery with which men and women adorned themselves. And the Ijo of the Niger delta became well known for their masks which represent various spirits.

Possibly the most impressive artistic discoveries to date are the large megaliths which have been found in Senegal, Sine-Saloum, parts of the Gambia and southern Sierra Leone. The megaliths are made of blocks of laterite which stand in circles. Sometimes there are two circles, one encompassing the other; stones standing on their own also occur in these circles. In Senegal, pottery, iron spear heads, copper bracelets and quartz beads have been found in the graves associated with these circles. Religious ceremonies might have been conducted at these circles, and they may have provided burial grounds for the privileged. We do not yet know for certain which people in Senegal built the circles, but some think that the Jola were the architects of these magnificent monuments to the past. When were they built? No one can yet give a firm date, but they might have been built around the fourteenth century—perhaps earlier.

8

THE FOREST ZONE

The forest zone stretches from Sierra Leone to the Cameroons, a distance of over three thousand miles. At its centre in southern Ghana and Togo the forest belt is just a few miles wide but in other areas it extends inland for over a hundred miles. It is an area of tall trees and dense undergrowth where fast growth is encouraged by the rains that fall from June to November. To the north, this dense forest gives way by imperceptible stages to open woodland often referred to as 'the bush'.

In prehistoric times, when West Africa experienced periods of exceptional rainfall and the forest may have extended farther northwards, it may have been impossible for man to eke out a living in the present forest area. However, as time went on the forest became habitable and this was particularly true after Africans had learned to forge iron tools. With these, the process of clearing paths and farms became much easier. Thus by A.D. 1000 the forest area was inhabited by peoples who lived in wandering bands which gathered wild crops and hunted; or in small village communities each ruled by its own headman. The dense forest made travel difficult and prevented much contact between these groups.

Peoples
Forest dwellers can be divided into two main groups: those living in the western forest which faces the Atlantic ocean, and those living in the forest belt which looks towards the Gulf of Guinea. Western forest peoples include the Mende, Temne and Kru; those of the Guinea forest include the Baulé, Asante, Fon, Yoruba, Edo and Ibo. Many forest dwellers speak West Atlantic languages but one group, the Mende of Sierra Leone, speak a Mande tongue. Oral traditions suggest that the Mende migrated southwards from the savanna under pressure from Fulani enemies. In the Guinea forest, most languages are of the Kwa language group.

Economy
The first settled farmers were established in the forest before A.D. 1000. These peoples had experienced what is called the Neolithic revolution when man first learned to make polished stone tools, to cultivate the soil and domesticate animals. They probably

9

moved into the forest from areas to the north under pressure from their enemies or economic difficulties, bringing their new techniques with them. In the western forest they cultivated rice and in the Guinea forest, east of the food frontier, they grew the white and yellow Guinea yams. At some unidentifiable time, larger varieties of yam spread across Africa to the forest from Asia as did the banana and plantain. The guinea fowl and the pig, the goat and the chicken all formed part of an early farm. These early farmers also grew and gathered a variety of local vegetables and herbs; and the products of the pepper bush and the oil palm were at their disposal. Thus, the food resources of the neolithic forest dweller were much greater than was once thought possible. Nevertheless, the economy of these early peoples was a subsistence one: each group produced just enough food for its immediate needs and no more.

Gradually, however, improved agricultural techniques, especially better tools, enabled some peoples to have food surpluses available for trade. This process was much accelerated by the advent of the iron age which produced sharper hoes, knives, spears and arrows. Thus forest clearing, land cultivation and hunting were made easier so that food supplies could be increased and man had more leisure to engage in crafts, trade and politics.

By the eleventh century, some forest groups had already learned the use of iron. Archaeologists have found iron age settlements as far apart as Senegambia and southern Ghana, and they have discovered ancient bronze works at Igbo-Ukwu in eastern Nigeria where there is definite evidence of early iron-smelting and a fairly sophisticated technology. Bronze castings of great beauty have been found and it is thought that they were made around A.D. 600. These bronzes are in a completely different style from those produced by the craftsmen of Ife and Benin. It is thought likely that these craftsmen inherited their skills from forest peoples who worked metal and farmed before the migrant founders of the Yoruba peoples arrived, somewhere around A.D. 1000.

Political organization
In view of the difficult communications and farming conditions in the forest, it is not surprising that most forest settlements were small, fairly isolated and politically independent. A typical unit would be a single village. Within each village the main political

10

Fig. 1   Bronze works of art found in the River Niger area

and social bond was kinship, that is blood relationship. The heads of families, the kin group elders, led their people and saw that law and order were maintained. Working with and through the priests of the local cults, they saw that customs were followed and the year's activities planned in advance. When shortage of cultivable land or family quarrels produced migrations of small groups of individuals to found new settlements, these would usually recognize their kinship with their original home and the gods of its people. Thus, at least in times of mutual danger, trade and co-operation between them was quite common. Where this relationship was close, it might lead to steps to form a coherent political unit. In this way chiefdoms of groups of villages would come into existence under the headship of an individual chief or council of chiefs.

Small states and chiefdoms were the characteristic form of political organization until the eighteenth century. However, there were two major exceptions to this general rule, namely Benin and Oyo. In both cases, possession of iron and trading contact with the great Sudanic trading centres enabled growth on an imperial scale to take place from the fourteenth century onwards.

11

THE SUDAN

Geographical factors

The sudan belt stretches right across West Africa from the Atlantic coast to lake Chad and beyond. It is a region of tall savanna grasses and open woodland covering the vast, fertile plains that lie between the tropical forest and the Sahara desert. The area is drained by a network of rivers of which the mighty Niger, the Senegal, Gambia and Volta are the most noteworthy. Although the dust-laden Harmattan wind blows cold off the desert in December and January, temperatures are generally high. Rainfall is seasonal, the bulk of it falling between May and October. However, there are marked local variations and both the duration and volume of the rains is greater in the south than in the north.

Peoples

The sudan belt is the home of numerous peoples each with their own distinct language, customs, methods of government and area. Here we can but mention the Wolof, Tukulor and Fulani who speak what are known as West Atlantic languages; the Soninke, Malinke and Bambara branches of the Mande-speaking Mandingos; the Songhai, who together with the Kanuri of lake Chad speak a Nilo-Saharan language; and the Hausa whose languages belong to the Afro-Asiatic language group.

All these peoples are of Negroid stock but most of them have also an admixture of non-Negro blood. This is the result of centuries during which peoples of Berber, Tuareg or Arab stock penetrated the grasslands from the north and intermarried with indigenous peoples. In the main, such intruders came in small groups and were absorbed into the culture of existing societies.

Two factors worthy of special note are the widespread use of Mande languages and the scattered distribution of the Fulani people. Mande languages are spoken by peoples over practically the whole of the western Sudan and even by the Vai on the coast of Sierra Leone. Mande-speaking peoples were established over a wide area between the Senegal and Niger long before the beginning of our period. However, within our period, Mande-speaking peoples were to show such prowess as traders, colonizers and empire-builders that their influence and languages were to spread even farther.

Fig. 2 Women and children in a Fulani village today

The Fulani can today be found over the whole area of the western and central Sudan. Their main concentrations are however in the Futa Jallon, Masina, and northern Nigeria. Their West Atlantic language indicates that their primary dispersal centre was the Senegal valley where the Fulani racial types evolved through intermarriage between settled Negroes and immigrant Berbers. These early Fulani can be differentiated by occupation. Some of them lived as nomadic cattle-herders while others established themselves as sedentary farmers. Whereas settled Fulani

13

were generally quick to adopt and spread Islam, the pastoral Fulani have retained their traditional beliefs. The reasons why the Fulani have spread so far over the Sudan is veiled in obscurity, but fairly obvious answers suggest themselves. A pastoral people with increasing herds would always be searching for new or better pastures. And the settled Fulani are noted for their mobility in their effort to spread Islam. What is more, they have often shown themselves politically ambitious so that not only have they created states in the areas in which they have settled but they have also been driven from their homes into new areas by rulers who have distrusted them.

Economy

The peoples of the sudan belt enjoyed the most favourable conditions to be found in West Africa. The tall grasses of the undulating plains provided pasture for the large humped cattle and for other domesticated animals such as sheep, goats and fowls. The area also teemed with game both large and small and the rivers were no less productive of fish. In most areas the soil was relatively fertile and in some it was easy to work. Thus early sudan-dwellers were able to cultivate cereals and vegetables to supplement the herbs and fruits that grew wild. In the upper Niger, the Mandingos developed the cultivation of rice. Elsewhere, depending on the rainfall, Guinea corn or millet were the staple crops. Thus progressive peoples such as the Mandingos and Hausa, who developed heavy hoes for deep digging and ridging of their crops, were early able to produce food surpluses. As a result, sudanic peoples were able to become more complex in their economic and social organization. They tended to live in large compact settlements, many of which were surrounded by strong defensive walls. Within these towns, there were specialist craftsmen who wove and dyed cloth, worked in leather or metal, and made domestic utensils from clay or calabashes. There were administrators and warriors; there were markets for traders from near and far; and there were rulers descended from the founding heroes of the settlement.

The existence of gold in several parts of West Africa, particularly in areas of the upper Senegal and Niger, attracted merchants from North Africa. Using the camel, introduced to Africa after the fourth century A.D., these merchants developed a flourishing international commerce which provided the Sudan area with prosperity and cavalry horses. Wide areas of the savanna plains are free of the tsetse fly which kills horses elsewhere in West Africa; and so cavalry horses were successfully used in wars of conquest and to support imperial administration.

Another important factor in the evolution of Sudanic societies was the existence of deposits of iron. Long before A.D. 1000, peoples as diverse as the Soninke and the precursors of the Hausa peoples had learned to mine, smelt and forge the metal. With iron tools they had more control over their environment; with iron weapons they had military superiority over their neighbours.

Political organization
Although there were communities that were run by village elders and priests, the typical political unit was a kingdom. One man appointed by established laws of succession was the chief executive. With the advice of his principal officers of state, he governed an area containing a number of settlements of his people and his authority was bolstered by his headship of the local religion.

Aided by easy communications, an ambitious people could rise to imperial status in a comparatively short time. This presented problems, since the new emperor ruled over peoples for whom he was not the natural ruler. To overcome this difficulty, sudanic emperors were obliged to combine local autonomy with carefully organized central control. In their efforts to strengthen the central authority, they found support from the religion of Islam which established itself in the trading cities. However, just as the absence of physical barriers contributed to the rise of empires, so it left them always open to external attack. Thus the political history of the sudan belt is one of the rise and fall of successive empires, the first of which was the empire of Tekrur.

Questions

1 What do you understand by a life zone? Explain with examples taken from the major life zones of West Africa how geographical factors can affect the political and social life of its peoples.

2 Describe the leading characteristics of the three major life zones

of West Africa.

3 Find out the meanings of the terms 'kinship', 'lineage', 'association'. Illustrate your answers with examples from local history if possible.

4 What is the 'food frontier'? Outline the food resources available to neolithic man in both the savanna and the forest.

5 State why the idea of life zones can be useful in early history.

6 Suggest reasons why large empires grew up more easily in the savanna than the forest zone.

2

The states of the Senegal and Gambia valleys

ORIGINS OF THE PEOPLES

At the dawn of historic time the Senegal valley was the home of a number of scattered Negro communities. These were organized in rural village states, whose inhabitants early learned the use of copper and iron, in addition to the skills of pottery and cloth-manufacture. Being well watered and fertile, the Senegal valley attracted groups of nomads from the Sahara, including Berbers and possibly Jews. Because the desert was becoming increasingly arid and because of attacks from the north, groups of these nomads migrated into the Negro areas and settled there.

These immigrants, who were fairer-skinned than the Negroes, were always a minority in their areas of settlement. However, they often became the rulers of the indigenous peoples. Many theories have been advanced as to why this happened, such as the possibility of their having earlier knowledge of the use of iron, superior craft skills and more advanced powers of political organization. Whether or not they possessed all or any of these advantages is probably secondary to the fact that they were mounted nomads. In the absence of any land-hunger and large-scale trade, the indigenous peoples probably had little serious incentive to travel over wide areas and conquer large empires. The peoples of the desert on the other hand had been obliged to travel long distances, establish their authority over widely separated oases and to co-ordinate the activities of each band with those of their scattered kinsmen. They may also have been better informed on the possibilities of trade with North Africa and have entered the western Sudan with the intention of controlling its gold resources.

Whatever the truth may be, it is certain that inter-marriage between the immigrants and the peoples of the areas in which they settled produced new races such as the Tukulor, the Fulani, the Wolof and Serer peoples. The racial characteristics and customs of these new ethnic groups were a combination of both sides of their ancestry; but it is clear that in most cases their pre-Islamic customs and political systems owed more to the influence of the Negro majority than to that of the comparatively small number of immigrants.

EARLY SENEGAL KINGDOMS

When Arabic-writing historians first mentioned the western Sudan in the tenth and eleventh centuries A.D., they wrote of a series of Negro states along the river Senegal. On the coast north of the Senegal estuary was the town of Awlil which exported salt to the states along the river. Both banks of the Senegal near its estuary formed the kingdom of Saghana; and farther up-river were the kingdoms of Tekrur and Silla. These kingdoms were essentially negroid in culture and organization and bore no similarity to the homes of Moroccan travellers. It is equally interesting that these early kingdoms were associated with international trade; and this suggests that commerce was the most important motive for their foundation and growth. It is possible that at one time the major routes across the Sahara may have run along the coast or passed through Wadan. Thus, these Senegal states would have been the first to profit from the export of the abundant gold supplies of the upper Senegal.

Tekrur

Early importance   The first of these Negro states to attain imperial status was Tekrur. This kingdom, founded by the ancestors of the Tukulor people, was probably in existence as early as the birth of Christ. By the time the first surviving records in Arabic were written, its rulers were overlords of all peoples on both banks of the lower and middle Senegal and their authority stretched northwards into the desert and southwards towards the Gambia. Its importance is demonstrated by the fact that early Arabic writers on the western Sudan described the whole region as 'the land of Tekrur'.

18

North African merchants were extremely impressed by the Tekrur of the tenth and eleventh centuries. Its rulers were reported to rule firmly but justly, to have formidable armies at their disposal, and to maintain excellent law and order throughout their dominions. Their administrative capital, Tekrur, was an extensive city with quarters on both sides of the Senegal; and was an important centre of a brisk commerce. There, gold and slaves were exchanged with North Africans for wool, copper and beads; there came the salt of Awlil; and there the country people disposed of their ample production of grain, fish, cattle, milk products, vegetables and herbs. The prosperity of the people could be seen in their possession of large numbers of cattle, camels and goats and their clothing, made of wool or cotton according to rank. Most cloth was of local manufacture and the people of Tekrur enjoyed considerable fame for the quality of their weaving.

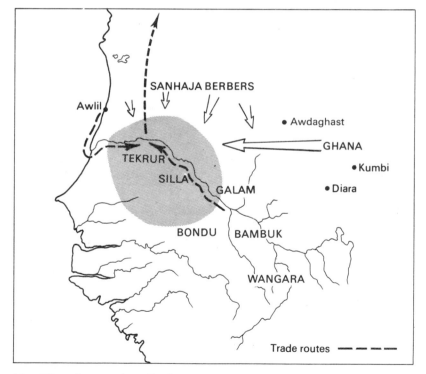

Map III The Empire of Tekrur

Political History   The greatest part of Tekrur's imperial expansion may have taken place under the Dya'ogo dynasty, which came to power in about A.D. 850 and is the first ruling family to earn a place in history. The Dya'ogo rulers were overthrown in about 980 by the Manna dynasty which came from Diara and probably consolidated the wealth and power of Tekrur. Little is known of individual rulers except that War-jabi, who died in about 1040, became one of the first Muslim rulers in West Africa. He compelled his leading subjects to become Muslims and also introduced Islamic law into his empire. Thus it was that when a great Muslim missionary, Abdullah ibn Yacin, fled from persecution by the Sanhaja Berbers, he sought refuge in the Senegal valley. From a base in the Senegal estuary, he taught the need for a jihad* against the infidel, and in preparation for this he built up a body of devoted supporters, mainly from the Lamtuna tribe of the Sanhaja Berbers, with the expressed intention of converting all the Sanhaja by force.

War-jabi's son, Lebi, saw clearly the political and economic advantages of supporting ibn Yacin. The Sanhaja Berbers, a confederation of the Goddala, Lamtuna and Mesufa peoples, controlled the desert trade routes northwards from both Tekrur and her more powerful neighbour to the east, the Soninke empire of Ghana. By this time, Ghana was the most powerful state of the western Sudan; it enjoyed the major share in the export of gold from the upper Senegal, and it had already forced Tekrur to become a semi-independent state of the Soninke empire. Alliance with ibn Yacin thus offered Lebi two valuable opportunities. If ibn Yacin were successful, a joint effort by the Sanhaja confederation and Tekrur to crush pagan Ghana's power might enable Tekrur to regain its independence and to win ascendancy in the gold trade. If ibn Yacin failed, the Sanhaja might be sufficiently weakened for Tekrur to extend its political authority over the Goddala to the north. Thus, Tekrur forces aided ibn Yacin in an unsuccessful attack on the Goddala in 1056; and, after he had converted the Sanhaja into a militant Islamic force known as the Almoravids, assisted the Berbers in a long campaign that led to the conquest of Kumbi, Ghana's capital, in 1076.

For a time, Tekrur enjoyed a period of independence but it could not replace Ghana as the imperial power of the western

*jihad = 'holy war'

Sudan. Although we know nothing of the internal reasons that may have weakened Tekrur, there are two external factors that militated against the growth of Tukulor power. One was that Ghana's former supremacy had permanently diverted the bulk of the gold trade along routes east of the Senegal and thus the successor states of Ghana, Susu and Mali, both arose in the area between the upper Senegal and Niger. Also, the Senegal area experienced partition by former tributary peoples and new immigrants. Fulani, Lamtuna and Wolof leaders at various times carved out their own kingdoms from Tekrur so that the area of its former empire became divided into a number of insignificant states, the rulers of which followed their ancestral religions. Thus Islam as a state religion died out, and those people who adhered to the Muslim faith lived impatiently under the government of a variety of ethnic religions.

The Wolof (Jolof) State
Today, the Wolof people form about thirty-five per cent of the population of modern Senegal, and they are closely related to the Serer who comprise a further sixteen per cent of the country's people. About eighty per cent of the Senegalese speak the Wolof language and it has been said that to be Senegalese is to be Wolof.

Tradition of origin The Wolof tradition of origin claims that the Wolof state was formed by the voluntary association of a number of small independent units. The story starts in Walo where the inhabitants of a number of village-states, each ruled by a king with the Serer title of Laman, quarrelled violently over the distribution of wood collected along the shores of a lake. Before bloodshed could occur, a mysterious figure arose from the lake, shared the wood fairly among the villages and then disappeared. The amazed people feigned a second quarrel and, when the stranger reappeared, they detained him and offered him the government of their states. At first their captive refused to eat but, tempted with the prospect of marriage to a beautiful girl, he became more human in his ways and accepted their offer of kingship.

When these peculiar happenings were reported to the ruler of Sine, who was himself the greatest magician in the land, he exclaimed '*Ndyadyane Ndyaye*', an expression of utter amazement.

21

He then suggested that all rulers between the Senegal and Gambia should make voluntary submission to the remarkable stranger. This they did; and the first ruler of the Wolof state became known as Ndyadyane Ndyaye with the title of Burba Jolof.

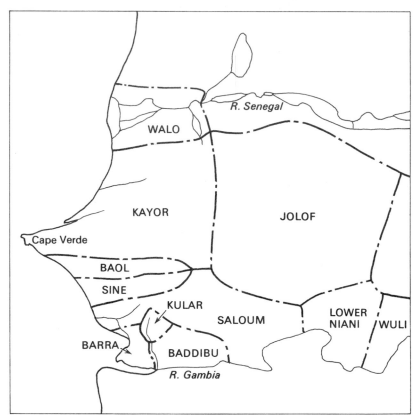

Map IV The Wolof Empire

The Wolof empire This story makes it clear that the original centre of Wolof power was the inland state of Jolof, and that its ruler, the Burba Jolof, governed all the land between the Senegal and the Gambia as far inland as the Mandingo state of Mali. The five major states of this area were Kayor, Baol, Walo, Sine and Saloum, each under rulers who acknowledged kinship with the Burba Jolof and accepted his overlordship. Thus, when the Portuguese arrived at the coast in the mid-fifteenth century, the Burba Jolof headed a small but powerful empire, and as late as the early sixteenth century could field an army of 10,000 horsemen and 100,000 infantry.

The political history of the Wolof states Although the Wolof have continued until the present day to be the dominant people of Senegal, and although they continued to venerate the Burba Jolof as the descendant of their founding ancestors and the religious head of their people, the imperial power of Jolof did not long survive the end of the sixteenth century. This empire like all others had to face internal dissensions and attacks from formidable external foes; and as we trace the outlines of Wolof history we shall notice how these two factors are inter-related in the destruction of the united empire. Internal tensions were the product of discontent among minority peoples not assimilated into the Wolof race, dynastic struggles within the ruling dynasty of Jolof and the ambitions of sub-rulers to exalt their own dignity and win political and economic independence. These separatist ambitions of sub-rulers, particularly those of the coastal states of Kayor and Baol, were encouraged by the growth of coastal trade with the Europeans, which provided a new profit motive and increasing resources for rejecting the authority of the Burba Jolof. Jolof itself had no port either at the coast or on the Senegal. External attacks were made either by desperate peoples displaced from their own homelands by more powerful enemies, or by the Moors of Mauretania whose own economic resources were slight.

Serious internal conflict occurred in the Wolof empire in 1481 when Burba Birain was deposed. This revolt was led by his half-brothers because he had advanced the interests of his full brother at their expense. The first serious blow to Wolof territorial integrity did not come until 1513. In that year, Dengella Koli, the son of an unsuccessful Fulani rebel against the mighty Askia Muhammad of Songhai, led a strong force of Fulani and Mandingo into Futa Toro. With the aid of its Serer and Tukulor inhabitants, he wrested Futa Toro from Wolof overlordship and set up a Fulani dynasty which lasted until 1776 when it was overthrown by a Tukulor muslim movement.

The first successful break-away movement by a Wolof state occurred in the mid-sixteenth century when the Damel of Kayor revolted, over-ran Baol and repulsed the efforts of the Burba Jolof to restore him to obedience. This division within the Wolof empire enabled the Moors of Mauretania to inflict a serious blow on the Wolof states in the next century. In about 1670, wandering Muslim clerics from Mauretania stirred up rebellions against Wolof rulers by promising their subjects that if they raised successful revolts they would be shown how to produce millet without the labour of planting. When the rebellions broke out, the Mauretanians moved in, killed the rulers of Walo and Kayor and defeated the Burba Jolof. After a period of severe famine, the disenchanted people expelled the Mauretanians and restored rulers of the Wolof dynasties in Walo and Kayor. However, the Mauretanians continued to make sporadic attacks on the northern Wolof, and Walo particularly suffered at their hands in the eighteenth century.

The power of Kayor, seriously damaged by the events of 1670, suffered a further set-back in 1686 when Baol successfully rebelled. This provided the opportunity for the Burba Jolof to attempt to recover his old imperial authority and he over-ran Kayor. However, Baol had not revolted in order to restore the authority of the Burba Jolof. Its Teny, Latir Fal Sukake, gave armed aid to the Kayor refugees, killed the Burba Jolof in battle and then imposed his own rule on Kayor. He maintained his authority by contriving the death of any powerful noblemen who stood in his way and by absorbing the traditional revenues of the nobility. However, the union of Baol and Kayor did not outlast his death in 1702 when one son became ruler of Baol and another of Kayor.

Kayor made one last impressive effort to master Senegambia in the late eighteenth century. In 1786, it again established control over Baol and then followed up this success by inflicting a serious defeat on the Muslim Al-mami of Futa Toro. Yet other forces were at work which were to end the independence of Kayor and all Wolof states in the late nineteenth century when the French advance into the interior absorbed them temporarily into a European empire. Until this time, in spite of their internal divisions, the Wolof had managed to preserve the independence of their states against all opponents.

The Wolof system of government   One of the prime functions of the Wolof tradition of origin would be to explain and sanctify the main features of their remarkable system of government. Each of the Wolof states was governed by its own ruler appointed from the descendants of the founder of the state. Each enjoyed practical autonomy in the administration of the affairs of his own kingdom but was expected to co-operate with the Burba Jolof in matters of common imperial interest such as defence, trade and the provision of imperial revenue. The authority of the Burba Jolof was bolstered by his traditional descent from Ndyadyene Ndyaye and the consequent divinity of his office.

An important feature of Wolof government was the strong position of the nobility. Neither the Burba Jolof nor the rulers of the other Wolof states held office by hereditary right alone. Although each had to be descended from the founder of his state in the male line of succession, and be born of a noble woman, actual appointment was made by elections conducted by the great nobility. Once appointed, the Burba Jolof, or the sub-ruler, went through elaborate religious rituals to inform him on the duties of his office and to elevate his status to that of a divine monarch. Thus sanctified, the Burba Jolof was expected to lead his people to victory and bring them prosperity. If he failed in these key functions, his exalted nature could not save him from deposition, although his personal army might.

Relations between Wolof sub-rulers and the Burba Jolof were based on voluntary co-operation, even the payment of tribute for the upkeep of the imperial dignity and power being voluntary. This voluntary element produced one of the most autocratic systems of government known in West Africa. As authority depended on personal wealth, prestige and power, the Burba Jolof, as did his sub-kings and other nobility, built up his own personal army of soldiers, political and commercial agents and praise-singers, as both a source and sign of his power. As a result, Wolof rulers were able to dispense with even the appearance of constitutional advice and to appoint at will district heads over groups of villages. Often they appointed men of non-noble origin, loyal to themselves, to those posts which were concerned with the preservation of law and order and the collection of royal revenue.

The strength of this system was that it reposed authority in the hands of men equipped to maintain it; its weakness was that it encouraged trials of strength between rivals when there was no over-riding common need to preserve a united front.

Women played an important role in Wolof government and

society. The *linger*, or Queen Mother, was the head of all Wolof women and was influential in the state. To maintain her dignity, she owned a number of dependent villages which cultivated her farms and paid her tribute. There were other female chiefs whose main task was to judge cases involving women. In the state of Walo, a woman could aspire to the office of Bur and rule the state.

Wolof society   The Wolof people were divided into a rigid caste system of royalty, nobility, freemen and slaves, and there were hierarchical subdivisions within each caste. People rarely married outside their caste and where a man of a superior order produced children by women of a lower one, these children did not inherit their father's position. Common freemen included peasant-farmers, smiths, leather-workers and *griots* (praise-singers). In spite of low birth, however, some of these people played key roles in the state. Smiths were indispensable because they produced the weapons of war and they often played a vital role as mediator in local disputes. *Griots* always commanded a respected place in society for each was attached to a man of considerable import-ance. Every important family retained the services of a *griot* and the office was usually hereditary. His function was not merely the public exaltation of his master by playing musical instruments in his honour, singing his praises and entertaining his guests, but above all of informing his master of the history of his house, its traditional rights and duties. Thus the *griot* was often the per-sonal adviser and private secretary of his employer and accomp-anied him to war with the specific duty of keeping up the morale of the troops and memorizing the details of his master's prowess. *Griots* were allowed a frankness of criticism of their superiors that a man would have resented from his equals. Consequently, their tongues were often feared, and discreet silence or outspokenness could earn a *griot* wealth far outstripping his rank. But for *griots,* West African history would be much poorer for it is they who have remembered the traditions of their own people.

Islam made little headway among the Wolof until the late nine-teenth century when many people adopted the religion as part of an anti-European movement. Knowledge of Islam had, how-ever, entered the Wolof area much earlier and between the eleventh and sixteenth centuries many of the Wolof chiefs nominally became Muslim. There is little evidence that many of them took Islam seriously although they patronized Muslim clerics whose miracles and charms they hoped to enlist in their own service. Neither the history, constitution nor organization of the society outlined above owe anything to Islam. Wolof achievement owed little to any outside influences.

The Serer

Although we have described Sine and Saloum as parts of the Wolof empire at its height, the leading people of these states were the Serer. These people also have traditions of migration into the Senegambia area, and are also the product of racial fusion between non-Negro immigrant groups and indigenous Negroes. Their customs and language bear considerable similarity to those of the Wolof. They appear to have settled originally to the north of the Senegal but under pressure from more powerful peoples moved into the Futa Toro area of Tekrur and became subjects of the Tukulor. Other invaders, including the Wolof, forced the Serer to migrate south-westwards until they finally established themselves in small states in the Sine-Saloum area probably in the twelfth century.

These states came under Wolof domination but remained Serer in character. However, both Tukulor and Mandingo groups rivalled the Wolof aristocracy for power in the Serer states; and before the Portuguese arrived at the coast in 1455, the Gelowar, a group of invaders, had won control of Sine and Saloum and a series of smaller states along the Gambia including Niani and Wuli. These Gelowar are generally believed to have been a Mandingo clan and it is from them that the ruling class of the Serer states descended.

Serer society   Serer society was stratified into a caste system similar to that of the Wolof and most people remained members of the group into which they were born. The highest class was the Tiedo or warrior caste which included rulers, soldiers, judges and tax-collectors. Of these, only men of pure Gelowar descent were eligible for election to the kingly office of Bur. Sons of Gelowar fathers by women of insufficient rank were known as Domibur; and although they could not inherit royal power, they were usually given lesser chieftainships in the kingdom. Slave members of the Bur's household could attain this status if they held important offices in the royal service.

Below this aristocracy was the Diambur class of freemen. Composed of peasants and craftsmen such as blacksmiths, leather-workers, weavers, woodcarvers and *griots*, it was at once the largest class in Serer society and the principal source of regular state revenue. At the very bottom of the social scale came domestic and agricultural slaves. Even these were divided into two categories: those captured in war by their owners, and those born into the service of their master. While the former were mere chattels of their owner and could be sold at will, the latter were regarded as members of their master's family and could own personal property and feel secure against the remote possibility of sale out of the household.

Serer government The head of the Serer state was the Bur, who was selected from among the Gelowar. On his accession, he was invested with divine status by important religious ceremonies but this did not safeguard him against lawful deposition if the Serer did not prosper under his rule. Consequently, the Bur, like Wolof rulers, built up a powerful following of his own which enabled him to rule despotically. He personally appointed leading state officials and district heads and could appoint people of servile origin whose loyalties were to himself alone.

The actual nomination of a new Bur was the function of a single king-maker known as the Diaraff Bundao. In strict theory, he had the sole right to select or depose a Bur but in practice always acted on the advice of a council of leading noblemen. The Diaraff Bundao himself could never have a claim to the throne for he was of non-royal blood, being the head of the Diambur caste. His own appointment was made by the reigning Bur, whose choice was influenced by the wishes of a council of Diambur chiefs. During the interval between the death of one Bur and the installation of another, the Diaraff Bundao actually governed the kingdom.

Other important men in Serer politics included the Burmi, the Grand Farba and the Farba Birkeur. The Burmi, the man named as the next Bur, was usually required to live away from the capital in order to prevent his becoming a source of serious political danger to the reigning Bur. The Grand Farba, chief of the royal slaves, and the Farba Birkeur, master of the royal household, were the great personal officials of the Bur on whom the success of royal administration largely depended. Another highly influential courtier was the *linger*, the Queen Mother, who played the same role as her Wolof counterpart.

The social and political systems of the Serer were maintained by the religious beliefs and practices of the people from which they largely derived. The strength of their ethnic religion was so strong that Islam did not become important among them until the twentieth century. The nature of the Serer constitution differed little from that of the Wolof, and both systems of government exhibited the same strengths and weaknesses. Equally, the resilience of their governmental systems enabled both Serer and Wolof to preserve their political identity and customary way of life against all external challenges until very recent times.

Questions

1 Name two ethnic groups which evolved in the Senegal valley. By what processes were these peoples formed and from whom did they inherit their most predominant cultural characteristics? Give a brief account of the social or political organizations of one of these peoples.

2 What factors enabled one of the earliest empires of West Africa to grow up in the Senegal valley? Why did it not preserve its early primacy?

3 Write a brief account of the history of Tekrur. Suggest reasons for its rise and fall.

4 Describe the political structure of the Wolof empire. What were the strengths and weaknesses of this system of government?

5 Give an account of an oral tradition of origin of any one people of the Senegambia area. Show what important factors in the history of its people the tradition illustrates.

29

6 Write a brief informative account on (a) Ndyadyane Ndyaye and (b) the *linger* in Wolof and Serer society.

3

The ancient empire of Ghana

In 1068, a learned Arab scholar of Cordoba in southern Spain wrote an important book on the savanna area south of the Sahara. His name was Al-Bakri (El-Bekri); his most remarkable information was an account of an empire of great wealth and power in the western Sudan—the ancient empire of Ghana. Although Al-Bakri never visited the western Sudan himself, his book was based on information supplied by Muslim merchants who traded across the Sahara from Morocco to purchase gold and other items of trade. Thus, his work forms our most important source on the empire of Ghana in the eleventh century.

By 1068, Ghana was the largest, wealthiest and most powerful state in West Africa. Situated in the vast savanna area between the Senegal and the Niger, its authority extended from the frontiers of Tekrur to the western banks of the Niger, and from the Mandingo area in the south to beyond the fringes of the desert in the north.

Its ruling people were the Soninke, the indigenous inhabitants of the area, who had established their capital at Kumbi, the greatest trading centre of the western Sudan. Their ruler at the time that Al-Bakri wrote was Tunkamenin, who commanded great devotion from his subjects and respect from foreign visitors. He had obtained the kingship because he was the son of the former ruler's sister: the Soninke followed the matrilineal system of inheritance.

The city of Kumbi
The imperial city of Kumbi was a twin city with two separate centres six miles apart. Although the two towns were linked by a continuous ribbon of housing, they were distinct in character

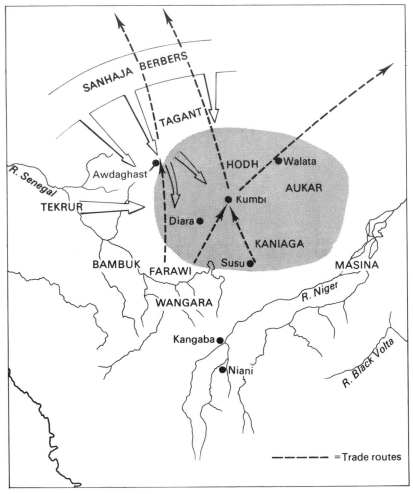

Map V   The Empire of Ghana

and function. The one formed a Muslim quarter where North African merchants resided during their trading missions to Ghana. This was the main commercial area and the influence of North Africa was apparent in the many stone-built houses, the twelve mosques for Muslim prayer and the presence of many scholars learned in Arabic, Islamic theology and Islamic law.

The other town, known as Al-Ghaba, was the more important for it was the administrative centre of the Soninke empire. Here lived the Ghana of Ghana on a lavish scale in his magnificent stone palace decorated with paintings and carvings and fitted with glass windows. Close to the royal palace there was a stone mosque for the use of Muslim visitors and officials. The rest of the buildings of Al-Ghaba were constructed of mud and thatch in the traditional manner, and around the whole quarter were defensive earthen walls. The exact location of Kumbi is a mystery historical researchers have worked hard to solve. Yet it seems likely that it was situated at Kumbi Saleh, about 200 miles north of modern Bamako. When archaeologists investigated local traditions that this was the site of ancient Kumbi, they unearthed the stone walls of houses built in the North African style and found many interesting fragments including glass weights used in the weighing of gold.

The Soninke religion

By 1068, Soninke's ruler and the vast majority of his people had not been converted to Islam, which was probably the religion of the commercial classes only. The Soninke people worshipped a variety of traditional gods and believed that the spirits of their ancestors guided the fortunes of the people. Each deity had its own cult and its own priests who cared for the cult-shrines and exercised great influence over the people. The Ghana himself acquired a semi-divine nature once he had undergone the necessary religious rituals at his accession and was regarded as the direct link between living man and the gods. Thus he was the chief priest of all the traditional cults. The most important cult-shrines were in the sacred groves which surrounded Al-Ghaba, and these were closely guarded by superintendent priests to prevent unauthorized access to the secrets of the cults. Within these groves, all the main religious ceremonies such as the offering of sacrifices and the consultation of oracles took place; here dwelt the spirits of Soninke ancestral heroes; here the Ghana had his dreaded prisons; and here the Soninke buried their dead rulers.

In common with all West African peoples, the Soninke believed in life after death. Therefore, when a ruler died great care was taken to see that he lacked for nothing on his journey to the spirit

33

world. A special hut was constructed for the dead Ghana's body and within it were placed comfortable rugs, his personal possessions, food and water and his domestic servants. Then the building was sealed off and completely covered with a thick layer of earth to form a huge mound. Later, sacrifices and libations would be made at shrines to the dead Ghana for he was now an ancestor who needed sustenance and whose aid was valuable to his people.

Court ceremonial
Both the sanctity and the splendour of the Soninke monarchy were amply demonstrated when the Ghana gave a public audience to settle disputes and hear grievances. On such occasions, the Ghana sat in a pavilion of state wearing gorgeous robes, golden ornaments and a cap of cloth of gold. Around the cap was wound a turban of finest quality cotton. Tethered outside the pavilion were ten fine horses, each with harness worked in gold; and behind the Ghana himself stood ten pages bearing shields and swords embossed with gold. The entrance to the pavilion was guarded by well-bred dogs wearing collars of gold and silver who were the constant companions of the Ghana. To the Ghana's right were assembled the sons of his tributary rulers expensively clad and with gold plaited into their hair. The royal councillors, with the exception of the governor of Kumbi whose position was in front of his ruler, sat on both sides of the Ghana.

Special drums known as *daba* were beaten to signify the beginning of an audience. Non-Muslim petitioners approaching their ruler proceeded on all fours and sprinkled earth upon their shoulders; Muslims showed their respect by clapping their hands politely. No petitioner was allowed to address the Ghana direct, conversations being carried on through a royal official known as the Interpreter. Not all the Ghana's business, however, was transacted in Kumbi and he frequently went on a tour of his kingdom. As he entered the towns of his empire, wild animals were driven before him to emphasize his mastery of man and beast.

The governmental system of Ghana
The display of majesty of the Ghana of Ghana derived from his overlordship of a wealthy and extensive empire. However, the exact political position of an individual Ghana could vary from

34

that of a dominating executive head of state to that of an impressive figurehead in whose name the government of the empire was carried on by the senior officials. The factors which determined the exact degree of personal authority he exercised were his own character and powers of leadership. There was great opportunity for full exercise of personal power. As a semi-divine ruler he could appeal to a vital combination of both the religious and political loyalties of his people. At the practical level, his semi-divine status made it possible for him to manipulate the pronouncements of the various religious cults which were the most important factor in determining the attitudes and actions of the Soninke people. On the other hand, where the Ghana lacked personal dynamism and political skill, these factors could practically exclude him from personal influence on imperial policy. Since his semi-divine nature required that he received all official communications second-hand through the medium of his Interpreter, who also transmitted his orders to his people, he could be kept largely ignorant of government business or policy could be changed by the officials applying it. Equally, if the cult priest gave political advice contrary to his personal wishes, he had little alternative but to follow it. Perhaps the glory of the Ghana system of government was that for such a long period it was able to provide stable and efficient administration irrespective of the character of the Ghanas.

✳The Ghana empire included many areas whose people were not Soninke and therefore had religious loyalties to gods of whom the Ghana was not the earthly representative. This, in the interests of imperial unity, produced a dual system of provincial government. In the Soninke areas, the head of local government was a Soninke governor, possibly a close relative or trusted companion of the Ghana. In the non-Soninke areas, the local ruler was the natural ruler of his own people selected by their customary procedures and confirmed in office by the Ghana. Possibly, there was a Soninke representative at the court of each of these tributary rulers to ensure that they did not avoid their obligations to the empire. Both provincial governors of Soninke areas and tributary rulers of conquered peoples had the duties of loyalty to the Ghana, provision of annual tribute and the contribution of bands of warriors to the imperial army when they were required for active service. In return, the Ghana provided protection against

35

external enemies, facilities for sharing in the prosperous trade of the empire and the provision of justice to settle serious quarrels that might arise within the empire. From his sub-rulers he was accustomed to receive wealthy presents; and in return he awarded honours and wealth for distinguished service to the empire.

We know little of the structure of the central government of Ghana although we have already noticed the personal position of its rulers. That there must have been a number of traditional dignitaries performing the duties of modern ministers is beyond doubt. The role of each would have been to supervise one or another branch of state activity such as, for example, finance or defence, plus the essential role of advising on the general conduct of imperial affairs. We know that two of the senior ministers were the Vizier (Waziri), whose role was similar to that of a modern prime minister, and the Interpreter, whose influence must have been great as he was the official means of direct communication between the Ghana and his people or foreign visitors. One remarkable feature of the central government was that by 1068, some of the leading officers of state were Muslim. The reasons for this must have been that the Muslims' literacy in Arabic was a valuable aid to government and that they were able to communicate directly with merchants and possibly rulers of North Africa.

The legal system of Ghana was not divorced from the executive. Each village head tried straightforward cases in his own village but people discontented with his judgement could appeal to the provincial governor or tributary state ruler. In the last resort, a man could appeal to the justice of the Ghana himself or of his trained judges. Serious law-suits could be judged according to Soninke custom or, if the discontented party was a Muslim, according to Islamic law.

✳ The empire of Ghana was of necessity organized to provide a colossal war-machine to maintain its position of wealth and authority. Although early historians do not mention the existence of any standing army, the Ghana must have possessed a considerable bodyguard of trained soldiers. This formed a nucleus of an army recruited from the provinces as occasion demanded. Through its requirement that any able-bodied man could be summoned to fight for the empire, Ghana could field an army of two hundred thousand men in the eleventh century. Yet size was far from being the sole source of Ghana's military success.

Through trade with North Africa, the Soninke had acquired large numbers of horses to mount a formidable body of cavalry and, also, the Soninke had early learned the use of iron. Thus their cavalrymen fought with metal spears, their considerable number of archers fired iron-tipped arrows and in close encounter with the enemy the army used sharp swords. It is possible that they possessed these valuable instruments of war earlier than other peoples in the area between the Niger and Senegal. Certainly, as late as the eleventh century, a people known as the Lemlem to the south of Ghana had only ebony staves and stones with which to attempt to repulse the might of Ghana.

Imperial revenues
It would have been impossible to maintain the royal style of the Ghana and to have provided for the upkeep of the imperial army without large resources of wealth. This was provided by the revenue system of the empire based on annual tribute in produce, taxes on trade and the spoils of war. As Ghana was in those days a fertile area, its people were able to supply abundant foodstuffs and useful materials such as grass-thatch for the upkeep of the Ghana and his hierarchy of officials. In addition, the strategic position of Kumbi between the goldfields of Wangara and the desert routes of the North African merchants gave the city an important position in the trans-Saharan trade. Thus Kumbi became an important commercial centre where the essential salt and horses plus luxury goods brought by North African merchants were exchanged for gold, slaves, ostrich feathers, ivory, gum and other commodities. On all these goods, the Ghana collected customs duties. Each donkey-load of salt imported into Ghana paid a duty of about ten shillings'-worth of gold; each donkey-load exported was taxed at a pound's-worth of gold. Import and export of other goods provided additional duties. Furthermore, any gold nugget unearthed by gold-miners automatically became the property of the Ghana whose treasury contained an enormous lump of solid gold. The value of this regulation lay not so much in its increase of the royal wealth as in its avoidance of undue increase in the amount of gold available in Ghana's markets; for this would have resulted in the North African merchants reducing the amount of goods they would give for a fixed measure of gold. It is evident that the income from

37

imperial revenue more than provided for the cost of imperial government and the needs of the royal court where luxury was the order of the day.

THE RISE OF ANCIENT GHANA

Very little is known about the stages by which Ghana grew into a powerful empire. Recorded tradition suggests that the Soninke lived in many small village-states and were predominantly agriculturalists until about A.D. 300. Then, according to Muslim historians, some 'white' people from the desert came and settled among the Soninke of Awkar. Such immigrants, possibly Berbers or Jews, may have brought with them horses and iron weapons and tools in significant numbers. Also, they probably maintained their semi-nomadic life, thus coming into contact with Soninke villages over a large area. Whether or not these assumptions are accurate, the immigrants are reputed to have made themselves rulers of Awkar, Bassikuna and Hodh. Some historians regard the Fulani and kindred peoples such as the Tukulor and Susu as their descendants.

Although these 'whites' intermarried with the Soninke and their descendants inherited many Negro physical and cultural characteristics, they remained a distinctive minority ruling class. In about A.D. 700, there was a serious Soninke reaction against their rule when Kaya Maghan led a successful rebellion, killed the last ruler of the 'white' dynasty and drove many of his race from the country. Kaya Maghan thus established a pure Soninke dynasty. He appears to have been a great warrior and diplomat who by a combination of persuasion and force united all Soninke people under his leadership. He is thought to have founded Kumbi as his capital and both he and his immediate successors achieved a great westward and southward expansion of the Soninke state. Thus, the empire described by Al-Bakri was largely a Soninke creation.

In the early ninth century, the new power and wealth of Ghana were endangered by the activities of the Sanhaja Berbers, who occupied the southern desert from the coast to the north-eastern frontiers of Ghana. The Sanhaja Berbers thus controlled all routes

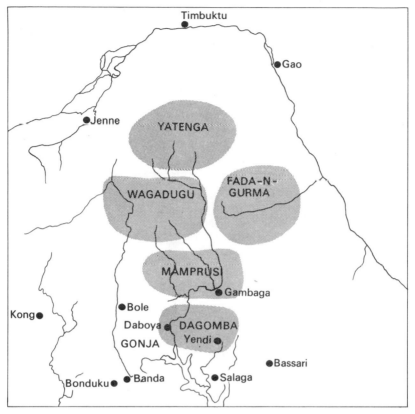

Map VI   The Mossi-Dagomba States (see pages 82–85)

crossing the desert from the western Sudan, and they enjoyed a profitable share in the trans-Saharan trade through their over-lordship of Awdaghast, a large and important commercial town east of Ghana. Possibly the foundation of Kumbi and the westward expansion of Ghana so challenged the pre-eminence of Audaghost in the gold trade that it forced temporary unity on the tribes of the Sanhaja federation. Thus united and under the leadership of a great warrior, Tilutane, the Sanhaja were able to field an army of ten thousand men mounted on camels and they made repeated raids on Ghana's northern provinces. However, Sanhaja unity did not long outlast Tilutane's death and the Soninke recovered control of their frontier areas. Indeed,

39

in 990, they conquered Awdaghast itself and became undisputed masters of the trade of the western Sudan. This conquest probably brought Ghana to the height of her power, possibly a power greater even than that recorded by Al-Bakri.

Reasons for the rise of Ghana
So far we have studied the available knowledge on Ghana up to the time that Al-Bakri wrote. It is an interesting story, and much of the interest of historical study derives from learning, in narrative and descriptive form, the achievements of the past. However, the most important aspect of historical studies is to analyse the past in order to find out the exact truth and thus ascertain why things happened as they did. Although this is a speculative process, it relies not on free use of the imagination but on scientific study of the known facts. Thus, although you may not have realized it, we have already touched on all the important factors that accounted for the rise of Ghana.

Geographical factors had much to do with the rise of Ghana. The presence of large supplies of gold in the upper Senegal and Niger valleys proved the main lure to North African merchants, whose ability to provide fine Arab horses from their homeland and salt from the mines of the desert formed the essential basis of a flourishing trade in the western Sudan. This trade was the source of Ghana's wealth and power. Although the Soninke did not themselves occupy the main goldfields of Wangara, the empire of Ghana stretched across the savanna area between the goldfields and the southern ends of the leading desert route. Kumbi itself had abundant supplies of pure water and foodstuffs farmed locally to meet the needs of the trans-Saharan travellers. Equally, the flat savanna plains made travel for trade, administration and conquest comparatively easy. Later empires were to make great use of the Niger valley as an important natural means of communication but there is no evidence that Ghana did so. To Kumbi, the Niger represented a distant boundary rather than a great artery of trade.

Geographical position alone cannot explain the rise of Ghana. Other villages and other peoples enjoyed the advantages of location utilized by the Soninke, yet it was the Soninke who built an empire. Part of the explanation may lie in the possibility that the Soninke were the first people in their area to develop the use

40

of iron and to amass large numbers of horses. These gave them economic and military superiority over less fortunate neighbours and enabled them in time to build up the largest and most formidable army of the western Sudan.

That Soninke commercial and military supremacy arose and' lasted for so long must, however, be attributed to the Soninke themselves. The nomadic impulse of their early 'white' dynasty provided the original initiative for the creation of an empire and this imperial ambition was increased by the growing importance of the trans-Saharan trade. Yet it was Soninke administrative genius that produced the governmental system necessary to control the vaster empire created by Kaya Maghan and his successors. The outstanding success of this system of government was its proved ability to provide justice and law and order of such a high quality that traders could travel safely and obtain remedies for their grievances. This was an essential condition for the prosperity and happiness of the Soninke people.

Although we have noted that the Soninke governmental system was capable of providing effective rule irrespective of the qualities of individual Ghanas, we must not underestimate the importance of the Ghana himself. Without effective leadership, both civil and military, no early states would have been able to attain or support imperial authority. Thus, although we know practically nothing of the lives of individual rulers of Ghana, they must have included several great men of the calibre of Kaya Maghan. The rise of Ghana, if we knew all the details, would clearly demonstrate how the Soninke, and not least their Ghanas, utilized their environment to create a state whose fame has continued long after it has ceased to exist.

THE DECLINE AND FALL OF ANCIENT GHANA

The first serious blow to Ghana's power was inflicted by the Sanhaja. Compelled by the serious economic loss of Awdaghast to re-unite against their common enemy, the tribes of the confederation received a new religious motive for total war with Ghana when, in about 1020, their ruler was converted to Islam. His successor, Yahya, made the pilgrimage to Mecca and on his return brought the puritanical Abdullah ibn Yacin to improve the quality of Islamic life among the Berbers. In spite of early reverses and exile, ibn Yacin imposed a strict Islamic life on the Berber tribesmen, now named the Almoravids, and led them on a jihad to eradicate paganism. This remarkable group, spurred on by devotion to God and lust for gold, conquered Morocco to the north and in 1055 recovered Awdaghast. Thus they completely controlled the western routes across the Sahara.

On ibn Yacin's death in 1057, the Almoravid empire split into two parts. His successor in the southern desert was Abu Bakr whose main political objective was the destruction of Ghana's power. This ambition was motivated by three considerations: only successful war producing ample booty could keep the Sanhaja Berbers united; conquest of Ghana would bring the Berbers complete control of the gold trade; and victory would produce the compulsory Islamization of the Soninke. In alliance with Tekrur, Abu Bakr began his assault on Ghana in 1062. Although some of Ghana's tributary states took advantage of the empire's difficulties to declare their independence, Ghana was not easily defeated and it was not until 1076 that Kumbi fell to the Almoravids. The Soninke were given the choice of Islam or death: many fled southwards and westwards, and others accepted the Muslim religion.

The rulers of Kumbi, however, did not long remain under Berber overlordship. On the death of Abu Bakr, the Sanhaja confederacy once again split into its component parts. The resilient Soninke reasserted their independence and tried once more to rebuild their political and economic ascendancy in the western Sudan. In this they failed, for their former tributary states to the south which had escaped Berber domination refused to return to their allegiance to Kumbi. In its weakened circumstances, Kumbi's military power was not sufficient to compel such states as Diara and Susu to do so. Thus the empire was reduced in extent to the areas of Hodh, Awkar and Bassikuna.

The power vacuum created by the military decline of Ghana was first filled by the rise of Susu, a nation famous for its blacksmiths and infantry. In about 1200, the Susu came under the rule of Sumanguru, a great war-leader whose position as leader of the Susu cults was reinforced by his reputation as an outstanding magician. He consolidated Susu domination over Diara and

Fig. 3 Kumbi-Saleh: niche of a house (twelfth–thirteenth century) in the capital of ancient Ghana

began the process of subordinating the small Mandingo states to the South. In 1203, he conquered Kumbi itself and soon completed its economic ruin. A cruel ruler, reputed to sit on the skins of chiefs he had defeated, he taxed the merchants of Kumbi so harshly that, in 1224, the wealthy Soninke and North African merchants fled northwards to found Walata. This town soon became one of the key centres in the trans-Saharan trade. In 1235, however, Susu was itself conquered by the rising Mandingo power of Mali, and in 1240 Kumbi was razed to the ground by the forces of Sundiata, first Mansa of Mali. Not until the twentieth century was the probable site of the once greatest city of the

43

western Sudan rediscovered.

The reasons for the decline of ancient Ghana
The later history of Ghana emphasizes two important reasons
for its decline and fall. One was increasingly effective competition
from the Sanhaja Berbers for control of the gold trade; another,
and more important, was the increasing pressure of attacks by
powerful enemies, notably the Almoravids and the Muslim state
of Tekrur, and later the Susu and the Mandingos. The attacks
of these people first broke the military power of the empire and
then ruined its economy. The campaigns of 1062 to 1076 and their
ultimate success also hint at another factor that was a source of
weakness to Ghana, namely the ambitions of local sub-kings to
escape the necessity of paying tribute to Kumbi and to win
political independence. Whether or not there was collusion
between internal malcontents and external enemies we may never
know. Yet at the time of the Almoravid attack, the tributary state of
Anbara, only six days' journey west of Kumbi, was in revolt. Also
the southern states of Ghana such   ra and Susu took
advantage of Almoravid success to break away permanently from
Ghana's rule.

Other contributory factors to Ghana's inability to resist external foes can be guessed at with some certainty. The enforcement
of Islam upon many of the northern Soninke in 1076 may have
sown serious discord between them and their non-Muslim
kinsmen. An even stronger possibility is that there were dynastic
struggles for the office of Ghana and constitutional struggles
by which the great chiefs sought to restrict the personal power
of their ruler. Such rivalries would have diminished loyalty to
the Ghana, weakened or destroyed his ability to lead his people,
and have increased separatist tendencies among both Soninke
and non-Soninke peoples within the empire. Ultimately, the
authority of the central government declined to the point where
it could no longer protect, control or tax the empire.

Today, the area of Kumbi is not the fertile well-watered area
it once was. Perhaps, even before the thirteenth century, wars and
increasing dryness in the area were producing famines destructive
of agriculture and population and undermining the economic
position of the capital. Thus, Ghana eventually fell before a combination of insuperable difficulties.

44

THE RESULTS OF THE FALL OF GHANA

The results of the fall of Ghana belong to the history of the western Sudan after 1240. The decline in Ghana's might produced a serious power vacuum in the western Sudan which other states struggled to fill. That this did not destroy the prosperity and law and order of the region was due to the rapid rise of other imperial powers, namely the short-lived empire of Susu and then the long-lasting colossus of Mali. One important result of this transference of power was that the main avenues of trade moved eastwards. In the river-based empire of Mali it was Timbuktu which became the *entrepôt* for trade from North Africa.

Furthermore, the successive attacks on Kumbi produced a great dispersal of Soninke people. Those fleeing from the Almoravids moved southwards and westwards and some of them may eventually have reached the middle Volta as co-founders of the Akan people. Those who fled from Sumanguru and Sundiata of Mali were often both Muslims and traders.

It is a great tragedy that historians cannot trace their movements, for these Soninke probably made a significant contribution to the spread of Islam among the Mandingos and peoples living along the upper Niger. They may even have taken the initiative in developing trade in Timbuktu and Jenne. But these are probabilities for which there is, as yet, no final proof.

Questions

1 Write an account of the social and political structure of the Soninke of ancient Ghana.

2 Outline the system of government of ancient Ghana and explain the strength of the Ghana's position.

3 Give a brief account of the rise and fall of the empire of ancient Ghana.

4 How do you account for the rise of Ghana's power? Why did the empire collapse?

5 Estimate the results of the fall of the empire of Ghana upon the western Sudan.

6 Write a descriptive account of the city of Kumbi, explain its importance and outline the main events in its history from 1076 to 1240.

7 Do personal research in your library to write short factual accounts of the Almoravids, Sumanguru of Susu, the goldfields of Wangara.

8 What most impressed North African travellers to the ancient empire of Ghana?

4

The ancient empire of Mali

The creators of the great empire of Mali were the Mandingo, a Negro people whose homeland was the Mandinka plateau between the upper streams of the Senegal and Niger. During the period of Ghana's ascendancy, they lived in scattered village-states about which little is known except that one Mandingo chief was persuaded to become a Muslim in return for the prayers of a Muslim cleric to end a serious drought; and that Mandingo political unity was brought about by a racial reaction against the oppressive rule of Sumanguru of Susu, who conquered the area after he had established his rule in Kumbi. The insurgent Mandingos found a national hero in Sundiata, a prince of Kangaba, under whose inspiring leadership they broke the might of Susu and founded the power and prosperity of the new empire of Mali.

The early life of Sundiata
According to one tradition, Sundiata (Mari Jata) was a son of Nare Maghan, ruler of Kangaba, by his second wife, Sogolon. The marriage of Nare Maghan and Sogolon is said to have taken place in mysterious circumstances and at the time it was prophesied that their son would become a great ruler. Yet Sundiata was a great disappointment to his parents for he was slow to talk and for most of his childhood was unable to walk. When Nare Maghan died, he was succeeded by Dankaran Touman, the son of his senior wife. Dankaran Touman was a man of weak character and the real power in Kangaba lay in the hands of the Queen Mother. She hated Sundiata's mother and humiliated her in every way, especially by jeering at the backwardness of Sundiata.

However, Sundiata suddenly gained the use of his legs and

47

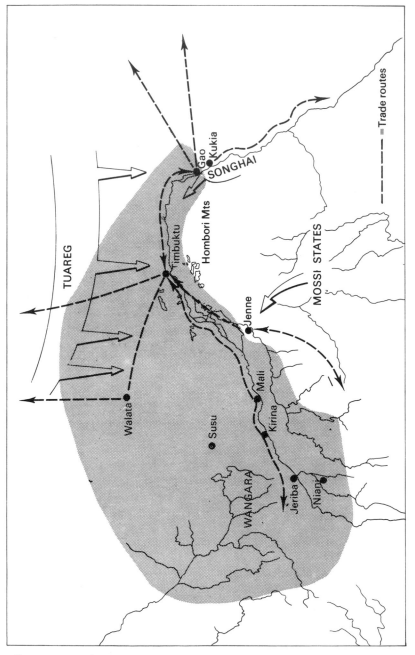

developed into a youth remarkable for his physical strength. His prowess in fighting and hunting made him extremely popular with the young people of Kangaba of whom he became undisputed leader. This so disturbed the Queen Mother, who feared Sundiata might plot to overthrow her son, that she planned his assassination. Consequently, Sogolon fled from Kangaba with her children.

Wherever Sogolon settled, the hatred of the Queen Mother pursued them and Sundiata's life was continually in danger. They moved from place to place until finally they were allowed to settle in Mema where their fortunes changed. By this time, Sundiata's physique and character were fully developed. He had amazing strength and courage and became a famous warrior. In addition, he possessed such a commanding personality that few people ever challenged instructions given by him. Although he was later to show himself a skilled diplomat, he had a fiery temperament that would brook no opposition from anyone. These qualities resulted in his appointment to the command of a cavalry division in Mema's army in which capacity he won notable victories for the local ruler. During absences of the ruler from his capital, Sundiata acted as viceroy of Mema, and was even named to succeed the childless ruler on his death.

Meanwhile, disaster had fallen upon Kangaba. The harshness of Sumanguru's rule had produced serious rebellions against Susu. The wrath of Sumanguru had been terrible: he had invaded Kangaba, laid waste the capital town of Jeriba, killed the royal princes and made himself the direct ruler of the state. Although Dankaran Touman fled, the Kangaba people were determined to regain their independence and in about 1230, they sent successful messengers to find Sundiata and ask him to be their leader.

Sundiata rose to the occasion. Accompanied by a small cavalry troop from Mema, he travelled westwards on a recruiting tour right across the Mandingo area. By a combination of diplomacy and a show of force, he persuaded Mandingo rulers to join him in war against Susu. Until his army was powerful enough, he skilfully evaded contact with the main Susu army; but at length, in 1235, he finally met the main Susu army, commanded by Sumanguru in person, at Kirina, near Kulikoro in the Niger valley.

Map VII   The Empire of Mali

49

Although the Susu outnumbered Sundiata's forces, his cavalry and superior generalship enabled him to win an overwhelming victory and Sumanguru was never seen again. Within a short time, Sundiata captured the strongly fortified and well garrisoned city of Susu itself and razed it to the ground. Over the next five years, he crushed all pockets of resistance in the Susu empire and, in 1240, destroyed the ancient city of Kumbi.

Having made himself master of the Susu empire, Sundiata's task was now to weld his allies and the conquered territories into an empire. At an impressive ceremony near the ruins of Jeriba one by one his allies surrendered the government of their kingdoms to Sundiata. Sundiata acknowledged their services in the wars of conquest and restored them to the rule of their own people not as independent monarchs but as sub-rulers under himself, the first Mansa of Mali. To each, he gave special titles, honours and privileges; to each he allotted particular duties in the new empire; and thus was born the empire of Mali.

Sundiata now set about the task of consolidating the power of his empire. He built a new capital at Niani near the confluence of the Niger and Sankarani and spent the rest of his life in developing its wealth. He encouraged agriculture, especially the growing of cotton, to supply the needs of the city; his generals conquered the gold-fields of Wangara and its supply of precious metal was diverted into Niani. Thus, aided by the excellent law and order enforced in his empire, Sundiata was able to attract North African merchants to Niani; and the prosperity which had once belonged to Ghana passed to Mali.

By the time Sundiata died mysteriously in 1255, he had conquered a vast area, laid the foundations of its wealth and established its system of government. He had successfully risen above the adversities of his early life to become one of the most heroic and constructive figures in West African history.

Mali after Sundiata's death
Sundiata was succeeded by his son, Mansa Uli (Wali), who reigned from 1255 to 1270 and conquered Bambuk and Bondu. However, between his death and the accession of Mansa Kankan Musa in 1312, there was a confused period in Mali's history. At least six different Mansas reigned during this short period due to a combination of dynastic disputes, struggles for power and a certain

amount of misrule. Oddly enough, the most successful ruler of this period was a usurper, Sakura (Sabakura), who reigned from about 1285 to 1300. This former chief of slaves was a notable warrior who made successful attacks on Tekrur and whose armies raided beyond Gao, the capital of the Songhai state. He may even have conquered the copper-mining centre of Takedda before he was eventually killed while returning from a pilgrimage to Mecca.

Mansa Musa the Magnificent, 1312–1337
Mansa Musa (Mansa Kankan Musa) used to be regarded as the great conqueror who founded the empire of Mali. This view, based on early Muslim writings, can no longer be held now that oral traditions have revealed the contributions of Sundiata and his successors. However, Mansa Musa could hardly have achieved his reputation had he not been a very successful ruler. Therefore it seems wisest to accept the old Muslim accounts of his victories but to put them into a different context. Thus, Mansa Musa occupied Timbuktu, and received the homage of Gao in 1325 after the victorious campaign of his great general, Sagmandir. But this was not the first time Mandingo forces had entered these cities. What Mansa Musa's forces did was to restore Mali's authority in areas that had repudiated its overlordship. It is possible that Walata and Taghaza came under Mali jurisdiction in his reign.

One of Mansa Musa's great contributions to Mali history was the spread of its fame and prestige abroad. He did this largely by his famous pilgrimage to Mecca between 1324 and 1326. He was not the first Mansa of Mali to go on a pilgrimage, but no West African ruler ever went to Mecca on such a lavish scale. He took an escort of about sixty thousand courtiers and servants, richly dressed and carrying three million pounds'-worth of gold in modern value. Everywhere he went, he became legendary for his generosity and the extravagant spending of his retinue. Wherever he halted on a Friday, he paid for the construction of a mosque; and his party spent so much gold in Cairo that the value of the precious metal fell there. So much did Mansa Musa disburse in charity, gifts and purchases that he had to borrow gold to pay the cost of his homeward journey. Every opportunity of advertising the great extent and power of his empire was taken. As a result, the power and wealth of Mali became known not only throughout the Islamic world but also in Europe.

Prestige has a practical value and Mansa Musa realized it and was able to develop friendly relations with North African rulers, especially the Sultan of the important Moroccan commercial centre of Fez. This, combined with the wealth, good government and growing Islamization of Mali, so encouraged trade between Mali and North Africa that Mansa Musa's reign was one of the greatest prosperity.

Mansa Musa is almost certainly the Mansa responsible for establishing Islam as the official religion of Mali cities. Famed for his personal piety, he was strict in observing the five pillars of Islam: prayers five times a day, attendance at congregational prayer on Friday, fasting during Ramadan, the giving of alms and the pilgrimage to Mecca. He made the Id celebrations at the end of Ramadan a national ceremony, built imposing mosques in several cities and probably insisted that Mali Muslims should worship and live according to true Muslim precepts as far as they were known and practicable. His encouragement of Islam extended into the field of education for he gave generous patronage to the *ulama**. This not only encouraged indigenous scholars in their study and teaching of Islamic sciences but also attracted Muslim scholars from other parts of the Islamic world. Thus, Timbuktu became one of the foremost centres of Islamic scholarship in the world. This had a number of practical advantages. Literacy in Arabic facilitated the transaction of government business and also improved political and commercial dealings with North Africa. And Islamic studies not only improved the quality of Islam in Mali but added immensely to its prestige abroad.

Mansa Musa's Islamic contact with North Africa also brought important development in architecture. On his return from Mecca, he was accompanied by an Andalusian poet and architect named Es-Saheli. Es-Saheli built Musa, a distinguished palace in Timbuktu, and a number of improved mosques in Mali cities including Timbuktu and Gao. The architectural style and materials used by Es-Saheli were new to Mali for he introduced the flat roof of North Africa, the pyramidal minaret and the use of burnt bricks.

Although there were limits to the depth of the Islam enforced by Mansa Musa, he firmly established the religion as the cult of

ulama = muslim scholars

the ruling and commercial classes. His motives for this were two-fold. In the first place, Islam demands that a good Muslim has the duty of spreading the faith and encouraging its proper observance. Secondly, Islam had an important political value for Mansa Musa. Within the western Sudan, the most important areas in politics and commerce were the great cities. Most of these were non-Mandingo cities and the Mansa of Mali, a semi-divine ruler with control of the Mandingo religious cults, could not command the religious loyalty of non-Mandingo peoples. Yet should these peoples become Muslim, they automatically acquired a religious bond with their Mandingo ruler and had a religious duty to obey him so long as he was a just Muslim ruler. It is also possible that Mansa Musa needed non-Mandingo political support because he was not a direct descendant of Sundiata and had only become ruler by chance.

Thus Mansa Musa still remains the greatest ruler of Mali, not because he was its greatest conqueror but because he was the great consolidator who built ably on the foundations laid by Sundiata and Sakura. He was its greatest ruler because he ruled Mali at its greatest point in history. He inherited a great empire; he preserved and extended its greatness. Above all, he spread its fame abroad by his conscious advertisement of its power and wealth, his work for Islam and his attempts to elevate the royal dignity in the cities of the empire. It is also probable that he improved government control over the non-Mandingo portions of the empire and encouraged the rise of Timbuktu from obscurity to primacy in the trans-Saharan trade.

THE DECLINE OF MALI

Whereas the rise of Mali was swift, its decline was gradual and not until the seventeenth century did Mali completely lose its political identity. However, by the mid-fifteenth century, it had lost its ability to dominate the affairs of the western Sudan. The first outward signs of Mali's weakness occurred in the reign of Mansa Musa's son, Maghan I, 1337 to 1341, when the Mossi of Upper Volta raided across Mali and devastated Timbuktu. At about the same time Songhai rebelled and gained its independence. Possibly Maghan I was handicapped in preserving Mali's unity by two adverse factors. One was the hostility of his uncle

Sulaiman, who as brother to Mansa Musa had a strong matrilineal claim to succeed him and who in fact became ruler of Mali on Maghan's death. The other was royal poverty: for although Mansa Musa's reign had been glorious, it had been extravagant of royal wealth; and a ruler who could not dispense generous patronage lost one of the essential cements of imperial unity.

Sulaiman, 1341 to 1359, had to face the same problems. His wise policy of retrenchment earned him an unenviable reputation for meanness; and he was obliged to imprison his senior wife for a plot involving army commanders to overthrow him in favour of Mari Jata, son of Maghan I and Sulaiman's successor in 1359. Thus it is not surprising that his reign saw the loss of Walata to the Berbers and successful raids upon Mali's western provinces by Tekrur. Yet the thrifty and capable Sulaiman consolidated his hold on the remainder of the empire, still large and powerful. As Ibn Battuta reported in 1352, he provided strict and honest justice, preserved excellent law and order and successfully continued the process of building Mali into an Islamic state. Trade with North Africa continued to flourish and strong ties of diplomatic friendship were maintained with Fez.

Sulaiman was the last great Mali ruler. After his death, Mali unity was shattered by dynastic struggles for power, effete rulers and the reduction of the Mansa's personal influence on politics. Sulaiman's son, Kamba (Qasa), was deposed and killed by Mari Jata II, who reigned from 1360 to 1374. He is said to have been an oppressive ruler, who ruined Mali by his extravagance. This forced him to sell cheaply the famous gold nugget of enormous size, which was the central reserve of the Mansa's treasury. Whether Mari Jata's bankruptcy and oppression were really the result of extravagance or a symptom of increasing royal poverty may never be known. What is certain is that serious illness for the last two years of his reign helped to remove the hand of the Mansa from control of Mali politics. Thus his successor, Musa II, 1374 to 1387, although a well-intentioned monarch, had to surrender real authority to his chief minister, another Mari Jata.

This able minister made determined efforts to restore Mali's military fortunes and was able to put down a Tuareg rebellion in Takedda. His raids however could never inflict a decisive defeat on Songhai and so the important trade of Gao contributed nothing to the Mansa's resources. However, his personal power had further contributed to cheapening the office of Mansa and destroying its authority. Between 1387 and 1390, three rulers— Maghan II, Sandiki and an unnamed relative of Mari Jata— perished in the struggle for power before Maghan III, 1390 to 1400, eventually became Mansa.

With Maghan III's accession in 1390, our knowledge of Mali rulers ends and interest focuses on the disastrous results of Mali's disunity. The Soninke state of Diara threw off the Mali yoke and the Mossi, Tuareg and Songhai mounted increasingly successful pressure on the empire. In about 1400, the Mossi plundered deep into Masina, while the Songhai at last emerged from their long struggle to preserve the independence of Gao and began to occupy Mali territory. The Tuareg seized the commercial towns of Arawan, Walata and Timbuktu in about 1433 and ruined Mali's control of the trans-Saharan trade. Finally, from 1464, the Songhai began their westward advance under the leadership first of Sunni Ali and then Askia Muhammad which robbed the Mansas of all their territories except the Mandingo homeland itself.

THE MANDINGO ACHIEVEMENT

The ultimate collapse of the empire of Mali must not blind us to the immensity of Mandingo achievement. Out of a number of unsophisticated and oppressed chieftaincies, they welded a nation whose appointed leaders dominated the affairs of the western Sudan for over a hundred and fifty years. At the death of Mansa Musa, the influence of Mali was felt as far west as the Atlantic coast; and in the east, its vague frontiers bordered on Hausaland. Except in the Volta region, where the stubbornly independent Mossi successfully resisted all foreign advances, its southern boundaries penetrated the forest belt. To the North, its control extended over an ill-defined area of the desert including the valuable salt mines of Taghaza and the copper mines of Takedda. Since Mali also monopolized the output of the Wangara gold mines, its position in the trans-Saharan trade was much more favourable than Ghana's had been.

Yet wealth and power are rarely the accidents of history. They rest on the character of a people: their initiative, resolution and ability to shape their environment to their purpose. Success largely depends upon the quality of the social and political institutions they evolve and the suitability of these institutions to the needs of the age they serve. On such firm foundations rested the Mandingo success until their state system failed to control or accommodate the private ambitions of its citizens.

Ibn Battuta's impression of Mali
Our most detailed account of life in the empire of Mali is that of Ibn Battuta, a Berber of Tangier, who visited Mali in 1532 when the empire had already passed the peak of its greatness. Accustomed to seeing African peoples only in the role of slaves, he was amazed to find them governing an empire which rivalled anything he had seen in North Africa and on his extensive travels in Asia. Ibn Battuta was immensely impressed by the ceremony and majesty that surrounded the Mansa, a true reflection of his exalted status and the wealth at his command. When the Mansa gave a public audience, he proceeded at a stately pace to a special three-tiered dais covered with silks and cushions and with its ceiling supported by elephant tusks. Before him came a throng of dancers and praise-singers; behind him advanced a bodyguard of three hundred warriors. Dressed in a scarlet gown over a voluminous pair of trousers, and wearing a golden skull-cap encircled with gold brocade, the Mansa took his seat on the audience platform. Beside him thirty Turkish *mamelukes* displayed his state umbrella and personal standards. Around him sat his army commanders; before him were his cavalry chiefs. Immediately beside him were his Executioner and Interpreter; while his bodyguard flanked the pavilion on both sides. Tethered to the pavilion were two fine horses and before its entrance were placed two goats to shield the ruler from the evil eye.

Once the business of the day began, the semi-divine status of the Mansa became apparent. Individuals addressed from the throne removed their gowns and put on a dirty cap and ragged clothing. With their trousers raised above the knees, they advanced on all fours sprinkling dirt on their head and shoulders. They remained in this position of humility until, their business completed, they returned to their place in the crowd. If remarks were addressed to the assembled throng, everybody removed his turban, and the entire dialogue was punctuated by the army

56

commanders twanging their bow-strings as a mark of respectful approval.

A Muslim himself, Ibn Battuta was also impressed by the apparent devotion of the people of Niani to Islam. They regularly observed the daily prayer times and on Fridays the mosque was so packed for congregational prayers that men sent their slaves early to reserve their places. Such emphasis was placed on koranic knowledge that children were assigned passages of the Koran to learn by heart and were kept chained up until they knew them. On the great Muslim festivals, such as Id al-Fitr after the fast of Ramadan, the people flocked with their ruler to the prayer ground to pray and listen to the sermon. Afterwards, the Imam addressed the people on the subject of their duty to God and to their ruler, whom they should obey and to whom they should loyally pay their taxes. Later, at court, there were dances and singing at which *griots* clothed in feathers and wearing bird masks sang the Mansa's praises and also whispered frank criticsm of his government in his ears.

Ibn Battuta hardly approved of the activities of these *griots*. Equally, he noted that Mali women enjoyed a freedom and importance not accorded to their sex in North Africa. Married women were not confined in purdah and were allowed to associate with other men besides their husbands. Young girls commonly walked about naked, something strictly taboo to Muslims. Not all meat was killed according to Muslim requirements and when a pagan Wangara delegation came to greet the Mansa, they were provided with a slave-girl for a cannibal feast. He also suggests that Islamic law was little followed although learned Muslim judges were highly respected.

Possibly, the thing that impressed Ibn Battuta most was the character of the people and the quality of their government. He records that the people were of exceptional honesty and that the government strictly punished anyone who engaged in dishonest practices. The corrupt governor of Walata, for example, was completely stripped of his possessions and privileges. Equally, law and order were so well maintained that a man laden with valuable goods could travel the length and breadth of the empire without fear of molestation. The whole atmosphere of the empire was one of peace and prosperity.

Whether he realized it or not Ibn Battuta had recorded im-

57

portant observations not only on Mali's wealth but also on the nature of the Mandingo religion and kingship.

Mandingo religion ˙
The Mali empire was founded by non-Muslims. For the Mandingos, like the Soninke, worshipped a number of ancestral gods who directly intervened in human affairs. Each deity had its own cult, its own shrines and its own cult priests. These conducted sacrifices and sought guidance on courses of action to be followed both by the state and private individuals. There were evil spirits to be protected against by charms and good ones to please. There were religious methods for detecting criminals and witches who brought affliction on others. There were religious cures to be applied for most illnesses which involved not only the invocation of spirits but also the application of efficacious herbal remedies. For everything in life there was a religious cause and a religious answer, and consequently the cult priests dominated every aspect of Mandingo life. The ceremonies and practices to which Ibn Battuta objected were the external manifestations of the deep-rooted traditional religion of the Mandingos. To have destroyed it would have destroyed their ethnic cohesion and broken the mainspring of the Mansa's authority over his Mandingo subjects. Right up until recent times, the vast majority of Mandingos adhered closely to their traditional beliefs.

Yet, Ibn Battuta spoke warmly of the quality and quantity of Islamic observance in Mali. The explanation of this apparent contradiction is twofold. Ibn Battuta visited the towns where, for commercial, political, and religious reasons, Islam was encouraged and enforced. But the bulk of the peoples of the Mali empire dwelt in the countryside where Islam was little practised. Secondly, the Mandingo religion was not an exclusive one; new cults could be founded to worship new or neglected gods. Thus, the acceptance of Islam meant the adoption of an imperial cult capable of being embraced within all the various ethnic religions. And a prestigious cult it was: with its magnificent mosques, its reputation for miracles and medicine and its sought-after koranic charms; with its mastery of the art of literacy, its contacts with the Islamic world and its fund of useful political value. Whether or not the Mansa themselves held a deeper Muslim faith than this will never be known.

The government of Mali
Basically, the governmental system of Mali was the same as that of Ghana. The Mansa was a semi-divine ruler whose political power was based on the spiritual headship of his people. His personal power depended on whether or not his character enabled him to control the pronouncements of the religious cults, all of which he headed. A weak ruler could be as easily dominated by the cults as a strong one could bend them to his will. Equally, the semi-divine status of the Mansa could be invoked to seclude him from effective contact with political life. The Mansa had an immensely strong position but only as long as he was forceful enough to use it.

The adoption of Islam strengthened the position of the Mansa as long as he did not neglect the traditional cults. Islam is a universal religion whereas ethnic cults are not. And Islam, while denying the validity of ruler-worship, does preach temporal obedience to earthly rulers as long as they are just Muslims. By careful conformity with the required externals of Islam and generous patronage of *ulama* and holy men, most Mansas could be assured of support from leading Muslims.

The Mansa also had considerable personal resources of his own. Both by inheritance and conquest, he acquired a number of slave villages. The peoples of these villages had the duty of providing the Mansa annually with fixed quantities of produce or service so that all the needs of the Mansa and his court were supplied. The most celebrated group of slave villagers were the *arbi*, who provided the Mansa's domestic servants, his personal bodyguard and royal messengers. Their personal relationship with the Mansa was so special that he could rely implicitly on their loyalty to his person.

The Mansa had a definite need for a personal military retinue. One of the weaknesses of the Mali constitution was that it was never clearly established whether or not succession was by patrilineal or matrilineal inheritance. Thus disputed successions were common and the fact that provincial governors were close relatives of the Mansa, with provincial forces at their command, further increased the danger of revolution.

Associated with the Mansa in the central government of Mali were a host of councillors and officials, some the inheritors of traditional titles from their forebears, others possibly the appoint-

59

ees of the Mansa; some non-Muslim, others Muslim. Unfortunately, we do not know the details of the various 'ministries' of Mali, but obviously no successful Mansa could ignore the advice of his leading noblemen.

Local government is more clearly defined. The Mandingo areas, being directly ruled by the Mansa, were divided into provinces each governed by a Dya-Mana-Tigi, who was either a relative or trusted friend of the Mansa. Each province was subdivided into districts composed of a number of villages, the district head being entitled Kafo-Tigi. At the bottom of the scale, but in some ways the most important, was the village community under a Dugu-Tigi who was head of the village cults. The duties of the local government officials were to see that the annual tithe on produce and livestock was properly assessed and collected, ensure that local levies were forthcoming for the army in time of need, preserve law and order and administer petty justice. Serious cases would be referred to higher authority and the Mansa himself was the supreme court of appeal.

The conquered peoples of tributary states were indirectly ruled. Their natural rulers, once appointed by their own people, were confirmed in office by the Mansa or his representative at investiture ceremonies where the tributary ruler did homage and took an oath of allegiance. The sub-ruler was responsible for the provision annually of a block tribute, the local assessment and collection of which was left to him. Tributary states also had the obligation of providing quotas for the imperial army and of accepting the Mansa's justice. In some cases, a tributary ruler had to accept at his court a Mandingo resident known as a Fari-ba whose function was to safeguard imperial interests. This was particularly true of commercial cities where the supervision of collection of taxes on trade was essential to the well-being of the imperial treasury.

Other sources of revenue were all gold nuggets found, tolls for using trade routes controlled by Mali, and the ample spoils of war. From revenue, the Mansa maintained his court, financed military expeditions, paid the cost of administration, and rewarded loyal service. The regular method of payment for officials was that each retained a fixed percentage of the revenue he collected. In addition, the Mansa was expected to make costly presents such as robes, horses, gold or grants of slave villages.

For valour in war, he awarded golden bracelets, necklaces and anklets. The highest award of all was an enormous pair of trousers; the wider they were, the more distinguished was the wearer. In the award of such honours the Mansa needed to be extremely judicious. To be a great Mansa was to be a great man.

THE REASONS FOR THE RISE AND FALL OF MALI

In the chapter on Ghana, we indicated the technique of ascertaining and illustrating historical causation. In applying this technique to Mali, we see that the first reason for the rise of Mali was the power vacuum created by Ghana's decline. The subsequent oppression of Sumanguru forced the Mandingo to unite and their latent military genius was brought to light and success by the inspiration of Sundiata. He proved capable not only of generalship and diplomacy but also of consolidating his newly won empire. The Keyta dynasty also produced other outstanding leaders such as Mansas Uli, Musa, Sulaiman and even the usurper Sakura. Yet leadership is only part, albeit an important part, of the story. For the Mandingo built a governmental system, based on religion, which provided authority to able rulers and continued to function when Mansas were ineffectual or involved in dynastic struggles. The combination of central control and local autonomy made vassaldom less irksome than it might have been; and the ability of the ethnic religions to absorb Islam provided a medium for uniting the great commercial cities under common rule. Once established, the vastness of its financial sources and military power enabled Mali to enjoy to the full the geographical advantages the western Sudan offered to people who took the initiative.

The decline of the empire can be accounted for firstly by dynastic struggles within the empire. Nurtured by personal ambitions that no state system can entirely hope to satisfy, dynastic rivalries were encouraged by the absence of a clearly defined law of succession and the official power held by many members of the royal family. Also contributing to a growing weakness in royal authority was the ambition of powerful noblemen to usurp royal authority by secluding the semi-divine ruler from human contact. These

61

factors, combined with the ineffectual government of some inadequate Mansas, weakened the central power. This process was further aided by the growing royal bankruptcy either through extravagance, maladministration or failing gold supplies.

This weakening of the centre gave the opportunity for ambitious individuals and tributary states to seek independence of the Mansa's control. These tendencies may have been encouraged by increased taxation and less central generosity as imperial wealth declined. Each unsuccessful rebellion, each palace coup, each successful independence movement made it increasingly difficult for Mali to withstand her external enemies, most notable of whom were the Tuareg, Mossi, and later the independent Songhai. Under such a combination of circumstances no empire could survive, and it is remarkable that the Mandingo preserved the integrity of their homeland from the even greater empire of Songhai that rose to take its place.

Questions

1 Write an account of the life and work of Sundiata.

2 Assess the role of Mansa Kankan Musa in the history of Mali.

3 Compare the character and achievements of Sundiata and Mansa Kankan Musa.

4 Outline the history of the Mandingos from 1230 to 1337, or from 1337 to 1390.

5 How do you account for (a) the rise and (b) the fall of Mali?

6 What were the main things that impressed Ibn Battuta about the empire of Mali? What important factors in Mali history are evident from his account of Mali under Sulaiman?

7 What were the main sources of political strength of the Mansas of Mali in the fourteenth century? What could weaken the position of a Mansa?

8 Give an account of Islam in Mali in the fourteenth century. What was its true position in Mali society?

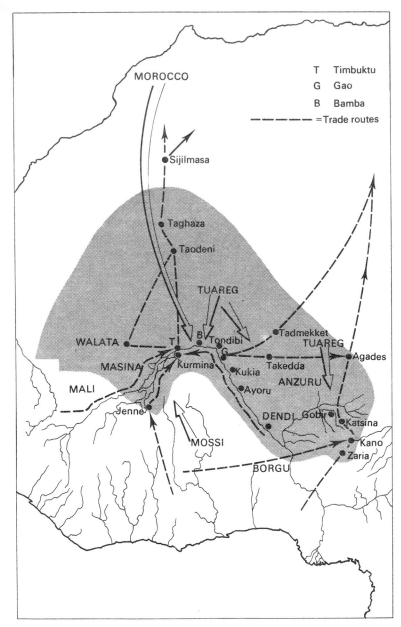

Map VIII   The Empire of Songhai

5

The Songhai empire

The Negro progenitors of the Songhai peoples were peoples living in small communities on both sides of the Niger in the Dendi area. The main factor differentiating these peoples from each other was occupation: the Da were sedentary farmers who rarely left the confines of their villages; the Gow were hunters; and the Sorko were skilled fishermen and canoe-men. Gradually, the Sorko established their rule over the other Songhai peoples. This was due to the growth of imperial ambition among the Sorko and even more to their great mobility along the Niger, which enabled them both to conquer and govern effectively a considerable riverain state. It is likely that they founded Gungia (Kukia) as a state capital from which centre they imposed an oppressive rule on the other Songhai peoples. Thus in Songhai mythology, the Sorko were depicted as a fierce river beast with a ring in the end of its nose.

The rule of the Sorko was brought to an end by an invasion of warrior bands from the north-east. These may have been the dark-skinned Zaghawa nomads from north of Lake Chad. The date of the actual arrival of these invaders is disputed between reputable historians: some suggest A.D. 690, others opt for A.D. 850. The exact date is not so important as the fact that a new ruling class was established under the leadership of Za Alieman and that not all the virile Sorko acquiesced in his rule. According to one tradition, a Sorko chief, Faran Maka, regrouped his forces and moved northwards to found Gao. Later, under further pressure from the south, the Sorko established colonies along the river as far as Lake Debo.

THE HISTORY OF THE ZA DYNASTY

Za Alieman and his companions intermarried with the indigenous population and gradually took on much of the physical appearance, language and customs of their subjects. After Za Alieman, no Za of particular note reigned until Za Kosoi, the fifteenth Za. He is famous as the first Muslim ruler of the Songhai. Converted by peaceful persuasion, he compelled the ruling classes of Songhai to accept the new imperial cult. He appointed Muslim officials and imposed the practice of circumcision upon them. Possibly more important, he moved the capital of Songhai northwards to Gao which was much better placed for sharing in the trans-Saharan trade. Thus once again we see the motive of international trade for the expansion of empire and the promotion of Islam. Historians also disagree on the dates of Za Kosoi: some favour A.D. 1009, others A.D. 1100. The authors of this book favour the earlier dates of 690 for the warrior invasion and 1009 for Za Kosoi, not least because they are those suggested by the famous seventeenth-century western Sudanic scholar, Al-Sadi.

Gao gradually became one of the foremost trading centres in West Africa, attracting merchants from Morocco and Tunis. But Songhai was not yet a great military power and the city itself was unfortified. Consequently, it was conquered by the Mandingos in the thirteenth century and incorporated in the Mali empire. However, the Songhai never willingly accepted Mali overlordship and won their independence, according to one account, on the death of Mansa Musa.

THE FOUNDATION OF THE SUNNI DYNASTY

The story runs that, in the reign of Za Yosiboi, Gao fell to the armies of Mansa Musa. On his return from Mecca, Mansa Musa received the homage of Gao and took two Songhai princes, Ali Kolon and Sulaiman Nar, as honoured hostages to his court. There was nothing peculiar about this: it was the custom for sons of tributary rulers to be brought up at their lord's court not only as guarantee of the loyalty of their father but also as an honourable and sought-after training for an administrative and military career. Ali Kolon distinguished himself in Mansa Musa's service and through military and diplomatic activities obtained a good knowledge of the highways and by-ways of Mali. On Mansa Musa's death, he put this knowledge to good account when with his brother Sulaiman he fled to Gao. There he organized a national rising which expelled the Mandingo garrison and proclaimed him ruler of independent Songhai with the title of Sunni, meaning 'liberator'.

This is but one tradition of how Songhai gained its independence. There is another theory which is very attractive and may be proved one day to be more correct. This is that Ali Kolon was in fact not the son of Yosiboi but was a discontented official of Mali who fled to Songhai and established himself as an independent ruler there in about 1275. This theory would fit in with the idea that Gao was first occupied by Sundiata's forces and that the ravages of Sakura were merely the suppression of Ali Kolon's rebellion. Thus Sagmandir's conquest of Gao would have been the suppression of yet another Songhai rebellion. It does not tell us, however, how the Sunni dynasty came into existence if Za Yosiboi was the ruler in 1325. At the moment sufficient research has not yet been done into the connections of this theory with the rest of the history of the western Sudan for us to fit it into a satisfactory pattern with other established facts.

Songhai under the Sunni dynasty
Independent Songhai was not a powerful state. Its main preoccupation was to preserve its independence against attacks by the Mandingo, Mossi and Tuareg. However, the decline of Mali provided Songhai rulers with the opportunity to build the greatest indigenous empire in the history of West Africa. By the reign of Sunni Ma Dogo, alias Muhammed Da'o, who reigned round about 1420, Songhai was powerful enough to force tribute from some of the Bambara in the Masina area. A later ruler, Sulaiman Dama (Dandi), who died in about 1464 or 1465, conquered the province of Mema which had recently won its independence of Mali. Thus the stage was set for the conquests of one of Songhai's greatest rulers, the brilliant but notorious Sunni Ali, 1464/5 to 1492.

The Character of Sunni Ali
Judging from the accounts of Muslim historians who hated him,

67

Sunni Ali was a man of unstable temperament. An arbitrary tyrant, he was sometimes savagely cruel, at others kind and generous. He had an ungovernable temper and when in a rage would condemn to death even his friends and loyal servants for trivial reasons. Afterwards, when his rage subsided, he would feel deep remorse for his conduct. Vengeful and vindictive to people who betrayed him or whom he did not trust, he treated the *ulama* of Timbuktu with brutal severity and hounded Fulani clans on the slightest provocation. Al-Sadi described him as a scoundrel, libertine and tyrant who gloried in the massacre of the learned and the pious. One story of Al-Sadi's is that Sunni Ali once ordered the *ulama* of Timbuktu to send thirty maidens to him at Kabara. When the girls collapsed with exhaustion on the way, he commanded that they all be executed. It is thus small wonder that few men dared to disobey Sunni Ali.

The *ulama* also classed Sunni Ali as an infidel who made a mockery of the worship of God. They related how he paid little attention to the prayer ritual in the mosque, frequently neglected to pray at the daily hours of prayer laid down by Islam, and, if he was very busy, contented himself with muttering the names of the prayers in the evening. Probably, Sunni Ali was not so hostile to Muslims as the *ulama* claimed and there are instances of his giving generous patronage to selected scholars. He was not prepared, however, to patronize or respect Muslim scholars and holy men who intrigued with the Tuareg and would not support his policies: policies which he refused to allow them to dictate. As a man of action, Sunni Ali was impatient at religious interruptions in his day's work. Also, as the semi-divine leader of a Songhai national movement, he had little need to placate the Muslims. His contempt for Muslim opposition was possibly Sunni Ali's greatest political weakness but it was based on the confidence that he could manage without Muslims.

The essential greatness of Sunni Ali lay in his martial qualities and strategic insight. A robust and warlike leader who devoted most of his life to conquest, he was both a great warrior himself and an inspiring war-leader. He employed his cavalry with such deadly effect that he never lost a single battle. In the words of his most hostile critic: he was always the conqueror, never the conquered. He saw clearly that the key to power lay in unchallenged control of the great trading cities and the desert route to North

68

Africa. Consequently he devoted much military effort to chastening the Tuareg and Mossi, who endangered his attempt to take over the role of Mali and threatened communications along the Niger, the lifeline between the eastern and western parts of his empire. To make maximum use of the Niger for imperial security and advance, he had constructed a large fleet of war canoes commanded by a Sorko, and he even planned to link Walata to the Niger by means of a canal.

Thus, Sunni Ali was no ignorant warrior dedicated to war for its own sake; and Songhai was fortunate to have a ruler of his calibre at a time when it was already poised for imperial expansion.

The achievements of Sunni Ali
Sunni Ali's first major achievement was the conquest of Timbuktu in 1468. Soon after his accession, the leading officials of the city appealed to him to rescue them from the oppression of the Tuareg. Expecting aid from the citizens, particularly in transport across the Niger, Sunni Ali advanced south of the river. By the time his forces lay opposite Kabara, however, the people of Timbuktu had realized that Sunni Ali might make a more powerful master than Akil the Tuareg. Consequently, they provided no transport and the furious Sunni Ali had to retire. Later he advanced north of the river, stormed the city and massacred many of its inhabitants, including *ulama*. As many of the *ulama* had fled towards Walata at his approach, he employed armed bands to hunt them down for three years. He never forgave Timbuktu, and his harsh rule caused many people to leave the city.

Sunni Ali's forces consolidated their hold on the Masina area and then attacked the proud city of Jenne with its history of semi-independence. The main value of Jenne at this time was that it had grown wealthy by tapping the gold resources of Bonduku and possibly Asante. Such a valuable prize, however, was not easy to secure for Jenne was surrounded on all sides by waterways and marshes which seriously handicapped Songhai cavalry. Added to these natural defences were imposing man-made fortifications and so the Songhai were forced to resort to siege tactics. According to tradition, Jenne held out for seven years, seven months and seven days before finally opening its gates to the Songhai in 1473. Yet its fall did not witness the brutality inflicted on Timbuktu. Its young ruler was treated with honour, his mother became a wife of Sunni Ali and the citizens found the Songhai generous victors. By this time, either Sunni Ali's temper had mellowed or he had learned greater political wisdom.

In about 1480, Sunni Ali began his fantastic scheme for constructing a canal to Walata. The project was never completed for work was interrupted by a Mossi raid across Masina which succeeded in reaching and sacking Walata. Sunni Ali's forces fell upon the returning Mossi at a place called Jiniki To'oi in 1483 and seriously defeated them. For three years, the Songhai raided deep into the Mossi area and shattered their offensive power. Although they failed to incorporate the Mossi within the empire, the Songhai were able to consolidate their grasp on Hombori and to conquer Gurma west of the Mossi states.

This is the last great military achievement recorded of Sunni Ali, who met his death by drowning in 1492 while returning from a successful expedition against the Fulani of Gurma. He had already allowed the Portuguese to establish a trading factory at Wadan in the far west. Whether his intention was to break Muslim domination of the trans-Saharan trade or whether he hoped to discourage Portuguese ambitions by allowing them to trade only in an insignificant oasis we shall never know. He had also provided for the government of his new empire by appointing provincial governors such as the Dendi-Fari and the Tondi-Fari (Hombori area) to govern sections of his vastly enlarged state; and he had laid down the terms by which rulers of conquered states accepted tributary status. A kingdom had grown into an empire, and the foundations had been laid for greater expansion under Askia Muhammad.

THE ACCESSION OF ASKIA MUHAMMAD

Soon after Sunni Ali's death his son, Abubakar Da'o (Sunni Baro), was deposed by his father's chief minister, Muhammad Towri ibn Abubakar, who took the title of Askia Muhammad. According to one tradition that is obviously intended to justify Muhammad's seizure of power, he thrice demanded that Abubakar Da'o should whole-heartedly accept Islam and when

Abubakar refused to abandon the Songhai religion he led a successful rebellion against him. The defeated supporters of Abubakar Da'o fled to the Ayoru region of Dendi taking with them most of the sacred treasures of the Songhai cults. There they established themselves as rulers of the Songhai homeland until finally defeated by Askia Muhammad in 1500, when they moved into obscurity in the arid Anzuru region.

Although there were strong religious undertones in Askia Muhammad's seizure of power, we must see his success as the result of a long and cleverly organized pursuit of personal power. As Sunni Ali's chief minister, he had played a key role in the government of the state and his caution and diplomacy had provided an excellent foil for the intemperate genius of his royal master. He is reputed to have won the gratitude of Sunni Ali by delays in carrying out hasty orders given in a fit of passion, thus enabling the orders to be reversed when Sunni Ali was in a more temperate mood. Since this often resulted in escape from execution for influential Songhai, Askia Muhammad must have built up a considerable reservoir of important gratitude. Also, he may well have ingratiated himself with the frustrated but influential Muslim elements embittered against the house of Sunni Ali.

Askia's measures to secure power
The ease with which Askia Muhammad displaced Abubakar Da'o did not alter the fact that he was a usurper who had to make his rule acceptable to survive as ruler of Songhai. He was not a member of the Songhai royal family, nor did he possess the sacred symbols of the national cults. He may not even have been Songhai and it is generally held that he was of Soninke lineage. With these constitutional disadvantages, it is little wonder that he sought the undivided loyalty of his Muslim co-religionists. *Ulama* and holy men were gratified to find themselves the recipients of bounteous patronage from a ruler who advanced the cause of Islam in every practicable way. They were flattered by consultation on the legality of Askia Muhammad's rule and on the correct exercise of executive and judicial power within the empire. In particular, Askia Muhammad was later to show great concern to secure the approbation of the distinguished cleric and scholar, Al-Maghili, who visited Songhai during his reign. But long before this, Askia

Muhammad had brought off a diplomatic triumph of the greatest magnitude. Between 1497 and 1498, he made an ostentatious pilgrimage to Mecca, during which he secured appointment as Kalif of West Africa from the exalted Sharif of Mecca. This title enabled him to claim the undivided loyalty and obedience of all West African Muslims.

Equally, Askia Muhammad must have done much to conciliate he non-Muslim Songhai. Although in the interests of his own security as well as military efficiency he formed a large standing army in place of Sunni Ali's complete reliance on provincial levies, he realized that government without a broad base of Songhai support was an insecure foundation for his rule. He therefore made no attempt to enforce Islam on the rural Songhai, and the head priest of the Songhai ethnic religion continued to hold high office in Songhai government. Thus we may assume that whatever his personal religious attitude to the Songhai cults, Askia Muhammad recognized their importance and won their support. Military success and the increasing prosperity of his reign both consolidated his position and enhanced the social standing of Islam.

Character of Askia Muhammad
The picture that emerges of Askia Muhammad from the recorded achievements of his life and the eulogies of Muslim historians is an impressive one. A war-leader of equal genius to that of Sunni Ali, he was more skilled in the arts of peace. Intelligent, wise, calculating, temperate and urbane, he realized fully the need for associating all the important elements of Songhai society in the work of government. He was a brilliant administrator who re-organized the system of government and strengthened the central power. A lover of justice and law and order, he provided Songhai with firm but equitable government. Trade and education he encouraged and, although not a scholar himself, he is reputed to have been the first Songhai ruler to send his children to koranic school. He was thus a far-sighted man of many skills and virtues and was to utilize the human and economic resources of Songhai to bring the empire to the peak of its achievement.

The Conquests of Askia Muhammad
Once Askia Muhammad had returned from his pilgrimage, he

72

began a career of imperial expansion. In 1498, using the refusal of Nassere of Yatenga to embrace Islam as an excuse, he ravaged the Mossi area. Although the Mossi were not conquered, their military strength was so weakened that Songhai was free of any immediate danger of attack from that quarter. Then, in 1499, Songhai armies began their great westward advance with the conquest of Bagana, even though its Mali defenders were aided by the Fulani. A successful campaign against the redoubtable Mali general, Fati Qualli, gave him control of Diara in 1502, and by 1507 Songhai forces had conquered Galam on the fringes of Tekrur. There the main advance of Songhai halted but the influence of the Askia must have been felt down the Senegal valley to the coast.

Meanwhile, Askia Muhammad had pushed his power down the Niger. As we have seen, he expelled his Sunni opponents from control of Ayoru south of Gungia in 1500; and in 1505, he invaded Borgu. There, difficult terrain, the tsetse menace to his horses, and the fortifications of Borgu towns made conquest impossible. Although the Songhai devastated a considerable area, their losses in men were enormous. Yet the cunning Askia Muhammad seems to have anticipated these casualties for the van of his attacking forces was composed of the descendants of the ancient Za dynasty, who might once again have sought mastery of Songhai now that Sunni's power was broken.

Askia Muhammad's frontiers now bordered on the Hausa states which had risen to prosperity in the previous century. In about 1513, Askia Muhammad ordered his forces to move into north-western Hausaland. Gobir, Katsina and Zaria offered little resistance; their rulers were killed, the cities plundered. Only Kano, behind its mighty walls, offered determined resistance and in recognition of the gallantry of its people their ruler was spared. However, he was brought into the Songhai orbit by marriage to a daughter of the Askia and obliged to pay one-third of his annual revenue as tribute to the Askia.

Songhai's attempt to dominate the trade of Hausaland brought the empire into conflict with the Tuareg of Aïr. From their commercial centre of Agades, they both controlled Hausaland's trade with North Africa and also frequently plundered the Hausa states. Therefore, Askia Muhammad decided to break Tuareg control of Agades. In alliance with Kanta of Kebbi, he invaded

73

Aïr, occupied Agades and expelled its Tuareg inhabitants in favour of Songhai colonists. However, Songhai power east of the Niger was of short duration; for Kebbi, feeling insufficiently rewarded for its aid to Songhai, rebelled in 1516 and soon established its own supremacy in Hausaland.

Songhai under the rule of Askia Muhammad

The conquest of Agades represents the height of Songhai power. At that time, Songhai power ran from Hausaland in the east to the Senegal in the west. Its southern boundaries ran north of the Mandingo and Mossi homelands except where they thrust down the Niger to tail out in Borgu. Most of the desert to the north was under Songhai influence including Taghaza which was only a month's journey from Morocco. Its economic resources were enormous: the gold of Wangara, Bonduku and possibly Asante passed through the cities of the empire; the copper mines of Takedda and the most important salt mines in the desert were directly under its control; and its victories provided slaves for labour and export. These were the essential bases of the prosperity that financed a magnificent court and a standing army notable for its cavalry power.

The opulence and power of the Songhai empire of Askia Muhammad is amply demonstrated in the writings of Leo Africanus, who started a long tour of the Sudan in 1510. Although he was not impressed by Songhai architecture, he wrote in wonderment of the Askia's collection of gold plate and sceptres, claiming that some pieces weighed 1300 pounds. He described the court ceremonial which was similar to that of earlier empires in the western Sudan and admired the imperial bodyguard of 3000 cavalrymen and numerous archers. The Askia had the right of first choice of imported Arab horses, a privilege he did not abuse by offering niggardly payment. Gold was so abundant in the markets of Gao that its owners could not always dispose of it. Justice, law and order prevailed; Islam was firmly established, its teachings faithfully observed, and its scholarship flourishing.

Askia Muhammad's domestic policies

At home, Askia Muhammad followed a policy of maintaining law and order, expanding trade and encouraging Islam. Law and order he enforced through the strictest central control of local

74

government yet seen in the western Sudan and by rigid insistence on honesty and justice in public administration. Peace and justice in themselves encouraged the growth of trade but Askia Muhammad, whose ambition was that life in Songhai cities should be similar to that in Cairo and Mecca, took direct measures to attract foreign merchants. Commercial justice was administered according to Muslim law and market superintendents were appointed to see that fair weights and measures were used. Even his decision to found a standing army freed other men for full-time economic production.

Although Askia Muhammad consciously used Islam to secure and increase his power, his encouragement of the religion was not merely the work of a cynical opportunist. By his own lights, he was a devout Muslim who upheld the five pillars of Islam and compelled his Muslim subjects to follow his example. During his reign the practices of keeping women in purdah and of making them wear the veil were both introduced for the first time. Thus, even though political wisdom prevented him trying to stamp out the Songhai religion, he improved both the quantity and quality of Islam in Songhai by royal example, persuasion and patronage.

As the proper observance of Islam requires familiarity with its theological and legal writings, a high level of Islamic life is rarely possible without a reasonable standard of Islamic learning. One of the glories of Askia Muhammad's empire was the high quality and range of Islamic studies conducted by the *ulama* of Timbuktu and Jenne. The Askia's patronage attracted scholars from all over the Muslim world, and *ulama* who had fled from Sunni Ali now returned. Islamic books flowed in with the North African merchants, and Songhai scholars exchanged ideas with those of Fez, Tunis and Cairo. Enormous private libraries were built up and Al-hajj Ahmad alone owned 700 books. So high was the standard of scholarship that a visiting Arabian lawyer found his knowledge inferior to that of the local dons.

THE LATER HISTORY OF SONGHAI

The greatest days of Songhai ended in 1528 when the aged Askia Muhammad was deposed by his son Musa. From then until the collapse of the empire in 1591, Songhai history was to be bedevilled by dynastic rivalries, independence movements and attacks from external foes. Nevertheless, Songhai remained the greatest state of the western Sudan until its destruction by the Moroccans, and was still to produce two rulers of considerable merit and authority in Askia Ishak I and Askia Daud.

Between 1528 and 1591, there were no less than eight different Askias. Most of them were so involved in putting down opposition to their rule and had such short reigns that they could not provide stable and effective government. Askia Musa, 1528 to 1531, turned out to be a blood-thirsty tyrant. He was overthrown by an army revolt under the leadership of Muhammad Bengan, 1531 to 1537, who banished the aged Askia Muhammad to a lonely and unhealthy island in the Niger. While Muhammad Bengan was absent on an unsuccessful invasion of Kebbi, Askia Muhammad's son Ismail organized a successful rebellion. Muhammad Bengan was overthrown and Ismail, 1537 to 1539, restored his father to the comforts of the royal palace. Ismail's short reign was spent in putting down one rebellion after another and so many captives were taken that the price of slaves fell in Songhai markets. His successor, Ishak I, 1539 to 1548, secured his position as Askia by killing all his rivals and did much to restore the power of Songhai. He successfully attacked Bonduku, raided Mali, put down a rebellion in Dendi and even ravaged southern Morocco. His work was continued by Askia Daud, 1548 to 1582, who succeeded in filling all key positions in the empire with his own supporters. His military successes included the sack of Bussa, an invasion of Mali and victories over the Tuareg that restored Songhai's waning control of the desert routes. He enhanced Songhai reputation by his devotion to Muslim studies for not only was he a scholar himself, but he also encouraged the growth of libraries and employed scribes to copy important manuscripts. He repaired and enlarged the Sankore mosque and erected many other spacious buildings. Unfortunately his death was followed by civil wars in which Muhammad II and Muhammad Bani both won and lost power before Ishak II finally became the Askia in 1588. He, however, had insufficient time to establish his authority and restore law and order in Songhai before he was attacked and totally defeated by the Moroccans who, in 1591, destroyed the Songhai empire for ever.

The Moroccan invasion

Moroccan rulers had long been envious of the rich resources of Songhai and resented its control of Taghaza. As early as 1546, Askia Ishak had to discourage Moroccan ambitions by despatching 2000 Tuareg to ravage southern Morocco. In the reign of Daud, the Moors actually occupied Taghaza but were obliged to withdraw as the Songhai labour force was merely moved to open alternative salt production at Taodeni.

However, circumstances began to change in 1578 with the accession of Sultan Muley Ahmad el Mansur. The Moroccans had recently defeated the Portuguese at the battle of El Ksar el Kebir and could turn more of their attention to Songhai. El Mansur sought to control not merely the salt mines but also the sources of Songhai's gold supply. He diplomatically hired the Taghaza mines from Songhai and then sent an impressive good will mission to Gao. Its real object was to prepare plans to march an army across the Sahara. As a result, a well equipped and carefully chosen force of 4000 men under the command of Judar Pasha crossed the desert and met the Songhai army at the battle of Tondibi in October 1591.

The actual arrival of Moroccan forces in the western Sudan clearly demonstrated the decline in the political condition of Songhai. Messengers despatched by Askia Ishak II to block the water-holes along the desert routes were waylaid by robbers and failed in their mission. Had they succeeded the Moroccans must have perished in the desert. It has also been suggested that a number of sub-rulers delayed to send local levies to support the imperial army so that the Songhai forces at Tondibi were not at maximum strength. Be that as it may, the Songhai forces outnumbered the Moroccans by over ten to one, and the victory of Judar Pasha was a triumph of superior weapons and superior generalship. Songhai attempts to destroy Moroccan morale by religious rituals having failed, Askia Ishak attempted to sow confusion in Judar's ranks by driving a maddened herd of cattle at them. The disciplined Moroccan forces broke ranks to allow the cattle to charge through their position and then rapidly regrouped. With their muskets, which the Songhai could only match with spears, bows and arrows, the Moroccans mowed down Askia Ishak's cavalry; then moving onto the offensive, they routed the Songhai army, slaughtering the imperial veterans who preferred death to flight. Ishak fled, the Moroccans occupied Timbuktu and Gao and soon the imperial unity of the western Sudan was no more.

THE GOVERNMENT OF SONGHAI

Thus came to an end the elaborate and successful government created by Sunni Ali and reorganized by Askia Muhammad. The masterpiece of Askia Muhammad's reorganization was his skilful blend of decentralization with maximum central control. In addition to the capital territory of Gao, Askia Muhammad created four major provinces: Dendi, south of Gungia; Bal, north of the Niger bend and including Taghaza; Benga in the lacustrine area; and Kurmina in the important grain-producing area south of the Niger from Timbuktu. There were also a number of smaller provinces.

There was enormous local power in the hands of governors of these provinces but they were carefully selected from the Askia's family and circle of friends to guarantee maximum loyalty. Furthermore, these offices were not hereditary but were in the gift of the Askia who could both appoint and remove governors at will. Another device to prevent provincial governors amassing excessive and dangerous personal power was the regulation that provincial governors could not hold office in the central administration. These provincial governors were at the head of the usual network of officers concerned with the collection of taxation, the preservation of law and order and the maintenance of imperial authority; and it is noteworthy that only at fairly low administrative levels were tributary rulers left in charge of their own people.

The central government was charged with advising the Askia on imperial policy and supervising the day to day administration of the great departments of state. Its ministers bore such titles as: Balama, the chief minister; Fari Mundyo, the chief tax-collector; Hi-Koy, commander of the war fleet, Korey-Farma, minister for problems relating to foreign merchants; and Kari-Farima, the chief priest of the Songhai traditional religion. Both central and local officials had a known position in the imperial hierarchy which helped to allocate responsibility and prevent quarrels over precedence. Each great official had his own distinctive dress, his own personal allocation of drums for use on ceremonial occasions and some distinguishing privilege. Such privileges included the right of the commander-in-chief (Dyina Koy) to sit on a carpet and sprinkle himself with flour instead of dust when prostrating before the Askia; the exemption of the governor of Gurma from removing his turban when kneeling before his ruler; and the distinction of the Governor of Benga who was allowed to enter the city of Gao with all his drums beating.

The exact nature of Songhai kingship under the Askia dynasty is hard to determine. On the one hand we see the great stress laid on the Islamic character of the towns with their crowded mosques, their flourishing scholarship, their Islamic judges and the personal piety of the Askia family. On the other, we have evidence of the sacred nature of the monarchy in the prostration before the Askia, the use of the Interpreter as an intermediary between ruler and people, and of traditional religious influence in the ministerial status of the Kari-Farima. The rural populace remained essentially non-Muslim and we are given a picture of Songhai magicians using local 'medicine', that is invocations to ethnic gods, to overcome the Moroccans. Equally, after the fall of Songhai, traditional cults dominated the religious thinking of peoples of the western Sudan. Thus it appears that the Askias were either essentially Muslims who for political reasons paid lip-service to the traditional religious forms to retain the loyalty of non-Muslim subjects, or they gradually became re-absorbed into the ethnic religion while maintaining a Muslim gloss that propitiated indigenous and foreign Muslims alike. Whichever was the true state of affairs, it is clear that successful Askias drew political support and religious approval from all quarters. This was a remarkable feat of statesmanship.

REASONS FOR THE RISE AND FALL OF SONGHAI

Songhai rose to imperial power through a combination of racial energy and brilliant leadership that enabled the Songhai to replace the waning might of Mali in spite of competition from

79

other peoples. They produced a system of government that utilized the energies and abilities of Muslims and non-Muslims alike and preserved a sense of justice and order which enabled trade, and through trade imperial wealth, to flourish. Thus their military and administrative talents gave them control of the favourable geography of the western Sudan. The destruction of the empire was due once again to the combination of dynastic rivalry and ethnic and personal ambitions for political and economic independence that weakened the central government and made the empire the prey of external foes. These tendencies were encouraged by an indistinct law of succession but were also modified by the strong authoritarian nature of the government once an Askia was firmly established in office. Thus, although by 1591 the empire was long past its peak, it still dominated the affairs of the western Sudan where no people had yet achieved sufficient military progress to offer serious challenge to Songhai. However, there had been a decline in the excellence of the Songhai enforcement of law and order which was fatal in that it allowed the forces of Morocco to reach the Niger bend. Once the Moroccans reached Tondibi, the Songhai had little chance against a foe well drilled in more advanced techniques of war and possessing fire-arms which the Songhai did not have.

THE RESULTS OF THE FALL OF SONGHAI

The immediate collapse of the Songhai empire after the destruction of its army at Tondibi was one of the most momentous events in West African history. At first its full effects were not apparent. The Moroccans occupied the great cities of Gao, Timbuktu and Jenne and established a Pashalic (viceroyalty) with its capital at Timbuktu. But although in the next few years successive Moroccan commanders pushed their forces across and down the Niger, they never succeeded in imposing their authority upon the western Sudan as a whole nor did they crush the hostile Songhai groups who established themselves as an independent state in Dendi.

There were a number of reasons why the Moroccans failed to rival Songhai achievement. South of the Niger bend, they found themselves fighting in unfamiliar, thick bush which impeded their military manoeuvres, exposed them to ambush and reduced their morale and numbers through fatal insect-born diseases. The Songhai soon found a patriotic leader in Askia Nuh, whose mastery of the art of guerrilla warfare reduced Moroccan resources in men and supplies. These were not easily replaced, for the transport of supplies and reinforcements across the desert was difficult. Also, as the areas conquered by the Moroccans did not yield large supplies of gold for their Sultans, these first resorted to high-handed treatment of their Pashas in the western Sudan and then lost interest in the Pashalic altogether. By 1610, the rulers of the Pashalic were independent of Morocco and had to rely upon their own resources. Struggles between the army commanders of the towns and even within each individual city, revolts by the people they oppressed, and decline into a life of indolence made the Moroccans an insignificant factor in western Sudanese politics by the end of the seventeenth century. By this time, they had been culturally assimilated through inter-marriage with West African peoples and were known as the Arma.

The failure of the Moroccans to gain control of the entire western Sudan broke its political unity with disastrous results. The former empire broke into a collection of independent and warring states, each trying unsuccessfully to establish its dominion over the others until the rise of the Bambara states in the early eighteenth century. Revolts provided opportunity for the former enemies of Songhai—the Tuareg, the Mossi, the Mandingos and the Fulani—to ravage the countryside. Thus perished the old tradition of law and order that had been so productive of peace, prosperity and human happiness. Constant war produced serious famines and drove land out of tillage.

The trans-Saharan trade of the western Sudan suffered a blow from which it never fully recovered. The predatory attitude of the Moors rapidly drained the Songhai cities of their available gold supplies and discouraged trade between the gold-producing areas and the gold marts of the Niger. The collapse of law and order rendered trade unsafe and failed to produce any single state with the resources to support large-scale commercial activity. For a time, the trans-Saharan trade stopped altogether until enterprising merchants reopened it, providing for their security by the hire of armed guards. But the damage was already done: the interruption of trade and endemic warfare encouraged the new tendency to export gold to the coast; and the central Sudan replaced the western in importance in the trans-Saharan trade.

Although the Moroccans were a Muslim people, their invasion did incalculable harm to Islam in West Africa. Out of greed, they stripped the *ulama* of their wealth; and in 1594, as a reprisal for political opposition, the Moroccans deported most of the leading *ulama* to North Africa. Many died through brutality and the hardships of life in the desert but a few, including the famous historian Ahmad Baba, reached North Africa alive where they celebrated deliverance by solemnly cursing Morocco. Meanwhile, the ignorant soldiery had destroyed their priceless libraries and pocketed their other possessions. Thus Islamic learning suffered a blow from which it did not recover until the nineteenth century; and with the decline of learning went the decline of Islam.

With the collapse of the imperial power of the Askias, the greatest political pressure for the acceptance of Islam was removed. Also, with the destruction of the political power associated in the popular mind with the worship of Allah, peoples turned whole-heartedly and exclusively to the worship of traditional gods whose benevolence was felt necessary for survival. True, many Muslims continued to practice the outward observances of Islam but as they lacked intellectual and moral sustenance from *ulama* and were subjects of non-Muslim rulers, their Islam was a token gesture which barely distinguished them from the non-Muslim cultures in which they lived and shared. It was not until the nineteenth century that a purer Islam finally dominated the political and religious life of the western Sudan.

The fall of Songhai thus greatly contributed to a serious retarding of economic growth, put back the clock on the progress of Islam and made it necessary to evolve once again an administrative structure capable of governing an influential state. Some people regard it as the greatest disaster in the history of the western Sudan; others see it as providing essential proof of the resilience and reconstructive ability of West African peoples. The two views are not incompatible.

STATES OF THE UPPER VOLTA

The Mossi, who so menaced Mali and Songhai with their quick-raiding cavalry, inhabited the vast plains of the upper Volta. They evolved a state system which was one of the most stable in Africa. Powerful foes such as Mali and Songhai could not rob them of their independence, nor did the Islamic religion make any converts among them. The constitutions of the Mossi states were so stable that right down to the end of the nineteenth century there were rulers who could claim unbroken descent from the founders of the states.

Traditions of origin
Traditions indicate that the ruling classes of the Mossi-Dagomba states are of common descent. Thus one major tradition records that they had a common ancestor, Tohajie, a red hunter who came from an area eight days east of Bawku. His grandson, Gbewa, built up a kingdom in the Bawku area and from this base his sons emigrated to found Dagomba, Mossi, Nanumba and Mamprusi.

Another story is that Nedega, an eleventh-century king of Gambaga, refused to allow his daughter Yennenga to marry because she was a great general. However, when her horse bolted into the forest she met and married Riale, a banished Mandingo prince. Their son, Widiraugo, was later given a troop of cavalry by his grandfather Nedega. With this military force, Widiraugo conquered an empire which he later split into three provinces, one for each of his sons. These became the states of Wagadugu, Yatenga and Gurma.

The state system
The principal states to emerge in the area were Wagadugu, Yatenga, Fada-n-Gurma, Mamprusi and Dagomba. These states were of early foundation. Wagadugu is said to have been founded in about A.D. 1050 and Yatenga round about 1170; and the others were in existence before 1500.

As far as historians can make out, the Mossi-Dagomba states were founded by an immigrant military aristocracy, probably cavalry bands from Hausaland. They imposed their political authority upon the indigenous peoples, most of whom spoke Gur or Mande. However, the invaders were a decided minority group and in time were culturally absorbed by their subjects. In particular, their treatment of the local religion is most interesting. On arrival they found that each small society had its own Tengdana

83

(Custodian of the Earth), who as head of the earth cult was both political and spiritual head of his people. In many areas, the invaders allowed the Tengdana to continue to exercise spiritual authority provided they accepted the political supremacy of their Mossi-Dagomba conquerors. In eastern Dagomba, however, the Tengdana were insufficiently pliable and consequently they were slaughtered and their places taken by the new conquerors. One conqueror even married the daughter of a Tengdana he had killed in order to claim authority from the ancestors of the local people.

The political success of the Mossi states was due to their evolution of a strongly centralized system of government and to their rejection of all divisive external influences. At the head of a Mossi state was a sacred king (the Nakomse) aided by ministers known as Naba. These held central offices and local governorships and were responsible both for internal security and external defence. The Mossi rulers seem to have been determined to preserve the cultural identity of their states. For, although they mounted successful plundering raids across the western Sudan, they never attempted to conquer lands and establish their rule over alien peoples. They sternly set their faces against Islam and made no direct contact with North African merchants. Indeed, the state kept a very watchful eye on immigrants such as Mandingo traders, Hausa craftsmen and Fulani herders. Their services were appreciated but they were to be given no chance of subversion. In fact a special minister, the Yar-naba, was appointed to control the activities of the Fulani.

The state of Gonja
Gonja was the creation of Mandingo invaders. In the third quarter of the sixteenth century, a ruler sent a squadron of cavalry to investigate why supplies of Akan gold no longer came northwards. These warriors founded seven little states in the Gonja area. Later, in about 1629, Jakpa, a Mande war-leader from the Jenne area, swept across the region of Gonja, defeated the main Dagomba army and set up his sons and relatives as rulers in the conquered areas. He built several new towns (he may have been the founder of Salaga), and he took the salt-making centre of Daboya from Dagomba. By his death, he ruled a state stretching from Bole in the west to Bassari, two hundred miles to the east. This state was

an important trade centre because of its production of kola and the availability of Akan gold from Bonduku.

Dagomba resented this new commercial and political rival and there were severe wars between the two. The struggle was settled in favour of Dagomba in about 1720 but, by the end of the century, both had fallen to the forces of the Asante.

With the exception of Fada-n-Gurma, which fell to a Fulani dynasty in about 1700, the other upper Volta states retained their independence until the end of the nineteenth century.

Questions

1 Trace the rise of Songhai from earliest times to the death of Askia Muhammad.

2 *Either* estimate the contribution of Sunni Ali and Askia Muhammad to the growth of Songhai power; *or* discuss the view that Sundiata and Sunni Ali, and Mansa Musa and Askia Muhammad, played identical roles in the development of Mali and Songhai.

3 Give an account of the character and achievements of either Sunni Ali or Askia Muhammad.

4 What problems were faced by the rulers of Songhai after the deposition of Askia Muhammad?

5 Why were the Moroccans successful in conquering Songhai? What were the limits of their success?

6 What were the effects of the fall of Songhai upon the history of the western Sudan?

7 Give an account of the Songhai empire at its height. Include a consideration of its extent, government system, economy and religion in your answer.

8 Write an historical account of the Mossi-Dagomba states.

6

The Hausa states

The Hausa speaking peoples have long occupied the plains of north-west and north-central Nigeria. Although the majority of Hausamen are of necessity farmers, they have a long history of city life and their craftsmen and traders are noted for their skill and industry. Their language is one of the great *lingua franca* of Africa and is spoken by many people with little or no Hausa blood.

Traditions of origin
Although each distinct Hausa community is marked by intense local patriotism, all Hausas are conscious of their ethnic and cultural unity and their separate traditions are very similar. All claim descent from Bayajidda (Abuyazida), reputedly a refugee prince from Baghdad. Having settled for a time in Kanem, where he married a daughter of the Mai, he had to flee westwards to escape the treachery of his father-in-law. At Biram-ta-Gabas, he abandoned his wife who stayed to give birth to a son; at Gaya, he met a community of skilled blacksmiths who forged him a special sword; and with this, he slew the evil snake 'Sarki' who prevented the villagers of Daura from drawing water except on Fridays. As a reward, he was allowed to marry Queen Daura and thus became the ruler of the state.

Bayajidda's legitimate descendants founded seven states which bore their names. These were Biram, Daura, Katsina, Zaria, Kano, Rano and Gobir, collectively known as the Hausa Bakwai, or pure Hausa states. Traditions vary as to whether their founding heroes were the sons or grandsons of Bayajidda. Each of these members of the Hausa family was allotted a special task. Gobir, the youngest, was appointed war-leader; Daura and Katsina were chiefs of trade; Kano and Rano were 'chiefs of indigo', responsible for industry; and Zaria was the chief of slaves. In addition, Bayajidda is said to have had seven illegitimate sons by a slave-girl named Gwari. These founded the states of Zamfara, Kebbi, Gwari, Yauri, Nupe, Yoruba and Kwararafa— the Banza Bakwai, or impure Hausa states.

How much historical accuracy such traditions contain is impossible to guess and is in any case irrelevant. The role of oral tradition is to explain dramatically important facts in the development of a people, its customs and constitution. Thus, the Bayajidda legend indicates that the Habe ruling classes immigrated from the east and north east. They found Hausaland populated by peoples long organized in settled village communities and skilled in the use of iron. The first wave of immigrants settled in the Daura area, where they obtained political control by diplomacy and service to the community.

The tradition that Bayajidda arrived alone mounted on a strange animal indicates that the immigrants were a minority group who intermarried with the indigenes and that they may have introduced the horse or donkey. Initially, some invading groups may have imposed some features of their culture on their hosts. For example, the slaying of the snake may well represent a change in religion, while the marriage to Daura and the importance of male descendants implies a constitutional change from matrilineal to patrilineal succession. However, the later history of the Hausa states shows clearly that indigenous culture triumphed.

The accounts of the foundation of the Hausa Bakwai and the Banza Bakwai attempt to explain the widespread use of the Hausa language and the cultural affinities between the peoples of the leading Hausa states and their neighbours. Equally, the division of labour between the founders of the Hausa Bakwai rationalizes the historical development of the Hausa states. By its northerly location, Gobir was faced with the perennial problem of resisting Tuareg incursions. Katsina developed into a great terminal of the trans-Saharan trade route from Tripoli; while Kano's reputation for the manufacture of cloth, leather goods and metal-work is of great antiquity. Zaria, at the height of its power, dominated great expanses southwards which provided large supplies of slaves and gave access to the kola-producing areas of the northern forest belt. There is also evidence to show that Daura was once an im-

D

portant trading centre although its economic importance long ago declined. The real importance of Daura was as the spiritual home of the Hausa people and, respected as such by all Hausas, it remained immune from attack by other Hausa states throughout its long history. Even today, when Habe traditional religion has been replaced by Islam, the relics of Bayajidda are proudly preserved there, including the famous well and distinguished sword.

HAUSA CITY-STATES

In spite of their consciousness of brotherhood, the Hausa people never formed a lasting political union. Each leading settlement grew into a strongly fortified city able to dominate the surrounding countryside and to offer staunch resistance to external attacks which were easy to mount across the flat countryside. Civic patriotism, enshrined in local deities and religious rites, provided the essential basis of fierce local independence and perpetual political and economic rivalries among the city-states. The main object of these rivalries was to control the trade and tribute of an area that became prosperous through the fertility of its soil, the craftsmanship of the people and a geographical location enabling Hausa cities to share in the valuable trade of both the desert and the forest belt. For long, however, the economic development of Hausaland was overshadowed by the might of Mali and Songhai to the west and Kanem-Bornu to the east. Lacking large supplies of gold or vast imperial resources, the area did not attract North African merchants until comparatively late in its history. Once contact was made with North Africa, however, prosperity grew quickly, and after the fall of Songhai there was very rapid economic growth.

Failure to create a strongly unified empire meant that throughout its history Hausaland was the prey of the imperial ambitions of Songhai and Bornu, and for most of their existence the Hausa states were tributary to the Sefawa*. Yet the Hausa states were sufficiently distant from the Niger bend and lake Chad to escape with no more than spasmodic direct interference from outside. Apart from the collection of reasonable tribute, Bornu rarely

*Sefawa = rulers of Bornu

88

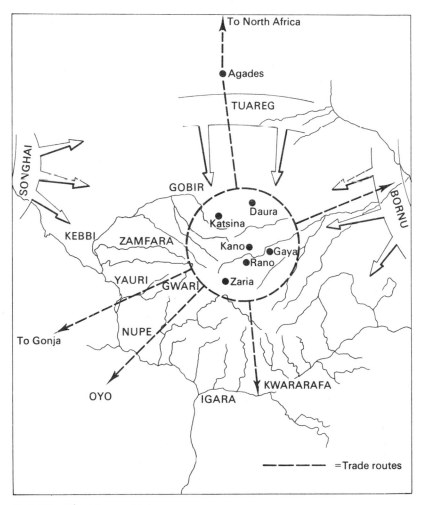

Map IX   The Hausa States

intervened in Hausa affairs. Thus the history of Hausaland remains the history not of a people but of its independent city-states of which Kano was the first to rise as a formidable power.

Kano

Pre-Habe Kano   The earliest known inhabitants of Kano were

89

the Negro Abagayawa, whose descendants still live in the city today. They were blacksmiths who had settled on Dala hill to work its supplies of ironstone. Their most famous ruler, possibly the founder of the settlement, was Barbushe, 'a black man of great stature and might, a hunter, who slew elephants with his stick and carried them on his head about nine miles'. As the high priest of the god Tchunburburai, whose shrine was the tree Shamuz, he exercised both political and religious authority over the Abaga-yawa. Once a year, he conducted the religious ceremonies at which sacrifices of black animals were made in the grove of Jakara, and after communing in secret with Tchunburburai foretold the events of the coming year.

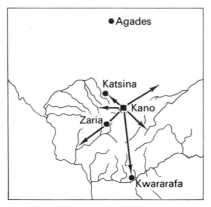

Map X   The Expansion of Kano

The establishment of Habe power   Kano tradition says that the Abagayawa were conquered in about A.D. 999 by Bagoda, grandson of Bayajidda. At that time, Kano was little more than a village but under Habe rule it began to increase in size and power. Defensive walls were finally completed in the reign of Yusa, the fifth Sarki, who also armed his warriors with shields of tough hides. These improvements in the art of war and Kano's ability to protect people of the surrounding countryside enabled Sarki Naguji, 1194–1247, to impose upon them an annual land-tax of one-eighth of each man's produce. Thus, there developed an administrative system capable of dealing with the affairs of a political unit larger than a village community.

Internal problems of early Habe rulers   However, these Habe rulers did not command the loyalty of the Abagayawa who excluded them from knowledge of the local religion. Sarki Tsamia, 1307–1343, therefore set out to develop civic patriotism and exalt the prestige of the monarchy. Successful steps in this direction were his forcible seizure of control of the Abagayawa religion, the introduction of long brazen horns to increase ceremonial pomp, and the playing of the new civic anthem: 'Stand firm, Kano is your city'.

A new source of religious discord arose under Ali Yaji, 1349–1385. Muslim missionaries from Mali persuaded him to accept Islam, declare it the state religion, appoint Muslim officials, and lay out a mosque beneath the tree Shamuz. Many citizens contemptuously used his mosque as a lavatory but were eventually obliged to yield.

The expansion of Kano   This imposition of Islam as the state religion of Kano was superficial and of temporary duration. Kanajcji, 1390–1410, Ali Yaji's son and a noted conqueror, devoted his reign to the expansion of Kano's power over large areas of Hausaland. He was the first ruler to equip Kano troops with chain-mail and iron helmets and to protect his war-horses with quilted padding. Frustrated in an early attempt to conquer Zaria, he reverted to the religion of his ancestors. Having thus enlisted the sympathies of the majority of Kano's citizens, he returned to the attack. Singing the song of Barbushe, his armies took Zaria by storm and later forced Kwararafa to pay tribute.

Under Kanajeji's successors, Kano enlarged its contacts abroad and its trade and wealth increased. Sarki Dauda, 1421–1438, was in touch with Bornu and had trouble with Dagachi, a Kanuri prince settled in Kano. Under Abdullahi Burja, 1438–1452, direct trade was opened up with Bornu and Gonja, and his possession of camels indicates that Kano was sharing in the trans-Saharan trade. His successor, Yakubu, 1452–1463, followed a policy of peace that enabled commerce to expand greatly. He also received Fulani Muslims from Mali bringing books and ideas unfamiliar in Hausaland. Thus the stage was set for the illustrious reign of Muhammad Rimfa (Rumfa).

The reign of Muhammad Rimfa   Muhammad Rimfa is remembered as the greatest of all Habe rulers of Kano. His long reign, lasting from 1463 to 1499, marks the zenith of Kano's military power and commercial prosperity under Habe rule. Although much credit for this must be attributed to his predecessors, the few glimpses we have of Muhammad Rimfa indicates that he was an extremely able Sarki, well fitted to exercise kingly responsibility. Although we know few details of his wars, he obviously enhanced Kano's military reputation. During his reign, the city walls were considerably strengthened and extended to protect a much larger area, an eloquent testimony to the remarkable growth of the capital city. The offensive menace of his armies in the field was increased by the introduction of *dawakin zaggi*, a method of advance in which the cavalry acted as a shield for the infantry. This new tactic was first used in the eleven years' war he provoked with Katsina in an effort to win control of the trade with Agades and North Africa. Although Muhammad Rimfa could not inflict a decisive defeat on Katsina, he nevertheless encouraged further expansion in Kano's trade. In particular, he laid out the site of the famous Kurmi market, capable of accommodating enormous numbers of merchants and still today the principal market within the city walls.

A considerable part of Muhammad Rimfa's reputation derives from his services to Islam. Under the influence of two great Muslim missionaries, Al-Maghili and Abd al-Rahman, he transformed Kano into an Islamic state. Not only did he cut down the tree Shamuz and build a minaret on its site but he also compelled Kano's leading citizens to become Muslim. The great Muslim festival of Id al-Fitr at the end of the fast of Ramadan was first celebrated in Kano during his reign, and the custom of keeping women in purdah was introduced. Al-Maghili wrote him a treatise on Islamic government entitled 'The Obligation of Princes', which laid down the principles of government to be followed by Islamic rulers and gave practical advice on safeguarding the security and authority of the ruler himself. In accordance with these teachings, Muhammad Rimfa appointed *qadis** to administer justice according to Islamic law and he also set up the Islamic system of taxation.

Closely linked with this advancement of Islam were Muhammad Rimfa's successful attempts to strengthen the personal authority of the monarchy. He exalted its ceremonial dignity by reserving for the Sarki alone the use of ostrich-feather

*qadis = muslim judges

fans and distinctive royal sandals; by increasing the numbers of the royal household; and by building a new and more imposing royal palace, known as Gidan Rimfa. Even today, a newly installed Emir must pass through the gate of Gidan Rimfa. To advance the authority of the Sarki over the power of the great hereditary chiefs of Kano, Muhammad Rimfa appointed to high office men of servile origin whose first loyalties were to himself. The treasury, the city-guard, the royal body-guard and the administration of the royal household were all placed under the control of his personal eunuchs. Even on the Council of Nine, an administrative council formed by Muhammad Rimfa to govern the expanding affairs of state, two great officers of slave birth shared authority with the old nobility. Thus the Kano chronicle justly claims for this remarkable ruler: 'He can have no equal in might, from the time of the founding of Kano, until it shall end . . .'.

Fig. 4   Gates into the old city of Kano

The later history of Kano   The wars against Katsina started by Muhammad Rimfa continued intermittently until 1706. Although Kano won its share of victories over the next two centuries, it was Katsina that became pre-eminent in the trans-Saharan trade.

93

There were also more powerful foes whose might Kano could not resist. In 1512 Kano fell to the army of Askia Muhammad, and Sarki Muhammad Kisoki became tributary first to Songhai and then to Kebbi; and in the second half of the seventeenth century, the Jukun of the Benue Valley twice broke into Kano and ravaged the city.

These conquests, however, were only temporary interludes. The power that most consistently exacted tribute from Kano was Bornu. In spite of temporary assertions of its independence, Kano generally had to acknowledge Kanuri overlordship down to the foundation of the Fulani empire in the early nineteenth century. Under Fulani rule, Kano was at last able to replace Katsina as the greatest commercial centre of Hausaland.

Katsina

Early rulers According to tradition, the people living in the Katsina area in the twelfth century were governed by an immigrant ruling class, the Durbawa. Katsina was little more than a village state under the rule of Janzama, whose wife Katsina, a princess of Daura, gave her name to the capital. In the same century, Kumayo, a descendant of Bayajidda, gained control over the Durbawa and became the first Habe ruler of Katsina, then a village eighteen miles south-east of the modern city. After his death, succession to the throne passed alternately to the descendants of Kumayo and Janzama until the thirteenth century. Then Sannau, the last of Kumayo's line, was treacherously stabbed by a rival named Korau during a wrestling match.

Accession of a Sarki One interesting peculiarity of the Katsina constitution was the transference of office from one ruler to another. The Sarki was obviously a divine ruler whose good health and strength were held to have an important bearing on fertility and the well-being of his people. Therefore, as soon as the ruler's physical or mental powers declined, a successor was named by a local selection process of which we have no knowledge. A black ox was then slaughtered over the Sarki-elect so that he was spattered with its blood. Meanwhile, the old Sarki was strangled by an official of the court, and his body was wrapped in the skin of the ox before being buried in an upright position.

94

Sixteenth century developments At first Katsina was an unwalled city and probably remained so until the middle of the sixteenth century. This may have been the reason why Askia Muhammad was able to conquer Katsina so easily. Yet, with or without walls, Katsina had already established its authority over the surrounding countryside and had preserved its independence from attacks by Gobir, Nupe and Kano. A knowledge of Islam had already reached Katsina where the religion was first embraced by the common people. In about 1493, Al-Maghili visited Katsina, converted the ruler, Muhammad Korau, and helped him to establish Islam firmly in the city. The spread of Islam was also encouraged by the growing trade with North African merchants and by the Songhai invasion. However, it was not until the second half of the sixteenth century that Islam was made obligatory for the citizens of Katsina and the religion became firmly established.

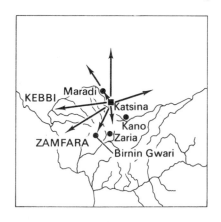

Map XI The Expansion of Katsina

By the middle of the sixteenth century, Katsina was a large city divided into about a hundred different residential quarters. People from Bornu, Gobir, Mali, Songhai and Asben had their separate quarters, as did Islamic teachers and craftsmen specializing in the various crafts such as leather-working and metalwork. Trade with Tunis was already brisk and bringing prosperity; and when in 1554 Katsina finally won its independence from Songhai, the problem of permanent defences for such a wealthy city could no longer be ignored. Consequently, Ali Murabus, one of its most famous rulers, ordered the building of the powerful outer walls of the city in about 1560.

95

The rivals of Katsina Even powerful walls and prosperous trade, however, could not obviate the fact that Katsina had many powerful enemies. We have already seen that her commercial pre-eminence, facilitated by her northerly position in Hausaland, evoked the long enmity of Kano. Although her northerly location enabled Katsina to avoid the worst of the ravages of the Jukun, they broke into the city in the 1670's and massacred many people. It was only saved from worse disaster when the Jukun general died from a kick by a horse and his men withdrew. Also, like Kano, Katsina could not resist the might of Bornu and paid tribute to the Sefawa.

The success of Katsina Yet, centuries of war and the overlordship of more powerful states did not seriously interfere with the economic development of Katsina. Throughout this period, it remained the leading centre of trade and Islamic culture in Hausaland. It became a noted centre of Islamic learning, famous for its local scholar Dan Marina in the seventeenth century, for its excellent government and legal system and for the politeness of its people. Until the second half of the eighteenth century, its rulers effectively controlled an area including Maradi, Zamfara and Birnin Gwari. Then, much of this territory fell to the rising power of Gobir, and finally Katsina city itself fell to the Fulani in 1807.

Zaria

Early history of Zaria Although Zaria grew into one of the largest Hausa states with valuable commercial links with the northern edge of the forest, we know less about its historical development than that of either Kano or Katsina. One of the peculiarities of the Zaria constitution was that even after it became a Habe state, it was occasionally ruled by women, two of whom are among its most famous rulers. Its first Habe ruler is said to have been Gunguma, grandson of Bayajidda, and Islam was traditionally introduced by Muhammad Abu, 1505 to 1530. It is thought likely that Islam did not take root in Zaria so firmly or so rapidly as it did in Kano and Katsina.

The rise of Zaria's power The rise of Zaria's military power is associated with the reigns of two formidable women rulers. The first was Bakwa Turunku, a woman of commanding personality and astute brain. She is reputed to have repulsed the Jukun and to have moved the capital city to roughly its present site in about 1536, as the former capital at Turunku had insufficient water to provide for the needs of a growing commercial centre. On her death, in about 1566, the succession reverted to the male Karama, a doughty warrior, who was accompanied on his campaigns by Princess Amina, the eldest daughter of Bakwa Turunku. In about 1576, she became queen of Zaria. Amina never married ever though she received a proposal from the ruler of Kano. For her, war was more interesting than life as a royal housewife and she commanded her troops in the field. Over a period of thirty-four years her armies won victory after victory, each being consolidated by the erection of walled forts as area garrisons. Thus the whole vast area between Zaria and the rivers Niger and Benue, including the Kwararafa and Nupe states, was forced to acknowledge her overlordship. This southern expansion provided not only abundant supplies of slave labour but also control of the trade route from Gonja. Consequently, by the time of Amina's death, Zaria had won a new and important share of Hausaland's trade and was at the height of its wealth and power.

The later history of Zaria Zaria's might did not go long unchallenged. In the seventeenth century, failing leadership and renewed raids by the Jukun reduced the extent of its territory, and in 1734 the city fell to the armies of Bornu. Although there is no positive proof, it is likely that Zaria paid tribute to the Sefawa before this event. However, the large extent of the modern province of Zaria and the activity of its commerce reveal that Zaria retained an important place in Hausaland even after her decline from the triumphs of Amina's reign.

The Nupe state

The Nupe people According to the Bayajidda tradition, the Nupe people have some distant kinship with the Hausas. Their main areas of concentration lie to the south of the states of the Hausa Bakwai and they enjoy a high reputation for the quality of their

97

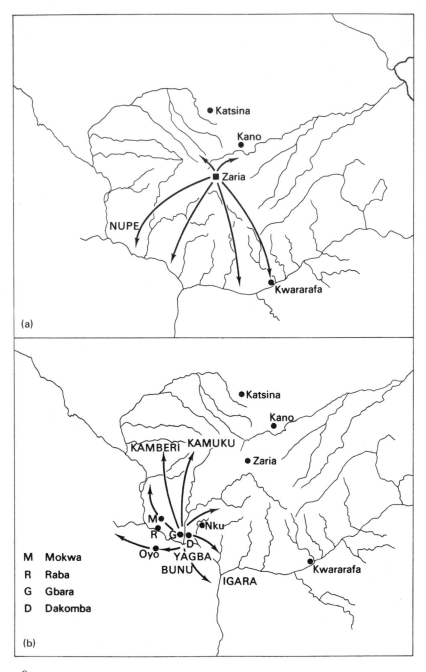

(a)

(b)

M   Mokwa
R   Raba
G   Gbara
D   Dakomba

work in brass, silver and glass. The skill of their boat-builders is also famous.

Until the late fifteenth century, the Nupe were not a united people but dwelt in eleven or twelve related though separate groups. Two of these had already achieved greater local predominance than the others: the Kyedye, centred on Mureji near the Niger-Kaduna confluence, had established a number of subordinate trading and fishing villages along the river valleys; and the Beni had founded twelve separate and independent towns. These small Beni states readily co-operated with each other to resist attacks from other ethnic groups, and for purposes of defence came to acknowledge the political leadership of Nku, near modern Bida, itself a Beni town. All these peoples were tributary to the Ata of Igala who controlled a large empire from his river base at Idah and exacted an annual tribute of one male slave from each Nupe family.

Tsoede and the founding of the Nupe state   The hero of the Nupe people is Tsoede, alias Edegi, who in the first half of the fifteenth century united all the Nupe peoples under his rule and won independence from Igala. He is said to have been the son of an Igala prince residing in Nupe and a daughter of the chief of Nku. Before Tsoede was born, his father was recalled to Idah to become Ata of Igala and on his departure left two presents for his unborn child—a charm and a distinctive ring. Many years later, these gifts enabled the Ata to identify his son when he was sent to Idah as the slave-tribute of the royal house of Nku.

The Ata, overjoyed at meeting his long-lost son, kept him at court and showed him every mark of favour. Tsoede on his part rendered the Ata many valuable services; and is said to have been the only one of his sons who could climb a very tall palm tree to pluck the only fruit that could cure his father of a serious illness. In doing so, he split his lip so badly that even today Nupe children born with a hare-lip bear his honourable name. Tsoede's increasing successes and the marked partiality of the Ata for his Nupe son rapidly incurred the jealousy of his Igala half-brothers. Consequently, the aging Ata advised Tsoede to flee to Nupe and conferred the government of that area upon

Map XII   (a) The Expansion of Zaria
(b) Nupe at the height of its Power

him. Tsoede left Idah laden with rich gifts from his father and various symbols of authority and royal rank including a bronze canoe, bronze ceremonial trumpets and heavy iron chains and fetters (the symbol of judicial authority).

Tsoede's flight from Idah was detected and his angry half-brothers and their men set off in pursuit. But for the aid of his twelve Nupe slaves, and two other men later appointed to rule the Kyedye, Tsoede might not have escaped capture. Having eluded his pursuers by hiding in the creek of Ega where he sank his bronze canoe, he fell upon Nupeko with a handful of men and made himself master of the town. From this base, he proceeded to conquer all the Nupe peoples, making his twelve companions sub-rulers of the Beni towns.

This great warrior, who built up considerable forces of cavalry, then led the united Nupe people on a career of territorial expansion. South of the river Niger, he subdued the Yagba, Bunu and Kakanda peoples and may even have driven the Yoruba dynasty of Old Oyo from its capital. To the north, he extended his authority over the Ebe, Kamberi and Kamuku areas. As Nupeko was too small to support his new imperial dignity, Tsoede founded a new large capital at Gbara on the lower Kaduna river. Even this town failed to serve the requirements of his court, warriors and war-horses and so the extensive new settlement of Dokomba was built on the opposite side of the river, originally as a stable for his thousands of horses.

In addition to his political services to Nupe, Tsoede is credited with the introduction of new and important skills to the Nupe area. He is said to have brought the first blacksmiths, bronze-casters and glass-manufacturers from Idah and to have introduced the technical knowledge necessary to build large canoes for war and trade. Other customs attributed to him are the payment of bride-price and the making of human sacrifices to the gods. Even the title 'Etsu Nupe', ruler of the Nupe, is derived from his name. Thus by his death, reputedly while on a military campaign in the north at the age of a hundred and twenty, he had not only created a powerful Nupe state but had introduced significant cultural advances.

Apart from the life of their founder-hero, Nupe traditions record little of Nupe achievements down to the nineteenth century. Four of Tsoede's sons are said to have ruled the kingdom in turn, one of whom founded Mokwa as a temporary capital. The dynasty is said to have become Muslim in the reign of Etsu Jibrin who died in about 1759, and to have reached the height of its power under Etsu Ma'aza who died in about 1795. On his death, however, there soon developed struggles for power and the kingdom was divided between rivals. One important outcome of these troubles was the founding of Raba in about 1796 which almost immediately grew into a flourishing trade centre where traders from as far as Adamawa came into contact with North African merchants.

Kebbi

The people of Kebbi   The well-watered Kebbi area has long been settled by populous groups of skilled fishermen. These peoples came under the leadership of the Lekawa, a group with traditions of migration from Egypt into the Kebbi area, then a remote part of the Habe state of Katsina. During the fifteenth century, a chief of the Lekawa is said to have made a marriage alliance with a princess of Katsina and thus formed a close bond between the Kebbi and Katsina peoples.

The Kebbi state: The achievement of Kanta of Kebbi   The state of Kebbi was not founded until the early sixteenth century and it then rose almost immediately to a position of pre-eminence in Hausaland. Its founder, Muhammad Kanta, often referred to as Kotal Kanta or merely Kanta of Kebbi, is reputed to have been the son of a ruler of the Lekawa and a Katsina princess. According to one tradition, he was so furious when his senior half-brother inherited his father's position and title of Magaji that he left home and joined a band of Fulani herdsmen. Among them, he gained such recognition for his prowess at boxing that he became the acknowledged leader of an aggressive and boisterous age-group association of young warriors; and with their aid took over the government of Kebbi. He disdained to take the family title of Magaji and styled himself Kanta of Kebbi. Whether or not this story is historically accurate, it admirably conveys a correct impression of Muhammad Kanta as a dynamic and rebellious young man of considerable physical power, leadership qualities and organizing abilities.

International politics gave this energetic and war-like young ruler of a village-state an opportunity for further advancement. When Askia Muhammad decided to conquer Hausaland, Kanta of Kebbi recognized the advantages of voluntary association with such a powerful neighbour. To oppose the Songhai army in the early stages of its campaign would be futile; whereas military assistance to the invading forces could be expected to bring Kebbi a valuable share of Songhai's plunder. Kanta may also have been hostile towards Katsina for not supporting his claim to leadership of the Kebbi people. In any case, Songhai military success would weaken the established Hausa powers and enable Kebbi to assume a new importance in Hausaland, especially as the main centres of Songhai power were so far distant that Songhai would hardly be able to exercise constant military pressure in Hausaland over a long period. Once Kebbi's power had been built up, the natural defences of its extensive marshes would enable it to resist the hostility of even the most powerful of rivals. Therefore, Kanta of Kebbi had no qualms about accepting the overlordship of Askia Muhammad.

Thus, when Songhai invaded Hausaland, the deceptively insignificant Kebbi was spared the fate of Gobir, Katsina, Zaria and Kano; and shortly after, Kebbi forces assisted in the Songhai conquest of Agades. However, Kanta's hopes of reward were rudely shattered when it was made clear to him that the Songhai had no intention of sharing the spoils of Agades. With the backing of his angry chiefs, he threw off his allegiance to Songhai and, in about 1516, seriously defeated a Songhai force near an unidentified place named Tara. This broke Songhai power in Hausaland; and, with both the Tuareg and the Hausa states seriously weakened by the recent Songhai attacks, Kanta's rapidly growing forces over-ran a vast area. Aïr, Gobir, Katsina, Kano, Daura, Zaria and possibly Nupe submitted to Kebbi and contributed tribute and man-power to support the new dignity of Kanta of Kebbi.

Kanta's reputation as a ruler equals his fame as a war-leader. He was a prolific city-builder, who used tributary labour to build such imposing centres as Surame, Gungu and Leka, the ruins of which still exist. Surame, his capital, was almost impregnable, being surrounded by a moat and seven concentric mud and stone walls; Gungu was a garrison town from which a large section of the enormous army he kept could repel invaders and police his empire; while Leka was a holiday centre for the royal family. A strict ruler, Kanta played an active personal part in the government of the Kebbi state, and is reputed to have owned a copper-sheathed canoe powered by fifty paddlers to enable him to tour Kebbi in the rainy season when most tracks were impassable.

The success of Kebbi antagonized Bornu, which already regarded Hausaland as tributary to the Mais. Kanuri forces laid siege to Surame but after a bitter struggle were forced to withdraw. Legend has it that Kebbi losses were so great that the city would have fallen if the defenders had not deceived the enemy by manning unguarded positions along the wall by dead bodies in defiant poses. Kanuri losses must have been equally heavy, for as the Bornu army withdrew, Kanta of Kebbi pursued them. At Nguru, he defeated the retreating Kanuri but was not sufficiently powerful to follow up his success with an invasion of Bornu. While returning from this campaign, Kanta was killed in a battle against

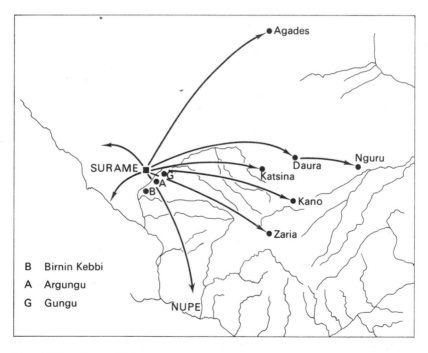

Map XIII   The Kebbi State

Katsina rebels, and his distressed but devoted followers solemnly carried his body to Surame for burial.

The decline of Kebbi Kanta's successors were unable to retain control of the whole of his conquests. The rise of Zaria in the south and the power of Bornu under Idris Alooma both whittled away Kebbi's sources of tribute. Yet, for a considerable time, Kebbi itself remained staunchly independent within its city walls and marshes, successfully defying Songhai attempts to conquer the area. However, internal dissensions within Surame and external attacks finally broke its power. In about 1700, Sarki Tomo abandoned Surame and made Birnin Kebbi his capital; and later in the eighteenth century, Kebbi became tributary to Gobir. The Fulani sacked Birnin Kebbi in 1805, but the Kebbi people re-established themselves at Argungu, and successfully defied all Fulani efforts to crush them.

Kwararafa

Origin of the Jukun Little is known of the Jukun state of Kwararafa, traditionally one of the Banza Bakwai. It is remarkable that the Jukun, who once raided at will across Hausaland, subjugated the states of the riverain area and menaced the power of Bornu, should have preserved little in the way of oral tradition.

Kingship among the Jukun The Jukun state system was very similar to that of other early Sudanic states. Their ruler, the Aku, was a divine king who controlled the secrets of the traditional cults and the destinies of his peoples. When he made a public appearance on ceremonial occasions, he sat behind a screen. As both religious and political head of his people, he enjoyed enormous prestige; but in the actual work of government his authority could be strictly limited. The religious nature of the monarchy could mean that a natural disaster such as harvest failure could destroy popular faith in the efficacy of his rule. His councillors, under the headship of the Abo, a kind of prime minister, possessed several constitutional weapons with which they could coerce the Aku. They could accuse him of breaking one of the many sacred regulations that controlled the daily life of the ruler; they could threaten to absent themselves from important religious

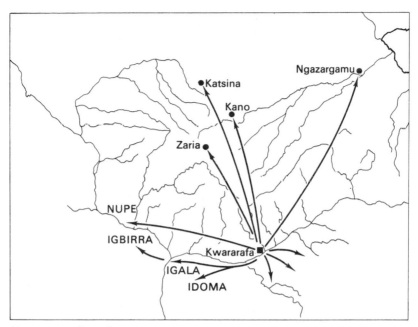

Map XIV   The Jukun State

ceremonies conducted by the Aku; or they could merely prevent government problems being brought to the notice of their secluded ruler. Equally, the priests of the Jukun cult could threaten to reveal the sacred objects of former Akus, thus destroying the air of mystery and divinity surrounding any particular ruler. Thus there were influential pressure groups which the Aku had to placate, and the extent of his influence on government depended on his personality and political ability.

The rise of Jukun power   Having been subject first to Kano and then to Zaria, the Jukun suddenly emerged in the second half of the sixteenth century as a dangerous military power. Mounted on horses and highly proficient with their long spears, they conquered and pillaged across Hausaland. During the reign of Muhammad Zaki, ruler of Kano from 1582 to 1618, they forced their way into Kano, massacred those citizens who did not flee to Daura, and 'ate up the country'. Their military efficiency and rapid striking power made them feared throughout the seven-

105

teenth century in the second half of which they again ravaged Kano and even forced their way into Katsina.

At about the same time, the Jukun appeared in force before Ngazargamu. However, the Mai of Bornu played them off against the Tuareg, who were attacking Bornu at the same time, and then defeated them. After this battle, peace was made between Bornu and Kwararafa; and the decline of Jukun power may date from this period. Although stories of competitions between the magic of the Jukun and the Islamic miracles of the Kanuri that always ended in a draw suggest a relationship of equality between the states, the title of 'Zanna' given to the Kanuri representative at the Jukun court was that usually given to the Kanuri official at the court of a tributary ruler. Thus by the end of the seventeenth century, Kwararafa may have become to some extent tributary to Bornu.

Yet, at the height of Jukun power, their influence had been felt in Kano and Zaria in the north and, along the rivers, they had controlled Idoma, Igbirra, Igala and Nupe. In northern Adamawa, their power had challenged that of Bornu; and it has even been suggested that their southward influence reached the Cross river, giving the Jukun access to the coastal trade with Europeans.

Reasons for the decline of Jukun power   The Jukun state rapidly declined in the eighteenth century and collapsed completely in the nineteenth. The reasons for this are not hard to surmise. Numerically a small people, they lived by plunder rather than by effective political control. Their capital was situated too far to the south to exercise effective power over the prosperous areas of northern Hausaland; and their cavalry was not of much effect in the forest to the south. Kwararafa did not sit astride any major trade route and it was blocked from direct access to the trans-Saharan trade by the ancient power of Bornu.

These difficulties might have been overcome had not religious ritual strangled the ability of the Aku to lead his people. Such a situation would almost certainly produce en-feebling struggles for power among the greater nobility. That there were also dynastic struggles is evidenced by the tradition that Wukari was founded by a newly-appointed Aku who fled from Kwararafa to escape the jealous wrath of his brothers.

Finally, the Jukun proved unable to survive the aggression of the Fulani in the nineteenth century at a time when they were also subject to military pressure from the advance into their homeland by the Chamba and the Tiv. It is greatly to be hoped that one day the full story of the Jukun past will be laid bare by research scholars.

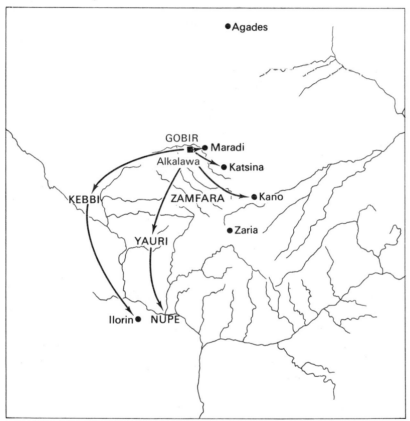

Map XV   Gobir at the Height of its Power

Gobir

Background of war   The Hausa peoples of Gobir, possibly the last of the Hausa Bakwai states to be founded, have always been noted for their martial qualities and the effectiveness of their heavy cavalry. A hardy people living along the fringes of the

107

desert, they were constantly subject to the attacks of the aggressive Tuareg. Thus only success in war enabled them to maintain their separate political identity.

The eighteenth-century rise of Gobir   The decline of Kebbi provided
Gobir with an opportunity for territorial expansion. Early in the
eighteenth century, Zamfara's determination to escape from
Kebbi overlordship became the occasion for an unusual alliance
between Gobir, the Tuareg of Aïr and Zamfara to partition
the Kebbi state. The three-pronged invasion was successful, the
leading Kebbi cities were destroyed and each aggressor annexed
the territory it had conquered. Sarki Soba, ninetieth ruler of
Gobir, raided as far south as Ilorin where a contingent of
Gobirawa settled permanently, and as for north as Maradi. But his
men wearied of constant campaigning and abandoned him
to the Tuareg.

After a brief period of dynastic struggle, Sarki Barbari, 1742 to
1770, achieved power in Gobir. His ambitions were directed
against Zamfara where a substantial number of Gobir people had
already settled peacefully on its rich farming land. In spite of the
existing diplomatic marriage between his sister and Mairoki of
Zamfara, Barbari invaded Zamfara several times. Finally, aided
by the disloyalty of a section of the Zamfara army, he destroyed
Mairoki's capital in about 1756. Barbari then built himself a new
capital at Alkalawa on lands formerly granted in friendship to
Gobir immigrants. From this more convenient base, Gobir
armies attacked in all directions in search of tribute. Maradi,
Katsina, Kano, Yauri and Nupe all felt the might of Gobir armies,
and in about 1770 Kano was compelled to pay tribute to the new
power in Hausaland.

The collapse of Gobir   Although Gobir gained spasmodic victories
over all her foes, she never achieved that political mastery won by
the great empires of the past. Mairoki put up a long and vigorous
resistance from Kiawa; Katsina and the Tuareg continuously har-
ried the Gobir state; and Zamfara and Kebbi made strenuous
attempts to regain their independence. The continuous pressure
on Gobir forces depleted its man-power and provoked political
tensions among the leaders of Gobir itself. Finally, in the last
quarter of the century, there grew up a Fulani-dominated Muslim

revival which came into serious conflict with the Hausa rulers. This broke into open rebellion in 1804 and eventually, in 1808, the Fulani stormed Alkalawa and extinguished the Habe dynasty of Gobir.

HAUSA GOVERNMENT

Pre-Islamic government of city-states
One reflection of the cultural unity of the Hausa peoples is the similarity of their systems of government. Early rulers were both political and religious heads of their people, their authority being enhanced by their sanctity, their key role in local religious ceremonies and their traditional descent from the founder of the state. Associated with them in the government of their states were members of the royal family, officials promoted on merit and loyalty and the natural rulers of tributary villages. Justice was given either by a district or village head or in special cases by the Sarki himself aided by the Master of the Royal Household. For particularly serious cases, the Sarki consulted others of his leading councillors. Revenue derived from a tithe on produce, tribute from subject peoples, customs duties, market dues and the spoils of war.

Hausa government under Islamic influence
On conversion to Islam, rulers naturally adopted some at least of the features of Islamic government. There was considerable advantage in this for the Sarki, as Islamic constitutional theory and practice tended to exalt the authority of the ruler over all lesser authorities. In particular, there was a tendency to remove real power from the hands of hereditary chiefs and transfer it to able men completely dependent on the ruler. Nevertheless, it would still be true to say that to maintain a commanding authority in his state, a Sarki had to display considerable qualities of leadership, adeptness in the management of men and a willingness to heed the advice of his councillors.

Central government   The post-Islamic Habe Council was composed of the great ministers of state and the most important officials of local government. The Councillors bore distinguished Islamic titles and enjoyed a definite position in state precedence. The Galadima was often the heir apparent but in some states he was a eunuch who deputized for the Sarki during his absence from the capital. The commander-in-chief rejoiced in the title of Madawaki. Second in importance to the Sarki, he was also responsible for important ceremonial duties, for advising the Sarki on appointments to high office and for summoning councillors to meetings. He was also on the panel of king-makers. In some states, the officer responsible for these duties was the Waziri (chief minister). Other important officials were the Magaji, Minister of Finance; the Yari, chief of prisons; the Sarkin Dogarai, head of the royal body-guard; and the Sarkin Yan Doka, the chief of police responsible for bringing wrong-doers to trial, the infliction of corporal punishment and keeping a general eye on social security.

Local government   Local government was in the hands of district and village heads. To these offices the Sarki could and did appoint members of the royal or other aristocratic families, yet often the appointments merely confirmed the authority of the natural rulers of the different areas. Each district head was under the supervision of one of the great officials of the capital, each of whom was responsible for a section of the kingdom.

Islamization of judicial matters tended to separate the executive and the judicature although the Sarki usually reserved cases with political implications for the judgement of himself and his Council. In such cases, the Sarki would seek the advice of his chief Muslim legal advisor, the *qadi* or Chief Alkali. The majority of trials, however, were conducted by Alkali administering Maliki law in the light of local custom. The Alkali usually had considerable knowledge of Islamic law and were able to consult Arabic law-books on the more tricky points. Appeals could be made from their courts to the Chief Alkali. Even so, much minor litigation at village level, particularly in the remoter areas, would be dealt with by the village head and possibly without reference to Islamic teachings.

The fiscal system   The revenue of Hausa states was obtained from taxes, mainly in kind, which had the approval of Islamic ideas of fiscal justice. *Zakat* was a tax on movable property to provide for the giving of alms to the poor; *jangali* a tax on live-stock; *kharaj* a land-tax based on annual production; while *jizyah* was a tax, usually on slaves, levied on subject peoples. In addition, there were excise taxes on the various skilled artisans and entertainers; tolls for the use of trade routes passing through the state; fees for the use of market facilities; and the traditional present-giving required of all men on visits to their superiors. An irregular, but at times considerable, source of revenue was plunder captured in war. Possibly the most important Muslim regulation on taxation was that it should be adjusted according to circumstance so that no free citizen would be saddled with an intolerable burden of tax.

People always grumble about paying taxes even when they are reasonable. There is much evidence, however, to show that the economic discontent of the peoples of Hausaland in the eighteenth century was the product of legitimate grievance over an excessive tax burden. This crushing weight of taxation can be explained by a combination of several factors. In the first place, growing state expenditure required an increasing yield from the established forms of taxation. The fact that privileged noblemen enjoyed exemption from taxation meant that a larger share of the required revenue had to be provided from the less privileged. Also, tax-collection was usually farmed out to important officials who sub-let the farms of their areas to men whose greed imposed arbitrary and unjust methods of taxation and extortion. Finally, the extent of corruption among officialdom in every Hausa state was such that it was difficult for a man to obtain even his just deserts without resort to bribery.

This perversion of the Islamic taxation system was the product of human weakness and the needs of the state. The same process can be seen in other spheres of government activity. In spite of their acceptance of Islam and their establishment of the formal structure of Muslim government, rulers continued to utilize their ancient political reputation as divine or semi-divine descendants of local gods. They observed the ancient ceremonies of their non-Muslim ancestors and made sacrifices to local deities whose existance Islam could not recognize; and one is tempted to wonder how much the authority of some of the great officials derived from their exalted Islamic titles and how much from their ancestral connection with the traditional heroes of their pre-Muslim

111

past. It was against all these divergences from the true path of Islamic orthodoxy that the Fulani Dan Fodio preached in the last quarter of the eighteenth century, and awakened a response in the breast of many Hausa and Fulani, Muslim and non-Muslim alike. For the ideal Islamic system he advocated appeared to offer a brand of justice unknown in the manipulated Islam of the Hausa states.

Questions

1 Describe briefly the tradition of origin of the Hausa people. Point out the difficulties of accepting this legend in its entirety but show the important contribution it makes to a study of the history of Hausaland.

2 Write a brief account of the rise of Kano until the death of Muhammad Rimfa.

3 How do you account for the great reputation of Muhammad Rimfa in the history of Kano?

4 Substantiate the view that Kanta of Kebbi was the greatest leader produced by the Hausa people.

5 Account for (a) the prosperity of Hausaland; (b) the failure of the Hausas to produce a united empire.

6 Give an account of (a) the pre-Habe occupants of Hausaland; (b) Queen Amina of Zaria; (c) the founding of the Nupe state; (d) the Jukun system of government.

7 Write an outline account of the Hausa system of government.

8 Write an historical account of any one Hausa state.

7

The Kanuri empires

The lake Chad basin early became the home of a virile people, accomplished in the arts of war and peace. These were the Kanuri, a race formed from inter-marriage between nomadic desert peoples and the more settled cultivators of the savanna belt. The predominant elements in this racial fusion were probably the dark-skinned, nomadic Zaghawa, forced southwards to the well-watered and fertile Chad area by the increasing dessication of the Sahara and political pressure from North Africa, and the So peoples who had built up a settled and organized society before Zaghawa intrusion.

THE SO CULTURE

Tradition records that the original stone age inhabitants of the Chad basin were little red men. In prehistoric times, they were either massacred, expelled or absorbed by a people of superior skills, physique and organizational gifts known as the So, whose language was akin to modern Hausa. The So established organized communities in Kanem and modern Bornu. We know little of their political history except that right up to the late sixteenth century independent So states fought many gallant and successful battles against the conquering Kanuri.

We know, however, that the So people possessed considerable political and artistic genius. Although they never combined effectively to form an empire, they developed city-states which were the centres of intense local patriotism. Each city was surrounded by strong defensive walls and dominated the life of

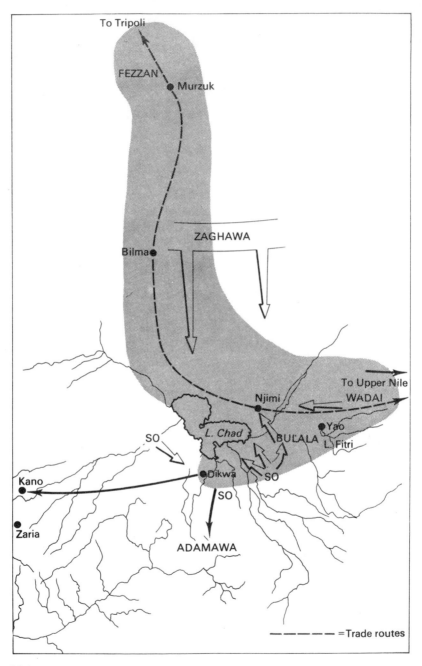

To Tripoli

FEZZAN
Murzuk

ZAGHAWA

Bilma

To Upper Nile

Njimi WADAI

Yao
L. Chad
BULALA L. Fitri
SO
Kano Dikwa SO

SO

Zaria

ADAMAWA

— — — — — — =Trade routes

the surrounding countryside which it both protected and governed. Government was by an elaborate hierarchy, headed by a divine ruler who as a god was worshipped by his people and held to control their destinies. Except on ceremonial occasions, the rulers made few public appearances and even then remained concealed from the common gaze by a screen. Women occupied a respected position in society and the Queen Mother and senior sister of the ruler exercised considerable political influence on the government of the state.

The So people were mainly settled farmers but among them were craftsmen of considerable industrial and artistic merit. They were able to work in both clay and metals to manufacture household utensils, tools, and works of art for religious purposes. Impressive objects found by archaeologists include burial urns and naturalistic figures of animals and human beings both in clay and bronze.

All this had been achieved by the So people before about A.D. 700, the earliest date used by modern historians in the political history of the Chad area. The vigour of their government and civilization is best demonstrated by their long resistance to the empires of Kanem and Bornu and by the fact that many cultural characteristics of the Kanuri have been adopted from the So.

THE FOUNDING OF THE KANURI STATE

According to tradition, the first ruler of Kanem was Sef (Saif), the leader of a small family group of Zaghawa who were allowed to settle peacefully among the peoples east of lake Chad in about A.D. 700. These immigrants obtained political dominance over the local inhabitants by a trick and either Sef or his son Dugu founded N'jimi, which was to grow into the capital of Kanem and become the centre of a thriving trade with North Africa. The early Sefawa rulers of N'jimi did not have firm control over a wide area but exercised spasmodic authority wherever they stopped on semi-nomadic wanderings. However, as time went on, they adopted the social and political attitudes of the indigenous people and developed a more unified and permanent form of government.

Map XVI The First Kanuri Empire

The rise of the empire of Kanem
The factors responsible for the rise of the early empire of Kanem were personal leadership, growing military power, expanding trade with North Africa and the spread of Islam in the central Sudan. Accordingly, the only facts recalled in tradition about the great rulers of the Kanem empire are related to one or another of these important forces. Mai Umme (Hume), 1085–1097, is remembered as the first Muslim ruler of the Kanuri. He rewarded Muhammad Ibn Mani, the learned *mallam* who instructed him in Islam, with the hereditary *imamate* of Kanem and granted both him and his descendants exemption from taxation in perpetuity. The death of Umme in Egypt, while on the *hajj* to Mecca, testifies not only to his religious belief but also to the existence of diplomatic contact with North Africa, considerable financial resources and a system of government sufficiently stable to enable the ruler to leave his country.

His son, Dunama I, Mai from 1097 to 1150, is celebrated for the command of large cavalry forces with which he established the power of N'jimi over the whole of Kanem. His military reputation was so great outside the central Sudan that, when he made the *hajj* for the third time, the Egyptians became suspicious of his motives and murdered him. His work in building the wealth and power of the empire was continued by Mai Biri, 1151 to 1176, and Mai Salma, 1194 to 1220. They extended Sefawa power over the desert peoples north of Kanem and controlled the trade route to Tripoli as far north as the Fezzan. Their power was sufficient for them to carry on diplomatic relations with Tunisia on equal terms. This contact with North Africa was facilitated by the growing reputation of the Mais for Islamic piety. In the reign of Salma, in particular, Islam made considerable headway as the imperial cult. A learned *mallam* instructed the Mai's son in the contents of a hundred and fifty Islamic books; the reed mosque at N'jimi was replaced by a more permanent plastered building and the sacred snake of the Kanuri ancestral religion is reported to have been miraculously killed.

Dunama II
Dunama II, 1221 to 1259, raised Kanem to the height of its power by military conquest and firm government. By his reign, the economic and man-power resources of Kanem were sufficient for

116

him to field a force of over thirty thousand cavalry supported by even larger forces of infantry. Warriors mounted on camels were recruited to cope with the problems of warfare in the desert. Thus, it is not surprising that his reign saw a great military thrust to the north that conquered the entire Fezzan and made Kanem master of the trade route to Tripoli almost to the fringes of the North African coastal strip. To the east, he over-ran the Bulala, a kindred people governing the area around Lake Fitri, advanced through Wadai and made the influence of the Sefawa felt as far east as the Upper Nile. He pushed the frontiers of Kanem around the southern shores of lake Chad as far as Dikwa, raided deep into northern Adamawa and exacted tribute across Hausaland as far west as Kano. These conquests provided spoils of war and increased revenues on a scale that enabled Kanem to support a greater volume of trade with North Africa so that Dunama's reign was a period of great prosperity in Kanem.

Dunama II was also an ardent Muslim, pious and militant. Wherever he made effective conquests, he insisted on the adoption of Islam by the defeated ruling classes and the institution of Maliki law as the official standard of justice. Yet Dunama was concerned by the fact that even among the Kanuri, Islam was still little more than an influential cult existing alongside the ancestral religion of ruler-worship. He worked to increase the prestige of Islam and while on pilgrimage to Mecca founded a hostel for Kanuri pilgrims in Cairo. Finally, he determined to destroy Kanuri traditional religion by demonstrating that it was founded on sheer superstition. To this end, he opened the sacred *mune*, a sealed container believed to hold the spirit of victory and of such great sanctity that its secrets should never be revealed to men.

This was a political error of the greatest magnitude. Dunama was soon to learn that the unity and power of early Sudanic empires depended on harmony between Islam and the indigenous religions. His sacrilegious act alienated a large section of the Kanuri and added dangerously to existing tensions within the Kanem empire. Some of Dunama's own sons joined the serious rebellions against him, and the Bulala made a dangerous bid to seek independence of Kanem and to avenge the insult to a religion they shared with the Kanuri. Although Dunama was able to contain these attacks on the Mai's authority during his

117

lifetime, he had seriously endangered the unity of the Kanuri state.

The collapse of the first Kanuri empire, 1259–1472
After Dunama II's death, the Sefawa dynasty suffered a long period of political disasters. Struggles for power, embittered by the religious issue, undermined the authority of the Mais. Civil war shattered Kanuri military power with the result that tributary states sought and won independence and then inflicted serious defeats on their former overlords. Between 1342 and 1352, So forces killed four successive Mais in battle. Even more dangerous were the Bulala who drove the Kanuri from N'jimi in the reign of Mai Daud, 1366 to 1376, and expelled them from Kanem altogether in the reign of Mai Umar ibn Idris (1384–1388). The Kanuri migrated west of lake Chad and led a semi-nomadic life trying to establish themselves in Bornu against the attacks of So and Hausa peoples. Even bands of Arabs from North Africa successfully raided the Kanuri for slaves during this period. Yet, in spite of these dangers, the Kanuri still remained divided by internal feuds.

THE FOUNDATION OF THE EMPIRE OF BORNU

Sefawa power was revived by Mai Ali Ghaji, 1472 to 1504, who accurately diagnosed the causes of Kanuri misfortunes and provided the remedies. He saw that it was essential to restore the discredited authority of the Mai over his councillors, enforce unity on the ruling classes and reconstruct Kanuri power in Bornu itself rather than dream of a quick return to the ancestral capital of N'jimi.

His major achievement was to restore the balance of the Kanuri constitution. One of the main causes of sectional discord was that some of the great officers of state had acquired power and income disproportionate to their traditional position in Kanuri society. This was particularly true of the Kaigama, the commander-in-chief, whose restless ambition continually provoked serious trouble. Ali Ghaji's forceful personality, political shrewdness

118

and reputation as a warrior enabled him to build up the personal following of the Mai, and then by a mixture of force and diplomacy to impose his will on the nobility. He redistributed power and revenue more equitably among the great officials and thus ended the period of constitutional struggles.

Other examples of Ali Ghaji's statecraft can be seen in his decision to build a capital city and in his attitude to religion. On land obtained near the confluence of the Yobe and Komadugu, he ordered the construction of the walled city of Ngazargamu. This provided the Kanuri with a settled administrative centre, a strongly fortified place of refuge and a secure market to which North African merchants were soon attracted. Clearly understanding the value of Islam both as a diplomatic and commercial link with North Africa and a means of politically uniting the different peoples he now controlled, he cautiously encouraged the spread of the religion by his personal example. He studied the Koran, followed its teachings in his daily life and confined himself to the four wives allowed by Islam. Under their ruler's guidance, the Kanuri began to return to the religion they had neglected in their period of adversity.

The restoration of Kanuri unity brought considerable military success. Ali Ghaji repulsed formidable attacks by the Bulala and the Jukun; he also made considerable conquests. The whole of Bornu was brought under Sefawa rule; renewed expansion into the desert led to the conquest of Tibesti; and Kanuri overlordship once more stretched westwards to Kano. This growing empire, the wealth it brought the monarchy and court, and the security Sefawa rule provided for travellers rapidly built up the trade and prosperity of Bornu. Before Ali Ghaji died, the fame of Bornu's power had reached Europe and its name appeared for the first time on fanciful European maps of Africa. He had laid a firm foundation on which a line of worthy successors was to erect one of the most notable of West African empires.

The successors of Ali Ghaji
Unfortunately, we know little of the history of Bornu between the death of Ali Ghaji and the accession of Idris Alooma. The two main dangers to the rising power of Bornu during this period were the Bulala and the Hausa state of Kebbi. Mai Idris Katakar-

mabi, 1504 to 1526, and Mai Muhammad, 1526 to 1546, were both able rulers who proved more than equal to these challangers. Idris Katakarmabi's victorious forces entered N'jimi in 1505 and forced the Bulala to acknowledge the overlordship of Bornu; and later, both he and Muhammad were able to crush dangerous Bulala attempts to regain their independence. Although Idris Katakarmabi and possibly later Mais failed to crush the rising power of Kanta of Kebbi, they amply demonstrated that Kebbi could not hope to challenge Bornu except on the periphery of the empire.

Early life of Idris Alooma
This most famous of all Bornu rulers was Mai Idris Alooma, 1572 to 1603, under whose illustrious rule Bornu reached the zenith of its power. Yet, he was lucky to live long enough to become ruler of the Kanuri empire. Just before his birth, his father, Mai Ali, was killed in a battle against the Bulala, and the next two Mais, Dunama and Abdullah, both plotted against the life of the young prince. He survived only because of the determination and political skill of a remarkable woman, the Magira Aisa. She shielded him from all danger and in about 1562 secured the regency of Bornu until Idris Alooma should come of age. For ten years, she governed wisely and trained Idris Alooma in the duties of Islamic kingship. To shield him from the intrigues and vices of the court, she brought him up in the new and beautiful Gambaru palace built a safe distance away from Ngazargamu.

Character of Idris Alooma   The young Idris grew into a man of remarkable ability and character. He was a natural leader of men, imposing in physical appearance and able to win the confidence and respect of his subjects. A pious Muslim, he had absolute faith that God controlled his destiny; and this steadfast, religious conviction made him resolute in enforcing Islamic reforms within the empire and completely fearless in battle. At times, the unwavering courage of this great conqueror turned imminent defeat for the Kanuri forces into victory. Yet the secret of his political success lay as much in his administrative gifts as in his fatalistic resolution. Cautious and calculating, he was a good judge of what was politic-

Map XVII   The Second Kanuri Empire

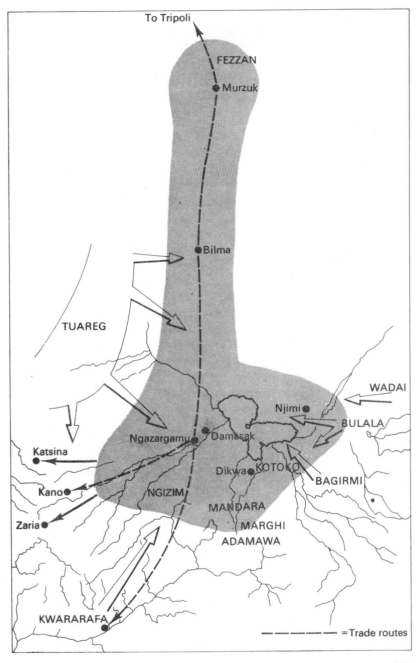

To Tripoli

FEZZAN

● Murzuk

● Bilma

TUAREG

WADAI

Njimi ●

BULALA

Ngazargamu ● ● Damasak

Katsina
●

Dikwa ● KOTOKO

BAGIRMI

Kano ●

NGIZIM

Zaria ●

MANDARA

MARGHI

ADAMAWA

KWARARAFA
●

— — — — — =Trade routes

ally possible and a master of the art of persuasion. He was a shrewd judge of character, and where he placed his trust, he placed it well and placed it completely. Thus he was well served by his great officials. Peoples who opposed him were out-manoeuvred by patient and painstaking diplomacy or brought to obedience by the swift and devastating onslaught of his redoubtable army.

Idris Alooma's military genius   Much of Bornu's success under Idris Alooma was achieved by war. Although he was well served by able commanders, it was Idris Alooma himself who was the leader and architect of Kanuri victories. During the three hundred and thirty campaigns of his reign, he developed into a master of strategy quick to seize upon any tactical error of the enemy. Making great demands upon the energies and courage of his men, he never pushed them beyond the limits of their endurance. If sudden victory eluded him, he resorted to siege warfare or to the systematic devastation of an area to deprive his foes of food and water. His forces on the march were compelled to erect stockades around their encampments as a precaution against surprise attack and pilfering by local scavengers.

Idris Alooma neglected nothing that could contribute to the military success of Bornu. He became the first Sudanic ruler to import firearms from North Africa and he hired Turkish musketeers to train his soldiers in effective use of these revolutionary weapons. Yet he realized that mounted warriors must continue to provide the main shock troops of Kanuri offensives. Accordingly, he encouraged his war-chiefs to increase the number of horses and camels at their disposal to strengthen the Kanuri war-machine in both the savanna and the desert. To facilitate the transport of his armies across the waterways of the Chad basin, a fleet of large boats capable of carrying great numbers of troops and their animals was constructed. By these means, Idris Alooma increased both the mobility and the striking capacity of his army.

The imperial policy of Idris Alooma   Idris Alooma's military policies were dictated by dynastic, imperial and religious ambitions. He set out to consolidate Sefawa power over existing parts of the Kanuri empire; to expand imperial frontiers so that greater revenue and wealth would accrue to Bornu through plunder, increased tribute and control of trade routes to North Africa;

and to weld his territories into a united and Islamic state. The extent of his success was great. Within Bornu itself, he reduced the fortress of Damasak and other semi-independent So city-states. Around the frontiers, he drove the anti-Muslim Tetala into the fastnesses of lake Chad with the aid of the Kotoko people; he subjugated the troublesome Ngizim people on the south-west frontier; he crushed a rebellion of the truculent Marghi; and he forced the Mandara people to restore a deposed ruler and to acknowledge his overlordship. Kanuri power was reasserted over northern Hausaland by a campaign which mastered all the strongholds of Kano except Dala itself. Thus the Kanuri were able to raid and exact tribute across Hausaland at will.

The main obstacles to the expansion of Kanuri power were the Bulala of Kanem and the Tuareg of Aïr. Neither was easy to defeat because of the problems of water supply and the difficulty of forcing the enemy into decisive engagements. In Kanem, he supported a rival to the usurping Sultan Abd al-Jelil, who was a determined enemy of Bornu and who sought control of several towns along the Kanem-Bornu border which had been ceded to Bornu by treaty. Several arduous campaigns and much tortuous diplomacy were necessary before Idris Alooma broke the power of Abd al-Jelil and annexed part of Kanem to Bornu. The conflict between Bornu and the Tuareg was a struggle for control of the trade route to Tripoli. Idris Alooma had conquered the Teda centre of Bilma, an important salt-producing and market centre on the trans-Saharan route. The Tuareg, concerned with establishing the economic supremacy of Agades over Bilma, proved stubborn foes capable of inflicting defeat on the Kanuri. Finally, however, the Kanuri, with the aid of Arab mercenaries, wore down Tuareg resistance and forced them to recognize Idris Alooma as their overlord.

Idris Alooma saw the spread of Islam as a religious duty and a political necessity. His own pious conduct set an example for his subjects and encouraged strict adherence to the tenets of Islam. He stamped out immorality in Ngazargamu, forbade the enslavement of Muslims captured in war and saw that e, his armies on the march punctiliously observed prayer times. On his pilgrimage to Mecca, he paid for the construction of a hostel for Kanuri pilgrims in the holy city itself; and within Bornu he replaced thatched mosques by others built of burnt bricks in the North

African style. He is said to have converted all the ruling classes within his empire to Islam and to have ruled in accordance with Islamic political theory. To ensure that Islamic law was genuinely applied in the trial of civil and criminal cases, he appointed Muslim *qadis* to the courts of local chiefs. These saw that judgements and penalties were those approved by Muslim law and were not based on customary or arbitrary procedures. Thus, by Idris Alooma's death, Bornu had developed most of the features of an Islamic state even if among the common people customary religions were far from destroyed. We are fortunate that his *imam*, Ahmad Ibn Fartua, wrote a chronicle of the early years of his reign as it enables us to evaluate the calibre of the most remarkable Sefawa ruler of Bornu.

THE DECLINE OF BORNU

Not a great deal is known of the Mais who ruled during the seventeenth and eighteenth centuries; and this is a sure indication that Bornu's expansion had halted. However, the Bornu state continued to present an appearance of strength to the outside world and to defend itself against its enemies until the late eighteenth century. It continued to receive tribute from a wide area and in the second half of the seventeenth century repulsed simultaneous attacks by the powerful Jukun and the Tuareg. As late as 1730, Kanuri forces successfully attacked Zaria. Yet it is probable that influences were already at work within the empire that were to render Bornu incapable of defending itself against the Fulani in the early nineteenth century.

The Mais who ruled after Idris Alooma are remembered almost exclusively as pious Muslims and patrons of Islamic learning. None of them seems to have possessed his personality, energy, political ability and martial enthusiasm; and few of them ever left their palaces. This means that during the seventeenth century the Mais were reduced to the position of heads of state with little executive authority. If this were so, then the unity of the empire would have been weakened by loss of leadership and a struggle for power among the great officials next to the Mai. The resultant ineffectiveness of the central government would have meant that tributaries and external enemies could challenge the might of Bornu and gradually erode its power. Thus by the end of the eighteenth century, the Tuareg of Aïr had established their control over the salt trade of the desert. One factor contributing to the loss of Kanuri control of the southern approaches of the trans-Saharan route was a series of famines, which may also have contributed to a general weakening of its economy and power. Finally, the forces of Bornu became increasingly so ineffectual through lack of cohesion and uninspired leadership that they were seriously defeated by the Mandara in the reign of Mai Ahmad, 1791 to 1808.

The collapse of Sefawa power came in the early nineteenth century. The Fulani occupied Ngazargamu in both 1808 and 1810 and only the intervention of the great Kanembu religious leader, Shehu Muhammad al-Amin al-Kanemi, saved Bornu from Fulani domination. Reduced to the position of puppet rulers in their own kingdom, successive Mais resorted to intrigues against the Shehu dynasty. This led to the final overthrow of the Sefawa dynasty in 1846 when Ali Dalatumi, the last Sefawa ruler of Bornu, was killed in battle.

Reasons for the success of the Sefawa dynasty
The Sefawa dynasty was one of the longest-lived in the history of the world, having ruled Kanuri states for about a thousand years. It is interesting to speculate on the reasons for their long supremacy. In the first place, there is the natural factor: the family did not die out through failure of heirs and many of the Mais enjoyed long reigns which enabled them to provide stable government and build up the power of the state. The family also produced men of outstanding political and military ability such as Dunama II, Ali Ghaji and Idris Alooma who provided the Kanuri with brilliant leadership.

Yet, important as is leadership in the annals of a people, it cannot alone account for national success. The Kanuri people early demonstrated martial qualities of a high order and produced a series of great warriors. Their political genius evolved a system of government which gratified the ambitions of the great officers of state for wealth and power but also kept firm central control over key matters of local administration. Rulers of newly conquered peoples were given sufficient local autonomy for them

125

to accept Kanuri overlordship and by a process of inter-marriage to become absorbed into the Kanuri governing classes. A vigilant central government, working mainly through freed men and slaves loyal to the Mai, watched that local powers were not abused. The suitability of the Kanuri system of government can best be gauged by the ease with which efficient rule could be restored after periods of political troubles.

Another important factor in the maintenance of Sefawa dominion was its early dominance of the trade route through Bilma. From North Africa were obtained not only luxuries to enhance the comfort and prestige of the court but also valuable supplies of war-horses and camels that enabled the Kanuri to build the most formidable war machine in the central Sudan. Equally, the trade of their successive capitals at N'jimi and Ngazargamu enabled them to establish their economic ascendancy over a wide and productive area.

Closely related to the growth of the trans-Saharan trade was the spread of Islam among the ruling classes. Although it is impossible to assess accurately the impact of Islam on imperial growth and stability, it is clear that Islam strengthened the power of rulers in two ways. It provided a religious basis for common loyalty to the Mai from people of many different ethnic groups; and it also encouraged the growth of central control over local government.

Finally, the Kanuri were lucky that, until late in their history, there rose no other empire to challenge their supremacy in the central Sudan. The other peoples of the central Sudan were too steeped in the traditions of the city-state to produce consolidated and lasting empires. The Tuareg to the north, the Bulala to the east and the Jukun to the south lacked sufficient economic resources of their own to establish permanent control over populous areas; and the might of Mali and Songhai was too far removed from lake Chad for serious clashes to occur between them and the Sefawa.

THE KANURI SYSTEM OF GOVERNMENT: ORIGINS

Little is known of the early Kanuri constitution. What is clear is that it gradually developed out of a combination of three important influences: the political and social practices of the original settled inhabitants of the Chad basin; the nomadic concepts of empire of the early Sefawa immigrants; and the centralizing and formalizing tendencies of Islam. It is probable that, throughout Kanuri imperial history, their dominant political ideas were those of the So and kindred peoples adapted to meet the requirements of empire and the precepts of Islam.

Fig. 5   Three Kanuri warriors

The position of the Mai   The head of the central government was the Mai, an hereditary sovereign chosen from the descendants of Sef. Originally divine rulers, the Mais preserved all the outward attributes of sacred monarchy long after their conversion to Islam. They ate in seclusion, appeared ceremonially before the public gaze on very rare occasions and gave audiences to strangers from behind a screen of curtaining. In strict theory, their position as both political and religious leader of their people gave them absolute power in all spheres of government. In practice, they were constitutional rulers who had to heed the advice and ambitions of their councillors.

The Mai and the council   The official organ of government was the Council of Twelve which advised the Mai on policy and saw to its implementation in his name. This council was composed of the great officials of state who were selected both from the royal family and influential men of servile origin. Without their co-operation, the Mai was practically powerless; they, on the other hand, could govern the country with little reference to his wishes. Thus the exact amount of influence exercised on the government of the Kanuri by any individual Mai depended on the strength of his personality, his administrative wisdom and ability to manage his councillors. The weak Mais could be practically excluded from contact with the problems of government, while strong ones could dominate their councillors, exploit differences of opinion among them and exercise a controlling influence on the administration of their empire.

The influence of women   Other important influences on royal government were the women who filled the highly respected offices of Magira, Magara and Gumsu. The Magira was the Queen Mother; the Magara the senior sister of the Mai; and the Gumsu the Mai's first wife. These ladies of the court had enjoyed privileged status from time immemorial. Their practical influence on politics probably stemmed from the fact that their household duties and special relationship with the Mai gave them easy access to his presence and made it possible for them to coerce him by the threat to withdraw their services. As the Magira had complete responsibility for the provision of royal food and the Magara for care of the royal children, such threats could never be taken lightly. The extent of the power of the Queen Mother can be seen in the fact that Mai Biri was imprisoned on the Magira's order and Magira Aisa controlled Kanuri political life before the accession of Idris Alooma.

Local government For administrative purposes, the Kanuri empire was divided into four great geographical subdivisions. The Kaigama was governor of the south; the Yerima controlled the north; the Mestrema ruled the east; and the west was the responsibility of the Galadima. These men were the four leading members of the Council of Twelve. Their functions were both administrative and military. They were responsible for the preservation of law and order, the collection of revenue and the mustering and command of local forces. They had to repel external attacks on the frontiers under their jurisdiction and to extend Kanuri influence beyond them. Yet in actual fact the day-to-day routine work of administration was delegated to officials known as Chima Gana, who were men born and respected in the areas they served.

The maintenance of imperial unity Great precautions were taken to avoid dynastic struggles, preserve the balance of the constitution and minimize rivalries within the ruling classes of the empire. As the Mai's sons reached manhood, they were despatched to the provinces to prevent them becoming centres of political rivalry and intrigue within the capital. Membership of the council was not hereditary and the four great officers in charge of the major sub-divisions of the kingdom were appointed to govern areas where their families had no vested interests. What is more, with the exception of the Galadima, they and other important noblemen were required to live in the capital under the eye of royal authority. Only in times of emergency did they visit the areas they governed and assume personal control. While this lessened the danger of their building up independent local power, it had the further value that as new areas were added to the empire, their natural rulers could be appointed Chima Gana to their own people. This reinforced their authority over their people, guaranteed a high degree of local autonomy and at the same time brought them under the supervision of one of the great Kanuri noblemen at Ngazargamu.

Fig. 6   A Kanuri warrior on horseback

Military organization   Although Kanuri rulers could field an army of many thousands when the occasion demanded, and this was often, the Mais did not keep large standing armies. The bulk of the troops on active service were local levies commanded by local officials. The four great sub-divisions of the kingdom were in fact four loose area commands. The Kaigama, Yerima,

130

Mestrema and Galadima were divisional commanders, and in addition the Kaigama was supreme commander of the entire army. Subordinate to the area commanders were high-ranking officers known as Kacella, each of whom controlled a regiment of cavalry and another of infantry. Smaller units were led by men of repute in their own area and thus the whole structure of military discipline depended on personal acquaintance of officers with their men, mutual respect and local pride.

Imperial finance The subjects of the Kanuri empires paid two main sorts of taxes, both paid in kind. One was a tax on the harvest to provide for the upkeep of the Mai and his court; the other was to supply the needs of local government officials. Both the Mai and important noblemen founded slave villages to further supplement their income. Equally, villages could be founded as a form of patronage to the *ulama* and these were usually exempted from imperial taxation. Other sources of revenue were the spoils of war, the profits of justice, the giving of presents to the Mai and taxes on trade.

Questions

1 Write an account of the So culture and point out the elements of similarity and dissimilarity between the political structure of the So and the Kanuri.

2 'The rulers of Kanem are remembered for their conquests and their contributions to the spread of Islam.' Illustrate this statement from the traditional accounts of the Mais of Kanem from the reign of Umme to the death of Dunama II.

3 Why was the reign of Dunama II followed by a disastrous period in Kanuri history?

4 Estimate the contribution of Ali Ghaji to the revival of Kanuri power.

5 Give an account of the character and achievements of Idris Alooma.

6 Account for the long survival of Sefawa power.

7 Describe the political system of the Kanuri. What were its strengths and weaknesses?

8

Islam in West Africa down to 1804

Knowledge of Islam and Arabic culture first came to West Africa along the desert routes from North Africa. By the early years of the eighth century, the Arabs had conquered the whole of the coastal strip of North Africa and they installed new Arab ruling families whose courts became the centres from which Islamisation spread. At this time, the trans-Saharan trade was conducted by the Berbers of the desert, particularly the Sanhaja. The lure of western Sudanese gold soon took Muslim Arabs across the desert and, when the Berbers accepted conversion to Islam, the entire traffic across the desert was in Muslim hands.

Early conversions
Muslim merchants and clerics, often one and the same person, made the spread of Islam an important part of their activities in West Africa. Most peoples of the savanna belt received their first knowledge of Islam from a wandering trader and most of the earliest conversions were effected through this agency. Thus Islam established its first roots in Sudanic cities by peaceful persuasion. All conversions, however, were not of equal value for the progress of Islam: to convert a Soninke or Mandingo trader was to gain another soul for Allah and possibly a useful missionary among his own people and kindred; the conversion of a ruler meant the imposition of Islam upon the ruling classes and the gradual introduction of the leading features of an Islamic state.

As early as the ninth century, there were probably indigenous Muslims in Tekrur, ancient Ghana and Kanem. By 1067, there was already a flourishing Muslim community in Kumbi, with its twelve stone mosques in the Muslim quarter and its leading members established as ministers of the Ghana. Islam, however, was not the religion of the Ghana himself nor of the vast majority of his subjects. But by then Islam had acquired a more official status in Tekrur where War-jabi had been converted and had already begun the process of establishing Islamic law among the Tukulor. Thus it was to the Senegal valley that the frustrated Abdullah ibn Yacin fled for refuge from the Sanhaja Berbers; and it was there that he built up his Almoravid movement that imposed its own form of Islam upon the western Sahara, Morocco and southern Spain.

The Role of Conquest

The conversion of the Sanhaja Berbers into the militant Almoravids was an important development in the spread of Islam in the western Sudan. On their conquest of Kumbi in 1076, they gave the Soninke inhabitants the choice of Islam or death. Many fled, but many others remained and joined the religion with which they were already familiar. Possibly more important for the early spread of Islam were the conquests of Kumbi first by Sumaguru and then Sundiata. These conquests caused Muslim Soninke to scatter over a wide area of the western Sudan and, wherever they went, they took their religion with them. The dual role of Soninke Muslims as merchants and missionaries gave them an influence out of proportion to their numbers in the spread of Islam along the upper Niger. The later conquests of the famous Muslim rulers of West African states expanded the influence of Islam and its culture to the ruling classes of conquered peoples.

Progress in the Western Sudan

Despite the early establishment of Islam as the imperial cult of Tekrur, political reverses were once more to bring the Senegal valley under non-Muslim rule. The key developments took place among the future empire-builders, the Mandingos and Songhai. During the eleventh century, a chief of a Mandingo village state, Baramendena by name, is said to have become a Muslim to save his country from drought through prayers to Allah after sacrifices to traditional gods had failed. Either at the beginning or the end of the same century, the peaceful conversion of Za Kosoi of Songhai was followed by the conversion of the Songhai ruling classes. Hopeful pointers as these events were to people wanting to build Islam in West Africa, they led to no immediate large-

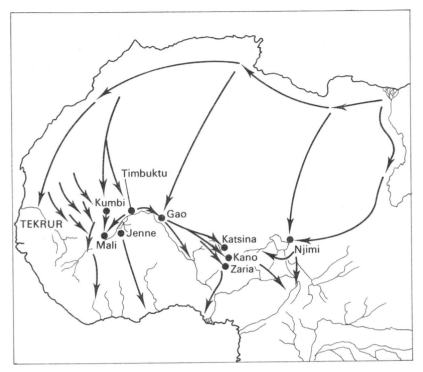

Map XVIII   The Advance of Islam

scale developments.

These large-scale developments came with the creation first of the empire of Mali and then that of Songhai. In both cases, the pattern was the same: first a founder-conqueror deriving his support and success mainly from indigenous religion and military leadership; then an imperial consolidator who worked to establish Islam. It was under Mansa Musa that the cities of the western Sudan took on an Islamic character. We saw in chapter 4 how he insisted on correct Muslim observances, went on the *hajj* to Mecca, patronised *ulama* and holy men and built new and imposing mosques. We also read, however, that not even Mansa Musa was fully aware of Muslim marriage laws, and that Ibn Battuta reported such non-Islamic customs as nudity among young women, the freedom and importance women enjoyed in

135

society and the provision of a cannibal feast for a Wangara delegation.

The fortunes of the *ulama* and Islam underwent a temporary
eclipse in Timbuktu and Jenne with the rise of Sunni Ali to imperial power. As we saw in Chapter 5, Sunni Ali had little time
for the *ulama*. Their cries against his persecution were bitter,
possibly even more bitter than the situation deserved. Under
his successor, however, the golden age of Islam dawned in the
cities of the western Sudan. Askia Muhammad threw the weight
of his influence behind conversion to Islam and stimulated
Muslims to proper observance of their religion. As mentioned
earlier, he gave such generous patronage to the *ulama* that refugees
from Sunni Ali and scholars from across the desert came to the
'university' cities of Jenne and Timbuktu, which became two of
the foremost centres of Islamic learning in the world. And so, it
would have seemed that Islam was securely established as an
imperial religion and that it was only a matter of time before it
spread beyond city walls to the masses occupying the rural villages.

Yet, at one stroke, the whole Islamic façade of the western
Sudan collapsed. The Moroccan conquest destroyed the imperial
character of the area, interfered with trade and drastically lowered
the standard of Islamic scholarship. The need for an international,
imperial religion disappeared. In their new dilemma, people
turned to their traditional gods for guidance and protection.
The new Bambara states which arose from the ruins of Songhai
owed their creation to the old dynamic impulse of rulers whose
power flowed from the dual politico-religious authority of a
sacred head of a people and their religion. It was not until the
nineteenth century that Muslim rulers were again to govern large
empires in the western Sudan.

Progress in the central Sudan
Islam filtered into the lake Chad area along the routes from Egypt
and Tripoli. Mai Umme's acceptance of the faith was the essential
prelude to the rapid growth of Islam among the ruling class, the
development of Muslim scholarship and the introduction of
Islamic law. However, the religious zeal of Dunama II, who
sought to destroy the indigenous religion of the Kanuri, brought
a serious reaction which not only broke the power of Kanem but
also relegated Islam to a minor position in Kanuri politics. It

was not until the reign of Ali Ghaji, as we saw in Chapter 7, that the restoration of Islam as an influential imperial cult was cautiously begun. His successors built upon the foundations he had laid until finally Idris Alooma was able to make Islam the state religion of Bornu. Under Idris Alooma, Muslim observances were strictly practised by the ruling classes, Islamic morality was imposed on the social life of towns, Islamic studies were encouraged and Islamic law penetrated the courts of sub-rulers. Even on military campaigns, the army faithfully observed Muslim hours of prayer; and the process of spreading Islam among non-Kanuri peoples was encouraged. Sefawa rulers after Idris Alooma were noted for their piety and devotion to learning; yet by the early nineteenth century, Usuman dan Fodio was able to use the imperfections of Kanuri Muslim worship as an excuse for a jihad against them. Even the pious Al-Kanemi, saviour and apologist of the Kanuri, admitted there were errors in their conception of Islam.

Islam did not enter Hausaland until late in its history. We are told of the arrival of forty Muslim missionaries who converted Sarki Ali Yaji of Kano in the fourteenth century. Although Ali Yaji appointed Muslim officials, founded a mosque and ordered his people to pray five times daily, Islam was not firmly founded in Kano. During his reign, it was necessary to resort to stern measures to crush resolute opposition from the devotees of Barbushe; and under his son Kanajeji, the cult of Barbushe became once more the official religion of Kano. Islam did not die out but it was not until the reign of Muhammad Rimfa that it became the state religion of the city. Elsewhere in Hausaland, Islam made even slower progress. Not until the early sixteenth century did the rulers of Katsina embrace Islam; and other Hausa states did not become Muslim until much later than that.

THE REASONS FOR THE SPREAD OF ISLAM IN WEST AFRICA

The key doctrine of Islam, namely that there is but one God, ran counter to the beliefs of all traditional religions in West Africa where religion was also a complete way of life. All peoples believed in a pantheon of gods—gods of the sky, of the earth, of

137

local sites, of the animal world. Their rulers possessed varying degrees of divinity through their descent from deified ancestors, who were worshipped and consulted by the people through oracles. Each god had his own cult; each cult its own secrets, shrines and priests. Each god was the centre of important ceremonies and the recipient of sacrifices; each cult was a vital cog in the working of the whole social system and a source of authority, political as well as religious. Offerings were made not only to the gods but also to appease or exorcize evil spirits. Where witchcraft was suspected, the supernatural was called upon to heal the sick, to discern the guilty or even to provide judicial remedy. For the Muslim, all these practices were irreligious and profane.

Yet during our period many West Africans became Muslims, and in the nineteenth and twentieth centuries Islam has become the religion of a majority of West Africa's people. The early spread of Islam was the result of a number of different factors, some social, some economic and some political. Obviously, one factor was the spiritual conversion of people who saw religion in a new light when the beliefs and achievements of Islam were explained to them. That this process took place in the trading cities is significant. There lived different peoples, removed from their own close village societies where the success of the harvest was held to depend on fertility rites and sacrifices to the local gods. In their non-traditional setting, these city dwellers were in a religious sense de-tribalized and thus more open to the influence of a new religion which seemed adapted to their urban mode of life. To them, Islam must have seemed very much like the cult of traders, and Allah the God of merchants.

The acceptance of Islam was also facilitated by the nature of West African religions. West Africans founded new cults to newly identified gods and, although they were polytheists, all of them acknowledged the existence of a supreme god who was usually the god of the sky. Thus, Muslim introduction of the worship of Allah must have seemed unobjectionable.

Although Islam did not make sacrifices to local gods, consult oracles nor approve of religious 'magic', its own rituals were recognizable as worship to traditional cults and could be interpreted in terms of local cult practices by the uninitiated. The Muslim prayer ritual, fasting, and in due course the building of

138

impressive mosques could be accepted as the peculiar but distinguishing features of a new cult. The required procedures for the slaughter of meat, the resort to prayer in times of danger, prayers for the souls of the dead and the sale of Koranic amulets to protect the owner against spirits and ill-health could be equated in non-Muslim minds with sacrifices, the consultation of oracles, ancestor worship and the efficacy of local 'medicines' which were essential parts of their own religions. As long as Islam did not attempt to destroy indigenous cults, there was no objection to it.

Another reason for the spread of Islam was the discretion of early Muslim 'missionaries' and even Muslim rulers. Muslims, both subjects and rulers, very rarely came into open conflict with traditional cults: to have done so would have been to invite disaster. Studies of modern Islamization of West African peoples have shown that Muslim clerics do not discredit existing customs but infiltrate them and change their nature. This almost certainly was the procedure in earlier times. Although Muslims could not accept the sacred nature of the ruler, they were prepared to share in non-Muslim ceremonies such as fertility rites and funerals. While observing local custom in these matters, they worked to gradually replace communion with the spirit world by prayers to Allah. If men could be brought to observe the externals of the five pillars of Islam, in time they or their descendants would come to believe exclusively that there is no God but Allah.

There were also a number of more positive factors that contributed to the acceptance of Islam in the early Sudanic states. These were mainly non-religious. In the first place, Muslims were associated with the wealth of the trans-Saharan trade and brought goods essential to West African economies and the increase of military power. Doubtless, too, early trans-Saharan traders told impressive stories of the Islamic civilizations in their home countries which gave practical expression to the glory of Allah. Their mode of dress, their new architecture and their possession of desirable luxuries added to the prestige of their religion. Their literacy in Arabic impressed non-literate peoples who assigned important supernatural qualities to the written word. This attitude was encouraged by the Muslim faith in the efficacy of Koranic amulets; and Muslim clerics have always found a ready sale for these among peoples who have remained aloof from Islamic teachings. The traditions of the conversion of the Mandingo chief Baramendena and the crushing of opposition to Ali Yaji in Kano are isolated instances which indicate the reputation established for the efficacy of Muslim prayers to Allah.

Islam had a special appeal for rulers of Sudanic empires, and once an emperor accepted the religion, his influence and authority were usually sufficient to impose it upon at least the ruling classes of his empire. Acceptance of Islam, correct observance of religious ceremonies and patronage of the *ulama* brought him the political support of urban Muslim communities influential for their role in commerce and for their learning. Their respect for the office of a just monarch, their authoritarian political theory and their literacy were valuable supports to the dignity and power of the monarchy: their connections with North Africa helped to develop the trade of the empire and establish diplomatic relations beyond the Sahara. But above all, the spread of Islam in imperial cities offered a new and necessary base for imperial unity. The authority of a ruler such as Sundiata or Sunni Ali rested mainly on headship of the traditional religious cults of his own people. But once an empire was established, he became the ruler of other peoples with their own religions in which he played no part. Therefore, he could not claim from all his subjects that dual loyalty, religious and political, which was the essential foundation of governmental authority in West Africa. Islam offered a means by which the ruler could claim a new dual loyalty from subjects of all nations. Not only would it form a bond between the emperor and all his Muslim subjects, but his political authority would be further reinforced by the Islamic teaching which imposed obedience to a just Muslim ruler on all Muslims irrespective of race. Thus rulers were quick to see the advantage of adopting an international religion in place of a local one; and it also seemed appropriate that the cult of the Almighty should be the personal religion of an almighty earthly ruler.

THE RESULTS OF THE SPREAD OF ISLAM

The most obvious result of the spread of Islam to West Africa was the introduction of a new and alien religion. Its monotheistic teachings and the idea that the souls of the dead do not participate in human affairs were completely novel to the societies into which they were introduced. With these doctrines came rituals and customs equally strange to West African peoples. The advent of Islam meant not only the profession of Allah but also the sight of Muslims praying and the sound of the *muezzin* call; it meant the introduction of the Ramadan fast, the building of mosques and the departure of leading citizens on the *hajj* to Mecca; it meant the marvel of scholars reading and writing. Not only did converts obey Muslim regulations on ablutions, on the slaughter of animals for food and on the seclusion of women, they also adopted Islamic styles of dress and architecture.

It is difficult, however, to estimate the exact religious impact of Islam on West African peoples. Early travellers and historians commented favourably on the standard of Islamic piety, scholarship and some features of government in the important trading cities. On the other hand, they record the continuance of traditional customs and ceremonial unacceptable to Islam. Also, nineteenth century Muslim reformers castigated nominally Muslim rulers for the travesty of Islam practised in their states. Possibly the efforts of Muslims to adapt ethnic customs and practices to Islamic purposes by stealth rebounded on them, and it was Islam that became assimilated into basically non-Muslim systems. It certainly seems that Islam in West Africa before 1800 was little more than an imperial cult of great prestige existing side by side with cults to other gods. Few rulers escaped the need to draw their power from ethnic religions; many people must have both worshipped in the mosque and sacrificed to local deities. Indeed, by 1800, Islam had barely made any converts outside the cities and although there were Muslim traders in the forest they had made no significant inroads on local religions. But West Africans knew of Islam and this is an important fact in itself.

With Islam came a new and important form of education Whereas indigenous education was purely local and concerned with initiating the young into knowledge of local custom, their duties within local society and the skills they needed for their livelihood, Muslim studies covered an international field of theology, politics, law, history, geography and the natural sciences. Above all, Islam introduced literacy in Arabic and

141

the art of academic criticism. Although Muslim knowledge and skills became the property only of an educated élite, the work of these scholars reached an outstanding level of academic achievement, especially in the 'university' cities of Timbuktu and Jenne. Scholars acquired large libraries and won enviable reputations in most fields of Islamic learning; and famous indigenous scholars such as Ahmad Baba, Al-Sadi and Mahmud Kati, all important historians, were in touch with leading Islamic scholars outside West Africa.

The acceptance of Islam as the official religion of Sudanic states brought political and economic advantages. Relations with North African merchants and rulers were placed on a friendlier and more equal basis. Arabic language and law became important in commercial dealings, and their introduction enhanced the prestige of rulers such as Mansa Musa, Askia Muhammad and Idris Alooma. The most practical demonstration of the value of these contacts was the ability of Idris Alooma to import firearms. Costly though pilgrimages were, they informed royal alhajis on the geography, politics and cultures of a wider world; they literally helped to put West African states upon the map.

The exact political results of the spread of Islam are difficult to estimate. When the early travellers and historians wrote of the spread of Islamic law, the appointment of *qadis* and of just Islamic government, we do not know exactly what they meant. Their favourite rulers certainly promoted the externals of Islam but whether or not their Muslim reforms constituted the creation of true Islamic states is very much in doubt. But in making the judgement that the Islam of these states was little more than a useful imperial cult and not the basis of a theological system of government, we need to be restrained by the fact that in Muslim political theory what is important is not the control of the entire political state but the application of law and government to its Muslim community.

The spread of Islam among his subjects definitely contributed to the strengthening of the constitutional position of a Sudanic ruler. The egalitarian nature of Muslim society weakened the position of great chiefs who had traditional rights to limit his authority. It may also have curbed the tendency for traditional officers of state to use the divinity of the monarch to gradually exclude him from direct control of governmental affairs. Muslim

142

respect for the authority and dignity of the temporal ruler, and its very limited right of lawful rebellion, contributed to the gradual building up of strong central control over the local interests that predominated in feudal empires. Much practical political cunning, useful in safeguarding a ruler's personal security and authority, was provided by Muslim politicians. The oft-quoted advice of Al-Maghili to Muhammad Rimfa is one example of this; and the practice of using people of servile origin in important government offices is another. Equally, Muslim literacy was a valuable aid to efficient government and accurate diplomacy.

Most important of all, however, was the value of Islam as a unifying factor in large empires containing many different peoples. We have seen that the successful spread of Islam, an international religion, could provide a common religious bond between the ruler and his various subjects and command their loyalty to him. Thus by encouraging Muslims in the observance of their religious duties, by patronizing the *ulama* and spreading the faith to the ruling classes of subject peoples, the ruler could strengthen imperial unity. That Islamic developments took place almost exclusively in the towns does not weaken the validity of this argument; for commercially, militarily and politically, the towns were the significant parts of early empires. That the spread of Islam in the towns could create a breach between the traditional religionists of the rural areas and their rulers in the cities did not create a serious problem. This was partly due to the fact that Islam accommodated many local customs and did not openly assault traditional beliefs; and partly due to the political and economic dominance of the towns. When, however, the towns lost their significance after the Moroccan conquest, it was the ethnic religions of the rural peoples that were to take the political initiative and gain ascendancy once more.

THE DECLINE OF ISLAMIC INFLUENCE

Sceptical as we may be about how far the spiritual life and the political arrangements of the Islamic empires really met the full demands of Islam upon its believers, it is still true that the sixteenth century represented a golden age in the history of Islam in

West Africa. With the fall of Songhai, politically organised Islam perished in the western Sudan. Apart from the decadent Pashalic of the Arma, the small successor states of Songhai did not maintain even an appearance of Islamic statehood. Rulers and people once more resorted exclusively to their own gods for social security and political guidance. Muslims there were, and they were allowed to continue their devotions unmolested throughout the western Sudan and also within the forest. Some of them enjoyed great prestige as political advisers of non-Muslim rulers, and their Koranic amulets were much prized as protection against ill-health and harmful spirits. Yet apart from their rituals there was little to distinguish them from the non-Muslims among whom they lived and whose social life they shared. They lacked positive encouragement to follow their religion properly and had to obey the orders of their non-Muslim superiors. Their religion thus became formalised, lacking in spiritual drive, and willing to play a secondary role to that of polytheistic religions.

In the central Sudan, there was no real political equivalent to the collapse of Songhai to influence religious affairs. However, here also, Islam was at a low ebb in the seventeenth and eighteenth centuries. In Hausaland, Kano and Katsina continued to preserve the Islamic character of their cities and Katsina even won some renown for its scholarship. But their Islam was of comparatively recent foundation and the process of submerging ethnic beliefs beneath an Islamic superstructure was less advanced than it had been even in the western Sudan. Other centres of Hausaland seem hardly to have merited the epithet 'Islamic' at all, and even in Kano, the *gidan tsafi*, 'house of idols', continued to exist. Throughout these difficult times, Bornu remained the one definitely Islamic state. Yet even here, the evidence of Usuman dan Fodio suggests that the religious process may have been one of Muslim readiness to share in non-Muslim practices forbidden by Islam.

THE BAMBARA STATES

The years of Islamic regression in the western Sudan witnessed the rise of the Bambara states of Segu and, later, Kaarta. At the

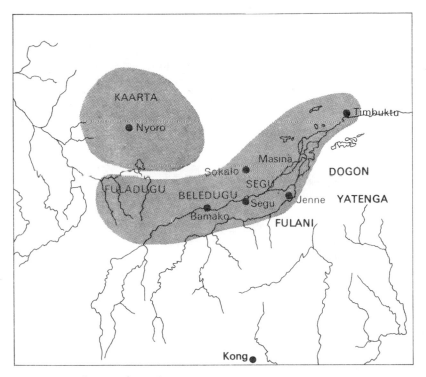

Map XIX   The Bambara States

time of the fall of Songhai, the Bambara were settled in a number
of disunited farming communities along the Niger valley southwards from Masina. In the political chaos resulting from the fall
of Songhai, Barama N'golo and Nia N'golo, two brothers living
in the Segu area, formed powerful war-bands of young Bambara
to raid neighbouring peoples. Successful plundering raids provided large booty and also captives who were incorporated into
the Bambara forces. Thus Kaladian Kulubali, who dominated the
Segu area from about 1652 to 1682, was powerful enough to raid
as far north as Timbuktu and exact tribute from the city. However,
Segu was as yet hardly recognizable as a state; rather it was the
base of a powerful war chief, whose personality alone kept his
followers together.

Kaladian's death was followed by a period of anarchy among
the Bambara caused by rivalries among war-chiefs. Order was

145

not restored until the reign of Biton Mamari Kulubali, a descendant of Kaladian. Mamari Kulubali did not inherit a state: he created it from slender resources. The original source of his power was no more than a group of boys of the same age who accepted his leadership because of his great physical strength, intelligence and commanding personality. When they reached manhood, he welded them into an effective fighting force and used them to establish his authority over the Bambara people. He then led his people in a series of campaigns which made him master of the Niger valley from south of Bamako to beyond Timbuktu.

But Mamari Kulubali was no mere warrior: he was also the organiser of a state. Fairly early in his reign, he transformed the settlement of Segu into a strongly fortified capital, which became a flourishing centre of trade. We are told that to invoke supernatural aid to make Segu impregnable he buried sixty young men alive in the foundations of the fortress and built sixty maidens into the walls; and that the strength of these fortifications enabled Segu to withstand a siege by the king of Kong in about 1730. To defend his state and to make new conquests he built a standing army known as the *tondion* which consisted of the cream of Bambara youth, captives taken in war and criminals who preferred military service to punishment. Mamari Kulubali also realized the importance of control of the Niger. In order to have water transport always available for his forces, he built up the power of the Somono people, a clan of skilled fishermen. In return for a monopoly of river transport including the right to charge tolls on other users of the river, the Somono had the duty of keeping a fleet of boats available for the king's use. They were also well supplied with slaves to service and power the canoes.

The state of Kaarta was founded during his reign. Mamari Kulubali, a descendant of Barama N'gola, quarrelled with the Masa-Si clan descended from Nia N'golo. He over-ran their settlements in Beledugu and killed their ruler. The surviving Masa-Si, under the leadership of Sey Bamama, moved northwestwards and made themselves masters of Kaarta. Kaarta remained a convinced rival of Segu until both fell prey to later conquerors, but Kaarta was never as powerful as Segu.

With the death of Mamari Kulubali, Segu once more became the scene of dramatic struggles for power. His eldest son Denkoro was strangled by members of the *tondion*, and his second was murdered when he adopted Islam. Several military men siezed power by force and lost it in the same way until N'golo Diara gained control in 1766. He restored order by reducing the power of the *tondion* and then restored wavering Bambara authority over its empire. The Fulani of Masina were subdued and Jenne, Sokalo and Timbuktu were forced to acknowledge his overlordship. His only serious reverse came when he attacked the Mossi state of Yatenga. Not only did the Mossi withstand the Bambara attack but they followed up their military success by a pillaging raid on Jenne.

His successor, Mansong, 1790 to 1808, was ruler when the famous explorer, Mungo Park, reached the area. He kept up the tradition of Bambara military success by raids on the Dogon and the Mossi, by restoring Timbuktu to obedience, and by ravaging Kaarta, Beledugu and Fuladugu. Yet the reign of Da Diara, 1808 to 1827, was to witness the collapse of Segu before the attacks of the Fulani of Masina and its incorporation in the new Islamic theocracy founded by a Muslim reformer named Ahmadu Lobo.

THE ISLAMIC REVIVAL

The jihad of Ahmadu Lobo was but one part of an Islamic revival which, starting in Futa Jallon in 1725, was to spread all over the west and central Sudan in the nineteenth century. The reasons for this revival were several. In the first place, Muslim subjects of non-Muslim rulers were never quite happy about their position no matter how decadent their personal version of Islam might be. They were very conscious of being the owners of a superior religious truth and of their ability to read or recite Arabic. Thus they were never willing subjects of non-Muslim rulers. Also, in the absence of Islamic law, Muslims could be forced to pay non-Islamic taxes or to fight against other Muslims. All too often, Muslim communities were of a different ethnic group—often Fulani—from the rulers of the states in which they lived, and this had the dual effect of making rulers suspicious of them and of adding an ethnic reason to the religious one for the overthrow of non-Muslim rulers.

What discontented Muslims long lacked, however, were leaders

147

not prepared to compromise with ethnic religions and non-Islamic rulers; leaders who could revitalize accommodating Muslims by passionate preaching of Islamic truth and who would be prepared if necessary to advance the cause of Islam with the sword. That the arrival of such inspired reformers had been prophesied for the eighteenth century meant that Muslims everywhere were tense with expectation of the rise of revivified Islam to political power. They awaited the call of new leaders; and in the eighteenth and nineteenth century such leaders appeared. These leaders came from clerical families devoted to the practice and study of Islam. Until the second half of the nineteenth century, these clerics were almost exclusively members of the Qadiriyya sect. This sect believed in mystical communion between their leaders and Allah, and taught the need for Muslims to lead a pure and simple Islamic way of life. The special grace of their leaders and the visions they received gave them great prestige with Muslims and non-Muslims alike. The logical result of their teachings was the formation of Islamic states which they would rule according to the will of Allah.

The creation of the theocracy of Futa Jallon
In the late seventeenth century, there was a considerable migration of Fulani from Masina and Hodh to the Solima area of Futa Jallon. Although the leaders of the migration were no more than nominal Muslims at the best, they were accompanied by Muslim clerics. These Fulani immigrants led semi-nomadic lives but two of their foremost leaders established a base at Fugumba where the Fulani clansmen met to discuss national business. There the Muslim clerics established their Koranic schools; and there grew up the two heroes of the Fulani Muslim movement in Futa Jallon, the pious Ibrahim Musa (Karamoko Alfa or Alfa Ba) and the warlike Ibrahim Sori. The interests of the Fulani immigrants and the ambitions of the handful of clerics coincided. The Fulani chieftains wanted to reverse the situation by which they paid tribute to the Dialonke (Jalonke) ruler of Solima; the pious clerics under the leadership of Ibrahim Musa wanted to forcibly convert non-Muslims and set up a Muslim state. Thus the clerics were able to convert Ardo Kikala, 1715 to 1720, to Islam: and in 1725, Ibrahim Musa was able to launch his jihad against surrounding peoples. The Solima Dialonke chiefs were invited to embrace

148

Islam and join in the jihad against their neighbours which they did to gain Fulani assistance against their rivals.

After initial success, Ibrahim Musa's jihad suffered serious defeats at the hands of the peoples of Sangaran and Wasulu; and when he died in 1751, the jihad was on the verge of failure. At this point the Fulani assembly, guided by their herald, Modi Mada, elected Ibrahim Sori as their war leader. He turned defeat into victory but became so dictatorial that Modi Mada rallied the former supporters of Ibrahim Musa to secure the appointment of the latter's son as Al-mami. However, this political triumph of the clerics over the military men was comparatively short-lived. The Solima Dialonke became alarmed at the religious aggressiveness and the political arrogance of their Fulani subjects and contemplated taking action against them. Therefore, in 1763, the Fulani executed a number of Solima chiefs and the Solima Dialonke joined with the Wasulu in the sack of the Fulani stronghold of Timbo. In 1767, Fugumba was only saved by the military genius of Ibrahim Sori who was then restored to power and became more dictatorial then ever. He showed his unwillingness to be controlled by the clerics by first moving his capital from Fugumba to Timbo in about 1780 and then by killing thirteen members of the assembly of Fugumba. After this, he formed a council more docile to his will and ruled Futa Jallon until his death in about 1784.

The death of Ibrahim Sori was the prelude to a century of struggles for power. The rivals for power were the Alfaya, the clerical supporters of the family of Ibrahim Musa, and the Soriya, the military party favouring Ibrahim Sori's descendants. As we have seen, the problem had arisen during Ibrahim Sori's lifetime. To keep the Fulani united, he had recognized Ibrahim Musa's son as co-rulers; but after his death, rivalry between co-Al-mamis became a constant source of civil war. In an effort to overcome this weakness of the constitution, it was decided in 1837 that co-Al-mamis should not both rule at the same time. Instead, they should alternately hold sole power for two-year periods. This created more problems than it solved, and it was not until French power was established in 1897 that peace returned to Futa Jallon.

The political system of Futa Jallon
The theocracy of Futa Jallon introduced a new form of political

149

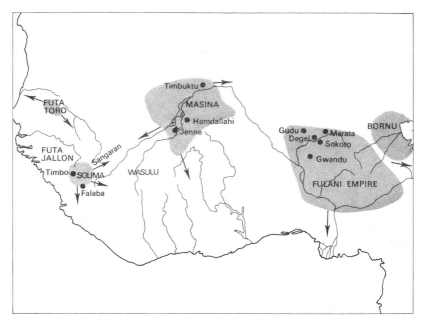

Map XX   The Islamic Revival

organization into West Africa, so new and idealistic that it could not continue in its original form. At the head of the state was the Al-mami, in strict theory the most suitable man in terms of Islamic virtue selected from among the Alfaya and Soriya. The Al-mamis were elected by a college of four king-makers descended from four clerical companions of Ibrahim Musa and Ibrahim Sori. Once nominated, an Al-mami had to be acclaimed by the assembly of the free Fulani. The elections actually took place at Timbo, the administrative capital, but turbaning of Al-mamis with due Muslim ceremony took place at the holy village of Fugumba. The Al-mamis, acting together or singly, were not absolute rulers but were presidents of a council of elders selected for their wisdom and piety. This council made all political, judicial and religious decisions and even had the right to depose an Al-mami. Its ability to do so, however, depended upon the strength of individual Al-mamis—for Al-mamis were supreme commanders of the armed forces.

The major units of local government were the provinces (*diwal*) each ruled by a Lamido nominated by the Al-mami of the day. Each Lamido had his own council on which sat a personal representative of the Al-mami. A Lamido appointed district heads whose main duty was the collection of taxes in their areas. These districts (*tekus*) were subdivided into *misidi*, each of which was a group of settlements served by a single mosque and administered by a local chief acting with the assent of a council of family heads.

You may well feel that there was nothing so very new about this system of government apart from the unintended duality of the Al-mami's office. What was new was the insistence on the religious qualification of all the leading officers of state and that all government decisions must be positively guided by the recorded word of Allah. On second thoughts, perhaps the only major novel feature for West Africa was the fact that the system was intended to be dominated by the word of one God.

However that may be, the system proved unworkable; and mainly for the same reasons that had destroyed earlier West African states. Almost from the foundation of the state, there were constitutional quarrels between Al-mamis and councils. These were nourished by the rivalry between the Alfaya and the Soriya, which produced first the unworkable institution of co-Al-mamis and secondly the impracticable idea of co-rulers alternating in executive office. The religious enthusiasm of the founders of the theocracy waned by the end of the eighteenth century and reduced political disagreements to squalid attempts to gratify personal ambition. Thus both the religious ideals and political efficiency of Futa Jallon rapidly declined.

Other Islamic revivals
The Islamic revival in Futa Jallon was the first successful challenge to the long ascendancy of traditional religions. It was not the last; nor even the most important. The example of Ibrahim Musa was followed in Futa Toro, where Sulaiman Bal, a Tukulor cleric, succeeded in overthrowing the non-Muslim Fulani rulers. He founded a theocratic state shortly before his death in 1776; and his successor Abd al-Qadir established his rule over the various groups of Wolof, Soninke, Bambara and Mandingo living in the area. One of his acts, based on purely political motives, was to create a special province for the Fulani ruling classes where

F

151

they were allowed to follow their traditional religion. Apart from this Fulani enclave, his state was run on the same theocratic principles as those of Futa Jallon. Yet the inherent weaknesses of the Futa Toro state were even greater than those of Futa Jallon. Struggles for power were even more endemic and involved as the Al-mami could be elected from the families of any of Sulaiman Bal's early companions in the jihad. Also the administration of Futa Toro was so decentralized that it did not even have a capital city. Thus, the state collapsed in complete anarchy in 1864 as the result of rivalries between a number of clerics.

The movement of Usuman dan Fodio
Possibly the outstanding figure of the Islamic renaissance in West Africa was Shehu Usuman dan Fodio. Born at Marata in about 1754, he was a Toronkawa (Torodbe) Fulani, whose scattered members provided most of the clerical reformers. His own ancestors had migrated from Futa Toro, possibly in the fifteenth century, and were a clerical clan devoted to Islamic learning, teaching and the manufacture of Koranic amulets. Shortly after Usuman's birth, his family moved to Degel in northern Gobir, and it was there that the young Usuman grew up.

Usuman dan Fodio developed into a young man noted for his deep piety and considerable academic brilliance. After his father had taught him to read the Koran and to write in Arabic, Usuman studied under a number of different *ulama* learning some specialist branch of knowledge from each. By the time he was twenty, he was an acknowledged expert in Arabic grammar; Islamic theology, history and law; the techniques of explanation and public-speaking; and the writing of poetry. The two teachers who had most effect in shaping the young man's character were his uncle Usuman Binduri and the revolutionary Jibril ibn Umar of Agades. Usuman Binduri convinced him of the necessity to 'enjoin the right and forbid the wrong'; Jibril ibn Umar insisted that if rulers would not voluntarily accept the pure way of Islam taught by the Qadiriyya sect then a jihad must be waged against them.

Usuman became famous as a scholar and a teacher, and many young men flocked to Degel to study under him and receive his spiritual guidance. He not only instructed them in the tenets of Islam but also preached the need for a purification and extension of Islam in Gobir in particular and the Hausa states in general. He was appalled by the fact that the nominally Muslim rulers engaged in sacrifices and ceremonies to traditional gods and that the common people did not follow truly Muslim lives. The main reason for this was, he believed, lack of knowledge of the true teachings of Islam. Therefore, he urged his disciples to return home and instruct the people of their areas in the true religious and moral life of Islam. He himself went on preaching tours, particularly in Zamfara and Kebbi. His work was aided by his personal character, for he was a very saintly man of great personal charm, patience and generosity who was able to influence people. He was also an outstanding teacher of remarkable clarity and eloquence. By the time he announced that he had seen visions, at the age of forty, he was already established as the most pious and learned Muslim in Hausaland and had built up a large body of supporters dedicated to the purification of Islam in the Hausa states.

Usuman dan Fodio's preachings were aimed first at converting the common people to a puritanical form of Islam and only later at compelling the rulers of Gobir to set up an Islamic state based on the teachings of the Qadiriyya sect. He enlightened people on Islamic doctrine and pointed out how wicked it was to make sacrifices to other gods and to be careless in observing prayer times, Islamic marriage laws, prohibitions on drinking alcohol and the need to give alms. He condemned the attitude of men whose prime concern was to live a life of luxury and ease, and he advocated the giving up of earthly pleasures that might tempt men into sin. Rulers were reminded that their duty was to rule according to the precepts of Islam and to encourage Muslim virtue. The government should conform to the requirements of the *Shari'a* (Muslim law): the law courts should follow Islamic law and apply Islamic remedies. Yet, claimed Usuman dan Fodio, rulers seriously neglected these duties and themselves engaged in idol worship and ceremonies to false gods.

Among his complaints against the administration of Gobir was the non-Islamic nature of the fiscal system. He claimed that taxes were too heavy and oppressed the people. There was no Islamic justification for the feudal custom of a man's property reverting to the ruler when the owner died; and the ruler's right to requisition transport animals to carry his own goods was an

153

unlawful imposition upon the people. The whole system was vitiated by corruption of officials that the rulers did nothing to suppress. Thus, citizens could not obtain administrative action nor even justice in the courts without the payment of bribes. Even market superintendents, charged with guaranteeing honest dealings in the market, corruptly relieved each trader of a portion of his wares.

Another grievance aired by Usuman dan Fodio was that the law courts administered customary instead of Islamic justice. The main penalties meted out were heavy fines which helped to swell the income of the state. Murderers were fined when they should have been beheaded and thieves were fined instead of having their hands cut off. Also the law was blind to many offences: drunkards, adulterers and cheats all too often went unpunished. Commercial laws to safeguard society against extortion were not enforced: traders who consistently gave short measure were not forced to give up trading; middlemen who cornered markets and artificially forced up prices neither had their goods confiscated nor were they banished from the kingdom. In all, the law courts did nothing to contribute to the establishment of good moral order.

Finally, Usuman dan Fodio condemned the prevalent attitude towards women. It was wrong, he said, to treat women as mere domestic animals whose sole concern in life was housekeeping and the bearing of children. They too were God's creatures with the duty to worship and serve their heavenly Master. Yet most husbands and fathers neglected to instruct their wives in knowledge of Allah. This was wrong. A woman had the duty to obey her husband, but this duty was only secondary to her duty to serve God; and a wife whose husband neglected her religious education had the right to leave him. Usuman dan Fodio himself taught mixed audiences of men and women, and for this was much critcized by Muslims.

Usuman dan Fodio's teachings challenged the entire administrative system and social order of Gobir in the late eighteenth century; and for that reason he won a large body of followers. Nominal Muslims (both settled Fulani and Hausa) responded to his call to reform their personal lives. Settled Fulani, discontented at their exclusion from the higher levels of government, saw the religious movement as a means of establishing their political power over the Hausa peoples. The people of Zamfara and Kebbi saw his movement as a means of embarrassing the Gobir government and enabling them to regain their independence. Peoples of all classes and races who suffered from the heavy taxation and corruption of the government saw the movement as a means of improving their economic condition. Finally, when conflict between Hausa rulers and the Fulani-led Muslim reformers broke out, the non-Muslim Fulani (Bororo) joined their settled kinsmen in an inter-tribal war between Fulani and Hausa.

Usuman dan Fodio himself was not at first a violent man nor a revolutionary. His object was to found by peaceful persuasion a Muslim state in which the rulers would be guided by the *ulama*. In time, it became clear that this would not be possible. The ruling dynasties could not dispense with the non-Muslim rites that buttressed their political authority and saw Usuman dan Fodio's group as a political movement aimed at transferring political power into the hands of Fulani clerics. A number of Gobir rulers therefore tried to stifle the movement before it became large enough to constitute a serious political danger.

Sarki Bawa, 1777 to 1796, tried to win over Usuman dan Fodio by flattery through consulting him on the doctrines of Islam. Usuman, however, was not prepared to compromise his principles and the fact that he had been consulted by Bawa increased his respectability and prestige with the people. Bawa therefore hoped to expose Usuman as the leader of a minority group and a schismatic by inviting all the scholars of the kingdom to the Id al-Fitr prayers of 1788/9. However, there it became apparent that, in spite of professional jealousies between scholars, the bulk of Gobir's scholars upheld the purity and excellence of Usuman's teachings. Finally, Bawa attempted to buy the support of the saintly Degel scholar with a present of 500 *mitkals* of gold. The incorruptible Usuman declined the offer and asked instead that he be allowed to preach freely in Gobir; that no-one should be prevented from joining his *jama'a* (body of companions); that anyone wearing the turban, as all his followers did, should be respected; that all prisoners, presumably opponents of the government and possibly Usuman's supporters, should be freed; and that the people of Gobir should not be over-burdened with taxation. The outmanoeuvred Bawa could hardly refuse these requests.

155

Usuman dan Fodio's movement continued to grow both in numbers and confidence. The younger men with political ambitions began to urge the use of force to create a Muslim state and also engaged in a campaign of civil disobedience to all government orders not justified by the *Shari'a*. Even Usuman became converted to the view that force might be necessary to establish a state and society of Islamic rectitude. In 1795, he began to preach that to equip oneself with arms was a duty incumbent upon all Muslims; and by this time, his personal prestige had been greatly enhanced by the fact that he had seen visions.

Thus Sarki Nafata, 1796 to 1802, faced a potentially dangerous situation. The Muslim-Fulani movement was determined to change the basis of the constitution and was obviously prepared to resort to force if the Sarki would not meet its demands. Usuman had himself become the rallying point for all sources of discontent within the Gobir state, yet his saintly reputation made it politically dangerous to take direct action against him personally. Nafata therefore attempted to avert the danger by restricting the movement's propaganda and removing the outward signs of the extent of the Shehu's following. He decreed that only Usuman dan Fodio, and none of his supporters, had the right to preach; that no more conversions to Islam were allowed; that people converted to Islam during their own lifetime should return to their former religion; and that nobody should be allowed to wear the turban or the veil which were respectively the required dress for men and women followers of the Shehu.

But it was too late for the movement to be halted by anything except successful use of force. This was the resort of Sarki Yunfa, in one tradition a former pupil of Usuman dan Fodio, who is said to have organized an unsuccessful attempt to assassinate the Shehu. Matters came to a head when Abd al-Salam, a non-Fulani cleric of Usuman dan Fodio's party, refused to bless a contingent of Gobir troops going to war. Yunfa, furious at this refusal to give moral support to his government, raided Abd al-Salam's village and took the inhabitants as slaves. When Usuman dan Fodio freed his unlucky supporters, Yunfa prepared to attack Degel. Usuman dan Fodio refused to save himself alone but led his followers to Gudu in 1804 and there declared a jihad against pagans. This was the beginning of the famous Sokoto jihad which created a large empire that was both Muslim and

Fulani-dominated. Although the jihad is part of the nineteenth century's story, its roots lay deep in the eighteenth century Muslim revulsion against the predominance of ethnic religious influences on the life of the West African Sudan.

Questions

1 Describe the spread of Islam in West Africa until the beginning of the sixteenth century

2 Give an account of the means by which Islam spread in West Africa.

3 Give an account of Islam in any one of the early empires of West Africa. To what extent do you feel that this empire was a truly Islamic state?

4 What was the importance of Islam in West Africa down to 1591?

5 How do you account for the rise of the Bambara states? What did Mamari Kulubali contribute to the rise of Segu?

6 What was the condition of Islam in West Africa in the seventeenth and eighteenth centuries? How do you account for the growth of Muslim revival movements?

7 Write a short account of the Muslim theocracy of Futa Jallon.

8 *Either* write a concise account of the early life of Usuman dan Fodio; *or* explain the reasons for the Fulani jihad of Usuman dan Fodio.

9

The economic history of West Africa down to about 1800

INTERNAL ECONOMIC ACTIVITIES

From time immemorial, the main occupations of West African peoples have been farming, hunting and fishing. These provided them with food, clothing, shelter and, in time, a surplus to exchange for things they did not produce themselves. Yet food producing has never been the sole preoccupation of all West African peoples since the days when new stone age peoples founded villages. Industries grew up to meet the growing needs of people for manufactured goods and these produced the basis first for local trade and then for commercial dealings involving peoples living far apart from each other. Unfortunately, it is not possible for us to date the beginnings of these industries nor to assess their growth rate until comparatively recent times. All we can do is to outline a generalized account of industry and trade in our period. In doing so we shall not repeat material on agriculture already studied in chapter 1.

The salt industry
One of the essentials of diet not available in most areas of West Africa was salt, and we shall see that this was one of the main imports of foreign merchants. Inland, only a very few areas such as Dendi could produce minute quantities for local consumption. Elsewhere the only source of salt was the washing of wood ashes, but an enormous pile of ashes produced only a limited trace of salt. Larger supplies of salt were produced all along the coast by the evaporation of sea water. The process was to trap the sea water in large holes at high tide and allow it to evaporate in the sun. The salt-encrusted mud was then scooped out, mixed with water, and strained through wickerwork funnels into calabashes,

or later brass pans, to remove the dirt. Further evaporation produced salt comparatively free of impurities. By this method, coastal peoples supplied their own needs and had a significant surplus for export inland.

The fishing industry

Both at the coast and around inland waterways, fishing was an important occupation. The demand for fish from people without their own local supplies led to the growth of a fish-curing industry. Fish of all kinds were either dried in the sun or smoked so that they could be preserved for transport to distant markets. An allied craft of great importance was the construction of canoes, both small and large.

Soap boiling

Forest peoples developed the manufacture of soap. The key ingredients were palm oil and ashes which when boiled together produced this valuable aid to hygiene. By the seventeenth century, the production of soap was on such a scale that Portugal banned imports of West African soap in order to protect its own soap-boiling industry.

The cloth industry

The earliest forms of clothing were made from animal skins, the bark of such trees as the baobab and the leaves of raffia palms. Allied crafts using these materials were the manufacture of ropes, matting and basket-work. However, the availability in some areas of wool and locally-grown cotton led to the development of a more sophisticated textile industry before A.D. 1000. The technical skill was provided by peoples who had learned the arts of spinning and weaving, and who knew how to extract dyes from the indigo plant or camwood tree. Such peoples early became famous for the quality of their cloth, and included the textile workers of Tekrur, Kano and Yorubaland. These, however, were not the only peoples to produce cloth.

The leather industry

The western Sudan was practically the sole source of the hides from which the famous leather of Morocco was manufactured. In addition to the export of hides, West African peoples also produced their own leather goods. This was done on a small scale in most places though leather manufacture reached its highest expression in the great cities of the Sudan area. The reasons for their lead in leather work was the existence of large herds of cattle owned by pastoralists, and the growing population of commercial centres which provided increasing demand for leather products. Urban sophistication called forth developments in the skills of curing hides, dyeing, shaping leather, and the stitching together of separate pieces to form a useful and attractive whole. The articles most in demand were shields for war, quivers for arrows, harness for horses, sandals and bags of various designs. Kano craftsmen had a high reputation for their work, and Leo Africanus commented on the skill of Gobir's leather workers.

The metal industries
West African peoples early learned to mine and utilize their supplies of three important metals—gold, iron, and copper. The production of gold must date from very early times, for Carthaginians are said to have bought gold at an unidentified place on the West African coast long before the birth of Christ. When iron was first worked, and also when it was first used on a large scale, is not really known. Yet it is certain that a knowledge of iron-smelting was gained before the beginning of the Christian era. Some historians believe the knowledge was transmitted from Libya in about 500 B.C. others that it came from the upper Nile around 300 B.C. We know that the rise of the early empires was partially due to their possession of abundant iron weapons and tools.

Gold   The main sources of West Africa's rich gold supply were the areas of the upper Senegal known to early historians as Wangara, the upper Niger, Bonduku and the area behind the coast at Elmina. Most of this gold was alluvial and was obtained by panning. In some areas, however, gold ore was mined from below the surface and then crushed to extract its valuable metal. Some of the gold was used within West Africa for the manufacture of jewellery and ornaments, a sample of which is a magnificent golden death mask of an Asante ruler. Yet the bulk of the gold, until the coming of the Portuguese, was exported to North Africa and from there passed on to Europe.

Iron   Iron was found at the surface in many places in West Africa. At first, it was mined by open-cast methods, but later by the sinking of shafts. Iron workers were organized in close communities of blacksmiths who jealously guarded their secrets of smelting, forging and tempering the metal. Their skills were directed mainly to the production of weapons and tools, and early European visitors were impressed by the quality of their work. Peoples who were noted for their early craftsmanship in iron were the Wolof, the Susu, the Kano Hausa, the Yoruba and the Awka blacksmiths of eastern Nigeria. One of the earliest people positively known to have used iron were the Nok of the plateau area of northern Nigeria, whose civilisation has been dated as lasting from 900 B.C. to A.D. 200.

Copper   Possibly knowledge of copper working did not predate knowledge of iron production in West Africa, for there is little evidence of a distinct bronze age between stone and iron age cultures. Possibly, also, copper was not so widely available in large quantities as iron, for the only important centre of copper mining mentioned by early historians was Takedda. That Takedda was not the only source of copper is evident from the fact that peoples so widely separated from each other as the Soninke, the Hausa, the So and the Bini processed the metal. Before the age of electricity, however, copper had little common utility as a pure metal, but in Africa, as elsewhere, it was combined with zinc to form brass or with tin to form bronze. Known centres of tin production existed on the Jos plateau of northern Nigeria and of zinc in the area bounded by the lower Niger and Benue rivers.

The use of copper alloys   Although we read of the copper-sheathed canoes of Kanta of Kebbi and Tsoede of Nupe, the main use of both brass and bronze was in the production of works of art which served some religious purpose or enhanced the magnificence of local monarchies. The most widely practised form of alloy casting was the famous 'lost wax' method which is still practised today. The method is beautiful in its simplicity, but success depends on the skill and artistic conception of the craftsman. A core of clay is surrounded by an ample layer of wax which is then moulded into the required shape by the craftsman. When he is satisfied with his sculpting, the whole is covered with a layer of wet clay in which

161

an opening is left at the bottom. The clay is then heated, the wax melts and runs out of the hole. Molten metal is then poured in to replace the 'lost' wax and the casting is put aside to cool. Later, all the clay is removed, the surface of the metal is cleaned and any roughnesses smoothed. Thus is born a work of art. Sheet brass or bronze was also beaten, cut and decorated with punch marks to make attractive bowls, ornaments and protective arm bands for use in battle.

Works of art
The most famous of all West African peoples in the use of brass and bronze were those of Ife and Benin. Although the craftsmen of Ife worked in bronze before those of Benin, it was at Benin that the art reached its peak of perfection. In skill, grace and beauty, the antique bronzes of Benin equal those produced in any age in any part of the world. It was once claimed that both the art of bronze casting, and its use to portray natural figures of humans and animals, was imported by Europeans. This view is no longer tenable. In the first place, although early European imports of brass and bronze enabled a great increase in Benin's artistic output to take place, much West African work in these alloys predates the arrival of Portuguese traders in the fifteenth century. Naturalistic figures are found in early So burial sites in the distant Chad area. Even more conclusive proof is the fact that early peoples not known to have worked in either brass or bronze produced similar figures in other media. For instance the ancient Nok people produced replicas of human heads and animals of high artistic merit in clay. It would seem that all over West Africa naturalistic art as well as stylised motifs were produced in wood, clay, gold, ivory and, among the Bulom of Sierra Leone, in soapstone; and that high artistic achievement—as a sincere expression of the artistic and religious temperament of the craftsman—is almost as old as the dance. Everyone knows that the rhythms of dancing are inborn in every West African and also what expressiveness the dances convey. At the practical level, these artistic skills are used to produce domestic utensils such as decorated calabashes, spoons made of gourds and a wide and shapely variety of pots and bottles fashioned in earthenware.

162

Other products

Other items of importance in West African economies both for domestic use and for export were kola and shea nuts. The former were gathered all along the northern edges of the forest belt where Gonja was a particularly important centre of their production. The kola nut's bitter taste is enjoyed by many African peoples and plays an important part in social life. Moreover, kola is a stimulant which keeps the mouth moist on long journeys and enables a man to keep going when he would otherwise be exhausted. The shea-nut tree is found in the savanna and when its nuts are boiled in water they yield a useful and palatable vegetable fat. Gum from the thorn trees of the northern savanna was much sought by North Africans.

THE ORGANIZATION OF INDUSTRY

By modern standards, all industry was on a very small scale during our period. The unit of production was a single craftsman and his apprentices. Each craftsman, however, was part of a larger society of fellow craftsmen engaged in the same industry. Similar organizations in Europe were known as craft gilds. In the towns and markets, the houses and stalls of the practitioners of a single craft were all located in the same area. Thus in one place would be found all the metal workers, in another the weavers, and in yet another the craftsmen in leather. Each craft had its own head who supervized the activities of his fellow craftsmen and chaired discussions on methods to advance their common interests. He might well be the high priest of a religious cult connected purely with the craft.

This specialization of labour had grown out of an earlier way of life in which each family had had to provide for its own needs. Certain men developed improved skills which enabled them to produce articles superior to those made by non-specialists. Demand for these higher quality products enabled the craftsman to concentrate almost entirely on his own type of manufacture, for he could readily exchange his goods for other things he needed but did not produce himself. Such economic conditions presuppose increasing productivity in other occupations to produce the wealth necessary to create the demand for the craftsman's products. It is probable that the first craftsmen to attain a high degree of specialization were the iron smelters and blacksmiths. References to good craftsmanship in the works of Leo Africanus, Ibn Battuta and even Al-Bakri clearly show that the industrial unit of the master craftsman within his local gild society existed before written records of West Africa began.

Internal trade
The earliest form of trade begins at the village level when the inhabitants exchange things among themselves. As social contacts widen, goods are exchanged with peoples of adjacent villages; and this process is facilitated by the establishment of fixed market places and market days. Gradually, trade takes place over ever-widening areas and some villages possessing an important strategic site, an abundant supply of particularly desirable products or a particularly powerful army grow into great commercial centres.

By A.D. 1000 most areas of West Africa had outgrown purely local trade, but not all were yet in contact with the international trade of the great cities of the Sudan area. Already people existed who were specialist traders travelling from one area to another buying and selling by barter. The details of trade within the forest are not known, and travel along the few main jungle tracks must have been excessively difficult. Yet already some east-west traffic must have taken place both along the coast and within the forest itself. Possibly already the main direction of trade was north-south along the rivers and established paths which were soon to link the trade of the forest with the trans-Saharan trade.

At what time and by what processes individual forest states engaged in active trade with areas north of the forest is not yet known. Yet there are important pointers that this was earlier rather than later. To start with, traditions of immigration from the north suggest cultural contact between the two areas from earliest times. The imperial expansion of Oyo and Benin produced two empires which had at least a footing in both life zones and a decided interest in trade. Possibly as early as the fourteenth century, Jenne's commercial contacts with Bonduku and beyond had already developed. In the traditions of Kano and Zaria, we have positive proof that the trade in kola nuts was being actively pursued in the late fifteenth and early sixteenth centuries; while the tradition of Tsoede shows the northward ramifications of Igara, itself closely connected with Benin, at roughly the same time.

It is likely that at first the main initiative for developing trade between the two life zones was taken by the merchants of the Sudan area. This was partly due to the stimulus to trade they received from North African merchants and partly because of the commercial instinct associated with Soninke and Mandingo Dyula and later with Hausamen. Through their activities, regular trade routes became established. Notable among these were: the route from Jenne through Bonduku to Asante; the route from Kano via Nupe to Asante; the route from Zaria to Yorubaland at Oyo; the routes up the Niger from Benin; and the routes from Oyo along the line of the river Ogun to the coast. The process of linking routes from the coast into the forest with those crossing the savanna belt must have been greatly encouraged by the growth of European trade at the coast. In this connection, it is important to notice that the Asante nation rose to power at the end of the seventeenth century in the area where the route from Jenne met the route from Hausaland at Tafo whence a path continued to the coast. Whatever the exact reasons and processes, long before 1800 the trade of the coast was linked with that of the savanna belt by a network of paths which were already the subject of intense political rivalries.

The trans-Saharan trade

Seen from the air, the Sahara desert appears as an enormous area of river valleys; yet throughout the whole vast drainage system there is rarely a drop of water. Appearances do not lie, for once the Sahara was a well-watered area. Archaeologists have shown that people who owned horses and used wheeled chariots once lived where now no life is possible. The ancient Greek historian Herodotus mentions the existence of wild animals living south of the coastal strip of North Africa. The estimated sites of Kumbi and N'jimi are now virtually desert when once they were well-watered centres of flourishing trade. Thus we are presented with a picture of a growing desert, already a desert before the birth of Christ but neither so large nor so arid as it was later to become. Once, trade goods may have crossed the Sahara region on the backs of oxen but long before the Christian era this had become impossible. Trade between North and West Africa was therefore practically severed until in about the fourth century A.D. the camel was introduced into North Africa and thus once again trans-Saharan trade became possible. Gradually commercial contacts were made and regular routes across the desert established.

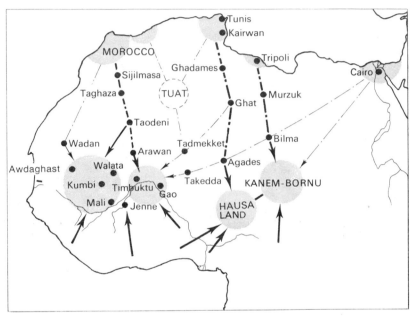

Map XXI   The Trans-Sahara Trade Routes

Dangers of the trade   Although the caravans of merchants travelled along known routes, their three-months' journey was one of great hardships and dangers. The routes were in fact no more than strings of oases supplied with food and water but separated by long stretches of featureless desert. To lose one's way was not a remote possibility, and to do so was to die of thirst. To counteract this danger the caravans hired desert guides known as *takshifs* from Saharan peoples such as the Berbers and Tuareg who knew the desert well. One remarkable fact noted by Ibn Battuta was that some of these guides were blind and found the way by their sense of smell and touch. Naturally such guides were costly, especially

166

as some of them had to go in advance of the caravan to the next oasis to arrange for water supplies to be sent to meet the travellers. Even hiring local guides was however not always proof against their predatory kinsmen who at times preferred the booty to be won by destroying a caravan to the fees and tolls they exacted from travellers crossing the desert. Another hazard was the danger of being caught in a sandstorm which was an unpleasant experience and could result in death. To survive all these dangers was to endure three months of torture from the sun, the cold nights and the shortage of water.

The desert routes At the height of the trans-Saharan trade, there were three main routes across the desert, running from Morocco, Tunis and Tripoli. These were linked by subsidiary routes and there was a fourth route running directly from Egypt to the lake Chad area. These routes made their way to whichever towns were the important commercial marts at any given time. Thus at various times, Tekrur, Awdaghast, Kumbi and N'jimi were all important centres of the trans-Saharan trade. However, during the fourteenth and fifteenth centuries, the routes developed fixed Sudanic termini.

The most westerly route was that from Morocco to the Niger bend. The caravans from Marrakesh and Fez assembled at the oasis of Sijilmasa and then proceeded via the saltmines of Taghaza to Taodeni, Walata (or Arawan) and thence to Timbuktu. Timbuktu was linked by the river Niger to Niani, Jenne and Gao, each of which were important trading centres. The central route from Tunis ran through Ghadames, Ghat and Agades to Gao or Hausaland. In Hausaland, Katsina and Kano were the leading rivals for control of the southern end of the trade and their southward extensions of the trade were to Gonja and Yorubaland. The third route from Tripoli passed through Murzuk and Bilma to Ngazargamu, which was the capital of the Bornu empire.

The Articles of Trade The most important items imported into the western and central Sudan were salt and horses. West Africa had a desperate need of salt and we are told that at times a North African merchant could sell his salt for an equivalent weight in gold. The salt was not brought from North Africa but was purchased from the salt mines in the desert, mainly at Taghaza and

167

Fig. 7   A desert caravan

Bilma. Taghaza itself was a horrible place, being little more than a stretch of desert with salt beneath it. The water was brackish, no food could be produced and the only building material was rock salt. If the caravans did not arrive at their customary times, the entire population could starve to death. Horses provided the mounts for imperial cavalry forces. Other items of trade were metal goods including swords of famous make, spices, perfumes, dried fruits, and luxury cloths such as brocades and silks. The most important exports to North Africa were gold and slaves, and the bulk of the gold passed along the western route to Morocco. Some of the slaves found their way to Europe but the majority of them became domestic slaves in North Africa or Arabia where they often led happy and sometimes distinguished lives. However, the death rate on the Sahara crossing was very high and a particularly vicious feature of the trade was the demand for eunuchs. Other West African goods highly prized in North Africa were hides, ivory, ostrich feathers, kola nuts, gum and the manufactured goods of Kano and Walata. The latter was famous for the delicate work of its goldsmiths.

The Organization of the Trade   At the height of the trans-Saharan trade, its volume and value were both very great. Each year, nine tons of gold alone were exported to North Africa to provide the basis of Moroccan prosperity and the bulk of the currency in Europe. What the value of other exports was we cannot even guess, but it cannot have been inconsiderable when some caravans numbered as many as a thousand camels. The capital for the trade was provided by wealthy North African merchants who owned large numbers of camels and had the resources to purchase the goods required in West Africa as well as to pay guides and protection money to desert tribes. As it was dangerous to cross the desert in small numbers, considerable organization must have been necessary to ensure that merchants met at the departure points at the right time. The usual departure dates were after the end of the rainy season when the danger of sandstorms was least. As the desert crossing took three months, a merchant could only travel one way in a year. Thus, he was committed to a year in West Africa during which he would engage personally in buying and selling from West African producers and merchants. Once he set off for home, he knew he could not return again for another year and so the great commercial houses of North Africa appointed resident agents who held stocks of goods on credit with which to trade on their master's behalf until the caravans returned. Also, merchants could obtain funds locally by bills of exchange payable in North Africa and some of these were for considerable sums.

The whole of the system depended on mutual trust which West Africans did not betray. An illustration of this is the famous story of how, when a North African merchant died in the empire of Mali, his goods were kept intact until his relatives could claim them. The southern extensions of the trade from such cities as Timbuktu probably lay mainly in the hands of their citizens, such as the Soninke and Mandingo Dyula. But we can be sure that a large number of people from the provinces also gravitated to the commercial centres with their little bags of gold, their lumps of gum, elephant tusks or handfuls of ostrich feathers. Occasionally, North African merchants may have been allowed to trade south of the trans-Saharan *entrepôts*, for Al-Bakri records a story of how the merchants purchased gold from the shy Wangara by dumb barter. What is certain is that North African merchants engaged in restrictive practices, for Leo Africanus tells us that merchants of the North African coast were debarred from crossing the Sahara by the merchants of the interior towns such as Marrakesh, Wargla and Tlemcen.

The decline of the trans-Saharan trade   The volume and value of this important trade began to decline from the end of the sixteenth century. One of the reasons for this was political events in both North Africa and the western Sudan. In the north, El Mansur's defeat of the Portuguese did not end military pressure from Christian Europe and, after the defeat of the Turkish fleet at the battle of Lepanto in 1571, Spanish naval power replaced that of the Ottoman empire in the Mediterranean. Also, Morocco became embroiled in quarrels within the state which were productive of disunity and political weakness.

As we have seen, El Mansur had tried to fight his way out of the dangers facing Morocco by the conquest of Songhai. This had brought little temporary, and no permanent, benefit to the declining fortunes of his state. The Moroccan conquest had produced such misrule in the trading centres of the western Sudan, and such unsettled conditions in the area as a whole, that conditions were never again favourable to the revival of large-scale trade along the western route. The great cities of Timbuktu, Jenne and Gao declined in economic importance and their former ascendancy passed to the cities of the central Sudan.

Yet powerful economic factors were at work which gradually undermined the trade of all Sudanic centres. The Portuguese exploration of the Gulf of Guinea inaugurated a period of growing trade with Europeans at the coast. Slight at first, this trade grew to immense proportions in the seventeenth and eighteenth centuries. In return for a declining trade in gold and a viciously expanding trade in slaves, Europeans brought such superficially attractive items as cloth from Manchester and India, bars of iron and brass, metal goods including knives, hatchets and metal dishes, trinkets such as pretty but cheap jewelry and mirrors, alcoholic spirits and, above all, guns. These goods attracted the merchants of the interior who began to turn their trading missions away from the Sahara towards the coast. By the eighteenth century, the dominant avenues of trade were oriented away from the Sahara towards the rising commercial ports on the Gulfs of Guinea and Biafra.

The total decline of the trade did not come until after the end of our period when European traders had penetrated the interior. By 1830, European explorers had traced out the main outlines of the Niger from its source to the delta, and European firms with large capital began slowly but surely to develop direct trade with the interior. Their efforts were brought to complete success when between 1885 and 1910 the whole of West Africa was carved up into European colonies. Colonial governments united strips of the coast with their hinterlands, sometimes up to the desert itself, into single states. The colonial administrations directly encouraged trade with their own nationals whose success depended on large-scale commerce. Moreover, they linked the coast to the interior with railways, motor roads and fleets of river-going vessels. Thus trade with European companies at the coast became at once cheaper, easier and more popular than the trade across the desert. By this time also, political and economic deterioration in North African states had weakened the commercial enterprise of their merchants. For these reasons died what had once been one of the most important trading relationships of all time.

Questions

1 Write an account of West African industries before 1800. Why did they not continue to expand into large-scale industries financed by large capital?

2 What minerals were mined in West Africa during our period? For each mineral give one area where it was mined and explain its importance in the West African economy.

3 Describe the main routes across the Sahara and name the main articles exchanged in the trans-Saharan trade. What was the importance of the trade routes in the history of West Africa down to 1591?

4 What dangers faced trans-Saharan traders and why did they brave these risks? How was the trade organized?

5 How important was the trans-Saharan trade and why did it decline?

6 Draw a map showing the main trans-Saharan routes and show how these routes became linked with those from the coast. Mark key trading centres both at the coast and in the interior.

10

The arrival of Europeans

Direct contact between West Africans and Europeans did not begin until the fifteenth century when the Portuguese pioneered the sea route between the two areas. Portugal, a small state of farmers and fishermen, was one of the first in Europe to enjoy national unity and was fortunate enough to be little involved in the major political conflicts that absorbed the energies of other European states. Although Portuguese rulers were ambitious, their country had neither the economic resources nor the man-power to engage in lengthy military adventures in Europe, nor did it have the financial capital, the geographical siting or the commercial expertise to oust the established leaders in European trade. On the other hand, existing European power struggles left Portugal comparatively free from immediate external dangers; and of southern European states only she was relatively safe from the threat of renewed aggression by Muslim states of the Mediterranean. Geographically she was more favourably placed than most European countries for direct contact with the western shores of Africa. Her hardy fishermen had long experience of sailing the Atlantic Ocean and politically she was in contact with Muslim North African states that marketed the valuable exports of West Africa. Thus, Portugal had nothing to lose and everything to gain by seeking economic wealth and power outside Europe.

King John I sought such expansion in North Africa. He set out to destroy piecemeal the power of the Muslim states there so that Portugal would not only gain control of the fabulous wealth of North African cities and of the trans-Saharan trade that underlay it, but would also serve Christianity by destroying Islam in the area. This ambition won a notable success when, in 1415, the Portuguese captured Ceuta. Yet more significant

173

for the future than the capture of the city was the young man who controlled the invasion fleet and became first Portuguese governor of Ceuta. This was Prince Henry, John's fourth son, known to history as Prince Henry the Navigator.

PRINCE HENRY THE NAVIGATOR

Henry's lasting fame derives from the fact that he dedicated his life to building up Portuguese wealth and power by systematic geographical exploration. Although some of the old text-books depict Henry as a recluse who shut himself away at Sagres to study astronomy, oceanography, cartography and religion, this is a grossly exaggerated picture. Henry, like most other princes of his day, was a man of action and involvement in politics. He won renown in the battle for Ceuta, ruled the city for a time, was patron of a religious order, governed the province of Algarve and played an active part in putting down a rebellion in Portugal. These facts do not detract from the traditional picture of the man dedicated to geographical exploration and conversion of the heathen; they merely serve to underline the greatness of his vision and the personal vitality behind his achievement.

Aims of Prince Henry
Prince Henry presented a sober appearance to the outside world but behind this mask lay a vivid imagination, a passionate desire for geographical knowledge and a deep religious fervour, both personal and crusading. All this he combined with qualities of leadership that were to drive men beyond the limits of terror and exhaustion to achieve greatness for Portugal. Of a studious nature, he developed during boyhood a thirst to know the geographical truths of the world, and throughout his life his appetite for knowledge of the peoples, climates, vegetations and geographical configuration of the world was never sated. Each explorer he sent out reported fully on his experiences and brought back specimens of people, birds, plants and trade goods. Each knew he would win recognition from his prince for his contribution to knowledge of the unknown and the exotic.

Yet keen though Henry was for knowledge for its own sake, he

Fig. 8   Prince Henry, 'The Navigator'

was a practical man alert to the needs of government and with the ambitions of contemporary ruling classes running through his veins. Expenditure could not be justified on the grounds of geographical research alone: that could never be more than an

175

intensely satisfying sideline. Knowledge had to be the hand-maiden of the administrator not his master: exploration must produce tangible benefits in the form of trade or empire, prefer-ably both.

First and foremost, Henry sought wealth and power for his country and its ruling family. His governorship of Ceuta had impressed upon him the great wealth of states south of the Sahara. He had learned that the Sudanic peoples were neither subject to North African rulers nor in military alliance with them. That many of these people were non-Muslims was witnessed by their sale in North African markets; equally, they were not Christian; and certainly their rulers were said to preside over impressive courts. He therefore conceived the plan of seeking a seaway to the gold supplies of the western Sudan so that Portugal, either by trade or conquest, would have a monopoly of West African gold exports. Later, he was also to wonder whether or not a seaway existed around Africa to the Far East. The discovery of such a route would enable Portugal to gain direct access to the valuable trade in Asian spices, silks and gems. This trade was dominated by the Muslim states of the Middle East, who jealously guarded the land routes between Asia and the Mediterranean, and by the merchants of Venice and Genoa who purchased sup-plies from the eastern Mediterranean and distributed them all over Europe.

Yet Henry's materialistic ambitions were also tempered by idealism. While he sought imperial status for Portugal, its achieve-ment was to be accompanied by the advance of Christianity. The peoples of the gold-bearing areas were heathen: it was his mission to convert them to Roman Catholicism by persuasion or force, even by enslavement if necessary. Thus would souls be brought to God, thus would the heathen escape damnation. There was also the prospect of crushing Islam if only Portugal could link up with the kingdom of Prester John, in European legend an immensely powerful Christian kingdom in Africa. The dis-covery of this kingdom would lead to a Christian alliance which would assault North Africa from both the north and the south. Thus at one blow Islam would be broken in North Africa and its territory and commerce transferred to the Christian conquerors. That this was a pipe-dream based upon exaggerated rumours of really Christian communities in Abyssinia does not affect the

176

fact that for Prince Henry it seemed a mission capable of achievement if his explorers and diplomats were equal to the task.

The work of Prince Henry
Somewhere about 1419, Prince Henry set up an observatory on a rocky peninsula at Sagres. Jutting out to sea, the peninsula was an ideal spot from which to observe the sea and the skies which must play such a large part in his ambitious plans. There he gathered together a group of able geographers, map-makers and astronomers. He also recruited intrepid captains capable of sailing ships into the unknown and recording their observations of tides, currents, coastlines and movements of the heavenly bodies so that their experiences would provide knowledge to guide and assist later voyagers. Shipwrights capable of modifying ship design to meet the needs of mariners sailing long distances in uncharted waters and tropical climates were also assembled. Men who had gleaned knowledge of the more advanced ship design and navigational science of the Arabs; men who had some knowledge or opinions on Africa, especially persecuted Jewish cartographers with contacts with the Sahara's past; all these Henry sought out and attracted to his service. Europe was scoured for maps to aid these men, and every detail of every discovery was to be systematically recorded to add to the sum total of Portugal's accumulating maritime knowledge. And over the whole operation was drawn the closest veil of secrecy lest Portuguese discoveries should be exploited by other European nations.

The earliest missions of Prince Henry's captains were directed into the Atlantic rather than southwards along the west coast of Africa. By 1431 they had rediscovered the Azores, Madeira and the Canary islands. The Azores and Madeira were later colonized, and Madeira in particular became valuable for its timber and wine. The Canary islands had later to be ceded to Spain as Castillian sailors had in fact visited the islands before the Portuguese arrival. So far, nothing of great moment had been achieved and Henry's dreams were far from realization. Still Cape Bojador was the farthest south any European sailor had travelled; still Henry's sailors were petrified by superstitious fears that boiling seas and dreadful monsters existed beyond the turbulent shallows off the dreaded cape; still his captains argued that their square-rigged vessels could not hope to return from the far south against

177

the full force of the north-east trade winds and the Canaries current.

Then finally in 1434 came the critical breakthrough. In response to Prince Henry's orders to pass Cape Bojador or never return, his cup-bearer Gil Eannes rounded Cape Bojador and returned alive. Although he had discovered nothing but desert, he brought back valuable information on navigation and above all proved that sailors could survive beyond the cape. A spate of voyages followed, not all worthy of recollection by history.

In 1435, Afonso Baldaya ventured over three hundred miles farther along the coast: his sole exciting discovery a footprint in the sand. Men obviously lived in this barren territory. The next exciting achievement was that of Antam Goncalves who was ordered in 1441 to hunt sea-lions along African shores for their valuable skins and oil. He, however, had greater ambitions and he ventured inland from the shores of the Rio de Oro in search of men. A few miles inland, he and nine companions came across a lone male with his camel. This Moor, probably a Sanhaja Berber, fought desperately until he was wounded and taken captive. Soon after, Goncalves' ship was joined by another commanded by Nuno Tristam and together they sought more captives. Altogether twelve desert people were captured and taken to Portugal to learn Portuguese and Christianity so that they could be used as interpreters and missionaries in future voyages. In a futile search for further human merchandise, Tristam extended Portuguese knowledge of the coast as far as Cape Blanco.

The original object of taking captives was to provide Henry with evidence of population and also to obtain African knowledge of geographical, political and commercial conditions in the interior. This would in time lead to location of the western Sudan's gold markets and the kingdom of Prester John. Yet, almost immediately, the baser motive of capturing men for profit became evident. It happened that one of Goncalves' captives was a man of noble birth and in response to his pleas it was agreed that Goncalves should return him to his homeland for a ransom of ten negro slaves. Other expeditions soon openly hunted for slaves to sell in Lisbon and, as early as 1443, Tristam returned from West Africa with a cargo of twenty-nine Africans.

Prince Henry was at first not pleased with this development

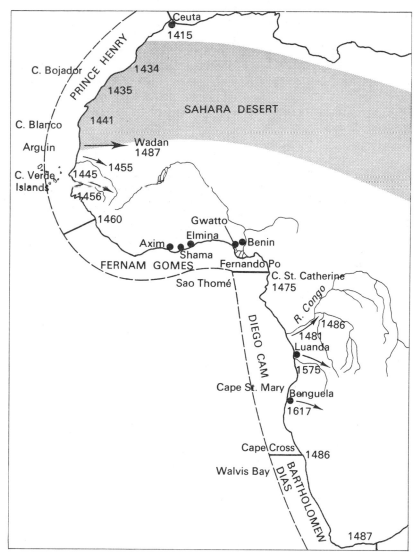

Map XXII The Portuguese Explorers

for it diverted attention from the main task of exploration. However, he was persuaded that enslavement was the only way of converting individual heathens and bringing them to spiritual salvation. Also, the commercial interest shown in this small-scale

179

slave trade was of great practical value to him. His work in encouraging exploration had always been hampered by the high cost of equipping ships and patronizing the sciences of navigation, astronomy and cartography. Apart from occasional contributions from the royal treasury, the bulk of the financial burden had been met from Henry's private resources and those of the religious order of which he was patron. Portuguese business men had not been inclined to speculate in such hazardous ventures, and had scornfully criticized Henry's expenditure of so much capital on enterprises unlikely to yield profit. When, however, they saw the profitable trickle of slaves landing in Lisbon, they changed their ideas and subscribed the capital for expeditions to West Africa.

1443 was certainly a year to encourage investment in exploration. For in that year, not only did Tristam bring his 29 slaves but Goncalves obtained the first small quantity of gold dust from the Rio de Oro. Tristam was also able to report that south of Arguin the mainland coast was green with vegetation. The desert had been by-passed. In 1445, Diniz Diaz rounded Cape Verde and demonstrated that from there on the coast ran south-east-wards. This exciting discovery suggested that a seaway around Africa to India might exist. Thus between 1445 and 1448, Tristam and Zarco pushed coastal exploration to the western borders of modern Sierra Leone.

Portuguese exploration never went beyond this point during Henry's life-time. For some years after 1445, he was preoccupied with political events in Portugal and North Africa, and it was not until 1455 that another significant voyage was made. In that year, Henry persuaded Cadamosto, a Venetian captain who had been shipwrecked off the Portuguese coast, to enter his service. Cadamosto's voyage showed where Henry's main interests lay. He took trade goods on a mission up the Senegal river with the duty of reporting on the area, its trade potential and its proximity to West Africa's leading markets. He sailed two hundred and fifty miles into the interior and spent some months with the peoples of the Senegal valley where he successfully traded cloth for small quantities of gold. During this time, he prepared an account of the Senegal valley and its peoples in which he said the Senegal was the dividing line between Moorish and Negro peoples. In the hope of establishing more profitable

Fig. 9   A Portuguese caravel of the fifteenth century

trading contact with the interior, he proceeded down the coast to the Gambia estuary. There mutiny forced him to return to Portugal; but in the following year he sailed sixty miles up the

Gambia. Again he did a little trade but did not find what he was looking for—contact with the gold market of Timbuktu. However, he made a further discovery when a violent storm blew him out to the Cape Verde islands. On similar voyages, Diego Gomez succeeded in profitably exchanging horses and Portuguese goods along the Senegal and Gambia. Yet when Henry died in 1460, none of his major objectives had been fulfilled.

The results of Prince Henry's work
Despite this, the direct achievements of Prince Henry the Navigator were considerable. Almost single-handed, he had driven Portugal to maritime exploration and raised the funds to finance it. His captains had established contact with West Africa and had explored over 1500 miles of coast from Cape Bojador to Sierra Leone. The coasts had been mapped, navigational hazards charted, astronomical data recorded. The rivers Senegal and Gambia had been explored to their navigable limits and small trade had been opened up. The voyages of his captains had provided invaluable experience and confidence in exploring uncharted waters, and Portugal had been converted to the view that systematic exploration must continue. The needs of his captains had led to important developments in the art of shipbuilding. The triangular lateen sail used by the Arabs was introduced to enable ships to tack against the wind. The Portuguese caravels became longer and more streamlined, and were equipped with more sails to increase their motive power. Astronomical and navigational charts were improved, and in time the sextant was introduced to enable sailors to fix their latitude from the sun. Even during his lifetime, Madeira and Arguin were colonized, and Arguin became a flourishing centre of trade with the African mainland. The entire right to trade and conquest in West Africa had been reserved to Portugal by papal order; and in Portugal these rights were a royal monopoly.

Yet the greatest results of Henry's work were not seen until after his death. Later generations of Portuguese were to discover the gold of Elmina, build up a trading empire along the coast of West Africa and round the Cape of Good Hope en route to India. They were to break the power of the Arabs in the Indian ocean, establish bases on the East African coast, build a Far Eastern trading empire and divert the spice trade to Portugal. This brought economic decline to the Italian republics and elevated Portugal for a time to imperial status and wealth. Such results exceeded Prince Henry's ambitions for Portugal, but without his original idea and persistence would any of it have happened in the way it did?

Later Portuguese exploration

After Henry's death, royal enthusiasm for costly exploration waned. But the mercantile community was interested in bidding for the royal monopoly of trade and exploration in the hope that great profits would ensue. In 1469, King Afonso granted a con tract to Fernam Gomes. In return for a cash consideration and a guarantee to explore about 300 miles of unknown coastline annually, Fernam Gomes was granted a monopoly of trade along the African coast. His captains, equipped with improved ships, made rapid progress. In 1471, they discovered the valuable gold supply of Elmina and within two years they had reached the eastern end of the Gulf of Guinea. Fernando Po discovered the island that bears his name, and Ruy de Sequeira reached Cape St Catherine, two degrees south of the equator.

Interest now turned away from exploration to exploitation of the discovered areas. New initiative was not forthcoming until the accession of John II in 1481. He resumed the royal monopoly and was obsessed with the idea of finding a sea passage to the Far East. In 1481, he despatched Diego Cam with orders to follow the African coast until he discovered a passage to the East. From Cape St Catherine, Cam pushed as far south as Cape St Mary, 13° 26' S. In the process he discovered the estuary of the Congo. On a second voyage, possibly in 1486, Diego sailed into the estuary and learned that the ruler of the area was a very powerful paramount chief entitled Manicongo whose authority was acknowledged over a wide area. Leaving four monks as ambassadors to the Manicongo's court, he continued southwards as far as Cape Cross. On his return, he could not trace his envoys so he seized some of the Manicongo's subjects as hostages. These were treated with honour in Portugal and, in 1487, Diego Cam took them back to the Congo as a gesture of goodwill. He was actually given an audience with the Manicongo, and friendly relations were established with this powerful African state. With this voyage, the exploration of the western shores

G

of Africa was virtually complete. The rest was accomplished by Bartholomew Diaz on his return from his epic journey around the southern tip of Africa. From then on, the emphasis of Portuguese efforts changed. Their objective was India: the successful explorer, Vasco da Gama.

THE PORTUGUESE EMPIRE IN WEST AFRICA

To use the word 'empire' is to suggest large-scale conquests. Nothing could be farther from the truth when we refer to the Portuguese empire in West Africa. The Portuguese conquered no territory, and the number of Portuguese settlers in West Africa was very small. The population of Portugal was too small to support large-scale emigration, and the African mainland was not a healthy home for Europeans. Also, the Portuguese were more interested in acquiring trade than farmland. But this is a one-sided view of the picture. In fact, the Portuguese did not have the resources nor experience to conquer coastal states which were formidable military units capable of resisting European aggression on their own territory. Indeed, even before Cadamosto's first voyage, the Portuguese had been forced to recognise that there was more profit to be had from peaceful, organized trade than from random plundering raids. What settlements the Portuguese founded on the mainland were created with the consent of local rulers, and Portuguese authority was confined within the walls of their forts. For the most part, their settlements were on healthy off-shore islands away from the main centres of African states.

The Portuguese West African empire consisted of a string of fortified bases on islands and at important mainland trading centres. These bases were to serve as collecting points for trade goods, ports-of-call for ships sailing along the coast and as bastions against encroachment by other European nations on their trading monopolies along the African coast and in the Far East. Although the Portuguese had papal blessing for their privileges; although they guarded their geographical secrets jealously from other Europeans; and although any interlopers, foreign or Portuguese, infringing the royal monopoly were brutally treated, the Portuguese could not prevent adventurous merchants from Spain, France and England risking their lives to obtain a share of the valuable Guinea trade.

The first Portuguese base in West African waters was Arguin, settled and fortified as early as 1448. Its function was to act as a port-of-call and also as a base from which to divert western Sudanese trade from the hands of North African merchants. Between 1487 and 1513, with Sunni Ali's consent, the Portuguese owned a trading factory at the oasis of Wadan which fed the markets of Arguin. The island's economy flourished on the purchase and export of gold dust, slaves, gum and ostrich feathers among other things. However, competition from Muslim merchants destroyed the Portuguese interest in Wadan, and this, combined with the opening-up of the trans-Atlantic slave trade, robbed Arguin of its wealth and importance.

'Upper Guinea' was the name the Portuguese applied to the coast stretching from the Senegal to Sherbro island. The most important Portuguese settlements in this area were the Cape Verde islands. These were colonized between 1460 and 1469, and an extremely powerful fort was built at Santiago. To encourage people to colonize these islands, settlers were granted the right of free trade with the mainland and even non-Portuguese Europeans were encouraged to go there. On the mainland, agents of merchants granted royal contracts so trade moved freely inland. Some penetrated into Bambuk and Cantor, and some married local girls and settled in the interior. Also at coastal towns such as Cacheu and Bissau there were settled Portuguese communities, but they were communities in African-controlled towns: they were not Portuguese colonies.

From Sherbro island to the eastern end of the Gulf of Guinea was known as 'Lower Guinea'. The Portuguese further sub-divided this coast into areas named according to the leading commodities available there. From Sherbro island to Cape Palmas was the pepper 'Grain Coast'; the 'Ivory Coast' stretched from Cape Palmas to Cape Three Points; and from there to the Volta was the 'Gold Coast'. The terms 'Oil Rivers', for the Niger delta, and 'Slave Coast', for the coast between the Volta and the Niger, were not used by the early Portuguese and are much later in origin.

The Portuguese did not make any permanent settlements along

the Grain and Ivory coasts where trade tended to be on a small and irregular scale. On the Gold Coast, however, they established their most important bases in West Africa. Elmina became the site of a powerful fort in 1582, and within twenty years others had been erected first at Axim and then at Shama. The gold supplies they guarded were initially worth as much as £100,000 per year in modern currency, and even when output declined they remained a valuable contribution to Portuguese trade. In the fifteenth century, these gold supplies amounted to something like ten per cent of known world production. Yet even here, where Portugal initially had most to gain, the authority of Portuguese governors was limited to their forts and even these stood on ground rented from local chiefs. All Portuguese attempts to visit the interior were frustrated by coastal rulers who were determined to control trade between the coast and its hinterland. All the gold the Portuguese exported was obtained by lengthy trade negotiations.

Apart from a temporary trading factory at Gwatto (Ughoton) at the mouth of the Benin river from 1487 to 1520, the Portuguese made little attempt to create land establishments between the Volta and the Cameroons. This did not mean that the Portuguese were uninterested in the area. Indeed, they could not initially afford to ignore the trading potential of such a powerful state as Benin with which they established diplomatic relations and which for a time they were confident of converting to Christianity. Pepper and slaves were the main commercial attraction of Benin, but with the development of the spice trade with the Far East the Portuguese lost interest in West African pepper. Slaves became their main objective and this trade could be easily carried on from the healthy islands of Fernando Po and Sao Thomé. These were colonized in the 1690's and Fernando Po was developed as an important producer of sugar. Sao Thomé became the slave emporium for the entire coast from lands immediately west of the delta to Angola.

Along the Congo, the Portuguese initially established with the Manicongo the most promising relationship created between African and European until very recent times. At first, respecting the Manicongo's power, the Portuguese dealt on terms of co-operative equality. Portuguese settlers and missionaries were welcomed and equitable trading relationships established. In return for these facilities, the Portuguese undertook to supply European tools, new food plants, teachers and artisans to develop the Manicongo's territory. The sons of rulers visited Portugal for educational purposes, and the Portuguese undertook not to trade in slaves. Portuguese settlements were founded and African Christianity numerically developed to the point where the Roman Catholic church could create a diocese of the Congo with its own cathedral town. However, the profits of co-operation were not great enough to maintain the interest of Portugal in aiding economic progress in the Congo. Portuguese diplomats, trading agents, and missionaries helped to subvert the Manicongo state by fomenting internal rivalries. Technical assistance from Portugal dried up as the Portuguese succeeded in breaking the might of a powerful nation. By the seventeenth century the Manicongo state had disintegrated into a number of petty chiefdoms, which acted as yet another reservoir of slaves to be sold across the Atlantic.

To the south, Angola did not even initially receive such fortunate treatment from early Portuguese ventures. Although its paramount chief, the Ngola, expressed the desire to receive European craftsmen and missionaries in the same way as the Manicongo, the Portuguese showed no interest in the area until 1575. Then a fortune-hunting grandson of Bartholomew Diaz was granted a concession by the Portuguese king to conquer and rule the area. He attracted a body of colonists equally interested in seeking for precious metals and founded Luanda in 1576. In 1617 another group of settlers founded the community of Benguela. Between these dates, fortified settlements were set up along river routes into the interior but the search for gold and silver was a vain one. Consequently, the Portuguese colonists resorted to the slave trade on a large scale. Possibly no comparable area of West Africa has suffered such lasting damage from the trans-Atlantic trade. Angola became the 'Black Mother' of many future rightless citizens of American mines and plantations.

The decline of the Portuguese Empire
The Portuguese empire both in Africa and the Far East collapsed suddenly in the early seventeenth century. It had never rested on really firm foundations. The empire was a series of isolated posts scattered over a wide area with long lines of maritime communi-

cations. The small numbers of defenders manning these bases meant that the empire was incapable of preservation against serious maritime competitors armed with weapons equivalent to those of the Portuguese. Such competition was forthcoming from European sources. Starting with individual interlopers, it developed into opposition on a national scale particularly from the Dutch and English. This reflected the development of both nations as major European maritime powers and also the changing political pattern in Europe.

In 1580, Portugal passed by inheritance under the rule of Philip II of Spain, who was also lord of the Netherlands. When his oppressive rule provoked the Netherlands' revolt, the Dutch saw their political and economic future in smashing Philip's naval and commercial strength. This provided an excuse for the efficient Dutch to fall upon ill-defended Portuguese possessions all over the world. The English, also at war with Spain, did likewise. In West Africa, it was the Dutch who took the initiative with the object of controlling the trade in slaves and sugar. By 1642, most Portuguese bases on the African mainland were in Dutch hands, so also were former Portuguese plantations and mines in Brazil. Although Portugal successfully rebelled against Spain in 1640 and later regained Brazil and Angola, the Dutch managed to retain the key forts on the Gold Coast. Equally, Holland and England absorbed the major Portuguese possessions in East Africa and the Far East. Portuguese imperial dignity was smashed for all time.

The Portuguese had contributed materially to their own downfall. Except in the Congo, they had done nothing to forge lasting bonds of loyalty between themselves and local peoples. They had been extremely arrogant and their policies had been governed by considerations of short term profits. Perhaps the Portuguese image in the West African's eyes is most aptly expressed by Benin bronzes of the grim, unfriendly, gun-wielding foreigner. In such conditions, the Portuguese could call upon few sources of local good-will to help them resist European enemies. Indeed, Africans welcomed Portugal's rivals as trade competitors, freeing them from commercial dependence on the unpopular Portuguese.

Portuguese influence on West Africa
The Portuguese made no lasting impression on the social and

political systems of West Africa. Such influence as they had was confined to the coast and was largely of a demoralizing character. For the most part, these Portuguese traders and government agents were men of the worst character. Ruthless, greedy and drunken, they felt free of the religious and legal sanctions they respected in Portugal. The pattern of living they set for the young African who was foolish enough to ape the stranger was one that no organized society would wish to embrace. Their half-caste offspring became a lawless and immoral element within local communities until in time tribal society absorbed them once more into traditional African life. Yet for a long time, Portuguese was the commercial *lingua franca* of much of West Africa, and it is only in linguistic survivals such as place-names and such expressions as 'to dash' and 'to sabby' that lasting social influence can be observed.

Except in Angola and Warri their attempts to convert Africans to Christianity were spasmodic and unsuccessful. African societies held to their traditional faiths and the social systems associated with them. A few temporary converts here and there remained nominal Christians merely so long as their adoption of Christianity was rewarded with effective political and military aid from the Portuguese. Even in Warri, in the long run their efforts were to leave not much more than a memory of Christianity.

Economically, the Portuguese influence on West Africa was more momentous. The Portuguese opened up new avenues of trade to Africans and introduced a new range of goods from Europe and the Far East. They introduced the enormity of the trans-Atlantic trade with results that will be examined in detail later. Then, we shall ask if there were any real economic benefits for Africa from centuries of commercial contact with Europeans. In doing so, we shall need to be aware that the Portuguese made an invaluable contribution to expanding the food resources of West Africa for they introduced new food crops from the Mediterranean, America and the Far East. In particular, the range of staple foods was extended by the introduction of maize, cassava, sweet potatoes and new varieties of yam. Sugar cane and coconuts, citrus fruits and pineapples, guavas and pawpaws were all introduced to feed Portuguese settlers. The result was the spread of their cultivation wherever conditions were favourable in West Africa. Thus food resources needed to support a larger population and to add variety to diet were made available.

OTHER EUROPEAN NATIONS

As we have seen, other European nations were not content to allow the Portuguese to enjoy a monopoly of the profits to be derived from West Africa. The Dutch, the English, the French, the Spanish, the Danes, the Swedes, and the Brandenburgers all tried to win a share of the prize. Although the conflicts among them for control of the trade were to take place partly along the West African coast and were to involve West African peoples, they were really part of larger European politics which we shall not examine here. Suffice it to say that these nations employed the same techniques as the Portuguese. They established forts from which to trade and to resist attacks upon their trading position. The forts of one nation were frequently in close proximity to those of others.

Frequent petty wars, aided by fleets from Europe, took place between rival establishments in an effort to expel commercial competition. Alliances with local rulers involved the coastal states in these struggles, and African rulers played upon European trade rivalries to obtain European aid in their own political rivalries. Piracy on the high seas was the order of the day. Yet fascinating though the stories are, they relate both to general European history and to intensely localized West African affairs. What is of general validity for West African history is their connection with the slave trade.

Questions

1 Account for the Portuguese lead in the exploration of West Africa and evaluate their contribution to European knowledge of West African geography.

2 What were the aims and achievements of Prince Henry the Navigator?

3 Write an account of the activities of Portuguese explorers down to 1487.

4 Describe the development and nature of the Portuguese empire in West Africa.

5 Write a short account of the extent of the Portuguese empire in West Africa and estimate its influence on West African affairs (see also chapter on the slave trade).

6 How do you account for the limited extent of the Portuguese empire in West Africa and why did it fall?

7 Evaluate the work of each of the following: (a) Prince Henry the Navigator; (b) Gil Eannes; (c) Cadamosto; (d) Diego Cam.

11

Peoples of the coastal zone

COASTAL HISTORY

The history of the coastal peoples during the centuries up to A.D. 1800 is little mentioned in text-books. Part of this unjustified neglect of the coastal areas may be due to the lack of straightforward information about exciting political events and brave leaders; part may be due to a common assumption that history is synonymous with political happenings, so that the dramas played out in the savanna states and the forest kingdoms attract all our attention. In the first chapter it was pointed out that history is not just concerned with powerful leaders and war making. It also includes such aspects of life as economic and social changes that influence the conduct of state affairs.

Now we have two kinds of evidence that can be used to reconstruct the history of the coastal peoples up to the nineteenth century. First of all there is the period leading up to the arrival of the European traders and explorers when we have to rely on oral traditions, archaeological, botanical and linguistic research. Secondly, there is the period after the fifteenth century when we can use the records of the early European traders, agents, explorers and missionaries. Here too there is the information provided by the work of linguists, archaeologists and anthropologists. And so our sources for the post-fifteenth century are richer than those for the preceding four hundred years.

Nevertheless, we still know far too little about what happened on the coast in comparison with our present knowledge of events in the savanna states or forest kingdoms where great leaders carved out empires for their people. On the coast, with the exception of the Niger delta, there has been pathetically little research into oral traditions. This is because no large kingdoms or empires were founded by the coastal peoples: so it is often

192

assumed that they could have had no great leaders. But, human nature being the same everywhere, there is no reason to doubt that if we did but know more we would unearth heroic leaders who were important in the history of their own people.

So we need to use our imagination. We need to read between the lines, so to speak, and to remember that men of ability and talent must have influenced the lives of those around them.

Three common factors

We saw in Chapter 1 that many peoples lived on the West Atlantic and Guinea coasts, and that they differed from each other in certain ways. Some, for instance, spoke West Atlantic languages while others of the Guinea coast spoke Kwa languages. Some, like the Sherbro of Sierra Leone, are thought to have lived in their present home since the twelfth century: others, like the Efik-speaking Ibibio, did not move to Calabar in the eastern Niger delta until the seventeenth century. There were also political differences among the coastal peoples: some were organized in petty chiefdoms or independent towns like those of the Ga of southern Ghana, and then there were of course the tiny self-governing fishing hamlets of the Ivory Coast lagoons.

But if we take a broader view and look back over the outstanding developments of our period, we can see something else. This is the fact that owing to events in the West African hinterland and in western Europe, the history of the coastal peoples is characterized by three common factors.

Firstly, there is the migratory factor. Throughout our period groups were moving towards the West Atlantic and Guinea coasts in search of new homes. Secondly, there is the economic factor. The commercial attractions of the salt trade drew migrants towards the coast, while ambitious men were eager to gain control of profitable waterways and to act as middlemen in the ever-expanding slave trade. Thirdly, but not least, there was the political-social factor. New forms of social and political organization emerged in response to the unsettling effects of the overseas slave trade, and the southward movement of forest peoples. Increasing wealth meant that society became more divided, people tended to live in larger political units and new leaders, self-made men, often rose to power.

Older books about West Africa used to look at its history from

193

the view-point of how the slave trade influenced the lives of people. Today, we emphasize the fact that, broadly speaking, there are two aspects to the history of the coast after the late fifteenth century: the external and the indigenous. The external factor is the overseas slave trade which had the radical effect of linking the coastal areas, particularly those on the Gulf of Guinea, with industrializing nations in western Europe. The Atlantic trade in slaves also speeded up the development of pre-existing trading patterns and of more centralized political institutions. The second aspect of coastal history, the indigenous aspect, is that kings, chiefs and village headmen did not just react to external events: they created and determined history in their own communities, chiefdoms and city-states.

THE WEST ATLANTIC COAST

On the whole, the West Atlantic coast was less affected by the slave trade than the coast of Guinea. The reasons for this are discussed in Chapter 12. Nonetheless, the eight centuries up to 1800 saw many changes in life.

History in the coastal plains of the West Atlantic area illustrates well how migratory, economic and political-social factors operated there. Regarding migration, coastal dwellers were continually subjected to invasions by forest peoples, either peaceful or warlike. Economically, different tribes fought for control of watering places where European ships took on water, food and cargo, or for the position of middlemen in the slave trade. And politically speaking, territorial units tended to grow in size as compact fortified villages and larger chiefdoms were established.

Migration
So far as we know, the general pattern and direction of migration on the West Atlantic coast was reasonably well established by the eleventh century: people generally moved in two directions, from north to south and from east to west. The same natural conditions, which facilitated easy movement in Senegambia but hindered it in Sierra Leone and Liberia, existed in A.D. 1000 as they did in 1800.

Linguistic studies and the accounts of European writers,

adventurers, and agents such as the Portuguese writer, Pacheco Pereira, and the Dutchman, Dapper, have shown us that all the principal peoples now living on the West Atlantic coast were already established there by the early eighteenth century. In Senegambia the Serer, who have a tradition of migration from Sine-Saloum, are thought to have dwelt on the coast since the twelfth century at the latest. The Pepel and Jola are ancient inhabitants who were encountered by the Portuguese in the late fifteenth century.

Further south, the Baga were displaced from the Futa Jallon mountains by incoming Mande; the Baga in about the eleventh century then moved towards the Atlantic coast. By about 1500 the Bulom and Temne were already living in their present habitat between the river Scarcies and Sherbro island, Sierra Leone. The Temne, who are a forest people, are thought to have only settled in large numbers on the coast after the early sixteenth century. The Mende, a Mande-speaking people, were probably the last group to move down from the forest to the Sierra Leonean coast. Their presence was not recorded on the plains opposite Sherbro island until the 1790's.

Reasons for migration
Since migration movements played such an important part in the history of the coastal peoples, we may well ask this question: why did men brave the unknown and endure incredible hardship to leave their homes and move to the coast?

There are three main reasons why men, women and children migrated to strange lands. Firstly, there was a tendency for the fertile lands of the Niger valley and Volta basin to become too populated for comfort. This may well be one reason why Mande-speaking peoples, who knew how to grow rice, settled in Senegambia so many centuries ago.

Secondly, there were political or religious crises when a defeated party, an unpopular minority or an oppressed community decided to seek refuge in other lands. The Muslim Fulani jihad of 1725 in the Futa Jallon is an example of how a conquering élite sparked off extensive migration movements which resulted in more people going south to find new homes on the coast.

The third reason for migration was economic. We cannot do more than touch on this point here since it is dealt with in more detail in connection with the slave trade. But it is important to mention that people did migrate in order to better themselves. Groups like the Lebu of Sierra Leone came to the coast because there was much profit to be made from the traditional salt industry. Other peoples like the Vai of Liberia had moved to the Cape Mount area by 1668, the year when Dapper published his account of life on the West African coast. It is probable that the Vai settled on the coast between 1500 and 1550 in order to obtain a firm hold over profitable watering places, and to get a share in the overseas slave trade. For the Vai, with the Kpelle, were to be the principal purveyors of slaves on the Liberian coast in the next two centuries. European ships had to pay a fee for mooring at watering places like those on Sherbro island and Cape Mount. These ports of call became very popular for their sweet water after captains learned that drinking water was extremely unhealthy along much of the Guinea coast. Local rivalries were probably furthered by the growth of the overseas slave trade since tribes often fought fiercely for control of these watering places and other strategic points on the coast-forest trade routes.

The Manes invasion of the sixteenth century
The outstanding political crisis on the West Atlantic coast between the fifteenth and eighteenth centuries was the Manes invasion. As far as we can tell, it was some time in the 1500's when an army of warriors entered what is now Sierra Leone from the east and decisively beat the Temne, Bulom and Sherbro.

Although the Manes invasion was such an important indigenous event, there is still a certain amount of argument among historians as to what exactly happened. However, it seems certain that the name 'Manes' was a nickname given to the invaders by the Portuguese. From the way in which Portuguese observers spoke about the Manes, it is clear that they were a section of the Mande-speaking people. What is not known exactly is where they came from. It is possible that the Manes were a sub-group of the Vai people who live to the south in Liberia, but this is not very certain and they may have originated in the forest-savanna borders of the western Sudan.

The Manes invasion seems to have taken place in two phases. The first and most significant phase began in the first half of the sixteenth century when a ruling élite of warriors moved towards the Liberian coast. After about 1550 the warrior élite picked up an army of infantry or foot soldiers from around Cape Mount. The soldiers, who were Vai, did most of the actual fighting for their leaders. The Manes then moved north up the coast and captured the Sierra Leone watering place which was the most important trading centre in the country. The Bulom and Temne could not stop the Manes. In fact the people were so terrified of these ferocious fighters that a Bulom king is said to have given himself up to the Portuguese as a slave rather than fall into their hands. The Portuguese helped the Manes because they could increase their influence on the coast by siding with the strongest group. They also profited from the war by following the Manes up the coast so that, guided by the light of blazing Bulom and Temne towns, the Portuguese captains could pick up fugitives as slaves.

Encouraged by their victories, the Manes then struck inland for the Futa Jallon. A Portuguese onlooker came with them, armed with a musket which was still a rarity in West Africa. But the Fulani and Soso combined forces against the Manes with an army which was led by a small detachment of Fulani cavalry. The Manes were defeated and driven back towards the coast.

The second phase of the Manes invasion took place in the late sixteenth century when other Manes groups made more military incursions into Sierra Leone. The Manes settled down on the Sierra Leone coast and became absorbed by the Temne and Bulom whom they had conquered so brutally. The warrior élite of the Manes army became the new ruling élite of the coast, for they set themselves up as rulers over the Temne, Bulom and other coastal peoples.

The effects of the Manes invasion
Until the fifteenth-century migrations, the Atlantic coast was usually fairly peaceful for there was game for all, plenty of land, and people did not know the art of defensive warfare. After the Manes invasion, military techniques spread among the coastal peoples and they became equipped to repulse invaders. In order to push their way to the coast, incoming groups had to be efficiently organized and so war became an integral part of life. Chiefs, many of them of alien stock well versed in the arts of war, were further encouraged to develop military organization because

197

of growing pressure in the coast and the forest from groups moving out of savanna kingdoms. Political crises in the savanna were one factor which led to increasing turbulence on the coast during the seventeenth and eighteenth centuries because forest peoples, displaced by savanna invaders, had to move southwards. Another reason for increasing instability on the coast was that chiefs were eager to enrich themselves and their people by fighting for a share in the overseas slave trade.

The Manes invaders taught the Temne and allied peoples how to defend themselves against attacks. They showed the defeated tribes how to enclose villages with palisades (strong wooden fences), so that villages remained in one place for many years. Previously, settlements had moved from site to site when the land, exhausted by shifting cultivation, was no longer productive. Now the people had to learn more efficient and intensive methods of agriculture. Thus it was that the Manes invasion contributed to a change in the settlement pattern of the coastal communities.

In addition to improvements in village defences, the Manes brought more advanced methods for manufacturing iron and cloth. Weapons became more effective. Although the spear, bow and arrow continued in use until the nineteenth century, muskets began to be imported from Europe in growing numbers after the seventeenth century.

Politically, there appears to have been a shift towards more centralized government, which can be interpreted as a natural response to unsettled conditions and more warfare following the Manes invasion. Chiefdoms became larger in size and there was more distinction between different kinds of chiefs. A village chief represented his village to a paramount chief who was often of alien stock with, for example, Manes ancestors. A paramount chief ruled over several villages. Another factor in the development of more sophisticated government on the coast was the growing power of secret societies during these troubled times. After the Manes invasion youths, who were the most active and eager fighters, became more important. On their initiation into the Poro secret society of Sierra Leone, for example, youths learnt the art of war. Organized by the Poro into military companies, youths from several villages launched attacks against neighbouring chiefdoms. Their aim was to get slaves or to forestall an attack on their village.

Trade was also affected by the Manes invasion. Until the up-heavals resulting from the invasion, Fulani and Susu used to go down to the Sierra Leonean coast to trade. But afterwards they took to going west towards the rivers Nunez and Pongas in Guinea in order to avoid their enemies. Some Mandingo traders became interested in trading on the Liberian coast around Cape Mount. Religious teachers followed in their wake, and so the Vai and Kru peoples who lived there became predominantly Muslim by the nineteenth century.

The Manes invasion and Mande influence
The Manes invasion represented yet another step in the spread of Mande culture on the West Atlantic coast. In Senegambia Mande-speaking peoples had introduced rice cultivation in the early iron age, and Mandingo as well as Dyula traders had long carried goods from the savanna to the mouth of the Senegal river. After the early fourteenth century Mande influence reached out towards the coast from the powerful savanna empire of Mali. Sometimes by peaceful infiltration, sometimes by force of arms, the peoples along the Gambia river and adjacent areas were brought into Mali's sphere of influence. In the fifteenth century, the Venetian explorer Cadamosto reported that Mandingo in the Gambian forest regarded the Mali emperor as their overlord. Titles such as Mansa were adopted by kings as were such Islamic titles as *Qadi*.

Thus it was that the coastal zone on the West Atlantic became more closely knit to the forest and savanna by trade in produce, the overseas trade in slaves, and military conquest. In a turbulent era in which there were many changes in life, chiefdoms became a well established feature of political organization.

Social and political organization 1500–1800
The following account of government among the Dyola of lower Senegal shows how some West Atlantic peoples may have run their political life. By the eighteenth century this kind of political organization is likely to have been characteristic.

The Dyola have lived for many centuries near the mouth of the river Casamance on the fertile plains of Senegal. They should not be confused with the Dyula, a Mande group, for the Dyola speak a

West Atlantic language.

One section of the Dyola have a system of fairly centralized government by kings and priests. But another section only obey one ruler when they are at war: here, secret societies, age-groups and petty chiefs maintain law and order during times of peace. In the former, the people appear to have opted for centralized administration, while in the latter they have chosen to live in semi-independent villages. It is difficult to explain why there should be this difference in political organization. Perhaps the centralized Dyola were influenced by a people from a savanna state, or perhaps a great Dyola king managed to strengthen his grasp on affairs, so that the powers of rulers were considerably increased and government became more centralized.

Among the centralized Dyola the king is appointed for life, while a secret council of chiefs help him to govern. There is a reasonably straightforward division of authority between the king who is a ruler and priest rolled into one—a divine king—and the secret council. The council deals with the affairs of state, but in theory the king has the final word. The council is solely concerned with administration, but the king has important religious duties in addition to his work as a political ruler. The kingship rotates between two to four royal clans: in this respect the Dyola resemble some of the savanna states where certain lineages take it in turns to provide a ruler. In theory, rebellions are less likely to occur when several lineages supply kings because power is more evenly distributed between the main contenders.

Among the less centralized Dyola, secret societies have an important part to play in governing the semi-independent villages. Secret societies worship spirits which sanction the authority of the society's members. In fact to become a member is like becoming a priest for life. There are also associations like age-groups which provide collective labour in the village as, for instance, the *compins* or work groups of the Gambian Wolof.

THE GUINEA COAST

In the first years of European exploration on the West African coast more white men traded in the lands facing the Atlantic ocean than on the coast of Guinea. For extended voyages to the

Bights of Benin and Biafra required some knowledge of local conditions, which could only be built up gradually. Europeans first sought out the Gulf of Guinea for its legendary supplies of gold, ivory and pepper. Then in the seventeenth century this part of the coastal zone became the most lucrative port of call for slaving vessels. It was in the seventeenth and eighteenth centuries that the Guinea coast was the scene of dramatic political upheavals, wars of conquest by forest kingdoms seeking a share in the overseas slave trade, and the full development of city-states in the Niger delta. As these coastal peoples were drawn inexorably into the Western commercial world, new forms of social and political organization were bound to emerge. Men had to adapt to conditions unknown to their forebears.

Migration

As on the West Atlantic coast, some people moved south to the Guinea coast to escape oppression; others sought a share in the salt trade and then the overseas slave trade. Yet other peoples were displaced by powerful forest kingdoms whose rulers were eager to control trade with European slave ships. Kingdoms like the Asante had been able to develop at leisure, unhindered by European intervention, building up their resources from the trans-Saharan trade in gold, ivory and kola. Because these peoples of the interior were relatively isolated from the coast, they had more chance to become strong, and were thus capable of subjugating weaker neighbours who barred the way to the coast.

To study some of the migration movements, we can work from west to east and begin with the lagoons and swamps of the southern Ivory Coast. Excavations by archaeologists indicate that the ancient inhabitants of the lagoons have lived there since at least the early iron age, and probably since the stone age. These people are called 'lagunaires', meaning lagoon folk; these fisher folk live in tiny hamlets on knolls of dry land bordering lagoons. According to an eighteenth century French missionary, the peaceful life of the lagunaires was disturbed in the early seventeenth century when fugitives from an Akan-speaking group sought refuge in the lagoons. In about 1670 there was a second great wave of migration when more people from the Akan bloc came to the coast. These new arrivals from the forest settled among the indigenous inhabitants of the lagoons, took up fishing and eventually absorbed some of them. Between 1690 and the early eighteenth century more Akan speakers migrated west, and in about 1750 some groups led by a queen arrived in the Ivory Coast where they met up with earlier Akan settlers, forming the Baulé people. These people then established powerful forest-based kingdoms.

By the 1480's a section of the Akan people were already living on the coast at Elmina. Elmina became an important trading station on the Gold Coast. To the east, the Portuguese governor of Elmina, Pacheco Pereira, found that the Itsekiri and Urhobo of the Niger delta were already living around the Forcados river in about 1500. He also saw a people he called 'Jos', meaning the Ijo, in the Rio Real area around the site of Bonny. The Itsekiri and Ijo do not claim to be the first inhabitants of the delta and they have many legends about an ancient folk whom they displaced: a small people who hated contact with the new arrivals, and disappeared miraculously into the ground. Such stories should be taken with a pinch of salt. But they do indicate that the Niger delta was probably long inhabited before the people we now know as the Itsekiri and Ijo emerged with their own distinctive identity, culture and social organization.

In the next two hundred years Ijo continued to settle new lands in the delta. By 1700 they had moved west towards the Benin river and eastwards into parts of the delta like Akassa, where they had not been seen before. It was during the seventeenth century that a section of the Ibibio people, the Efik, moved down from the forest to the creeks around the Calabar river. There they built the various settlements or 'towns' of Old Calabar, which became an important city-state during the eighteenth century.

Two coastal peoples: the Ga and Adangbe of southern Ghana
The Ga and Adangbe live on the coastal plain that runs from Accra in the west to the mouth of the Volta river at Ada in the east. Ga territory stretches for about forty miles from Accra to near Kpono; the Adangbe live in the area between Kpono and Ada. These peoples speak closely related dialects and are usually considered together because they live near one another, have a similar history, and come from the same stock. The map on p. 255 shows that the northern neighbours of the Ga-Adangbe are the Akwapim and Akyem peoples of the Akan group.

Ga tradition, which is generally accepted as correct, says that their ancestors and those of the Adangbe came from northern Nigeria to escape oppression. At one time it was thought that the Ga-Adangbe arrived in southern Ghana around the late sixteenth century. However, we now know that they must have settled on the coast by the fifteenth century at the latest. In our present state of knowledge, this date is accepted for two reasons. First of all, Portuguese agents in Ghana during the late 1400's observed that the Ga language was then already distinct from that of the Akan-speaking peoples, and from the Yoruba and other groups to the east. Secondly, the Ga city-state of Ayase or 'Great' Accra, which was situated about ten miles inland from 'Little' Accra (the site of modern Accra), was fully established by the 1480's.

When the Ga and Adangbe arrived on the coast they met an indigenous people called the Guan. The Guan are a lagoon folk who live in little fishing hamlets and villages. Some of them were absorbed by the Ga-Adangbe, who incorporated the fishing gods of the Guan into their own religion. At this time the Ga lived in small farming settlements. They had no centralized government or military organization, but gradually formed six 'towns' which were like large villages. Each town was independent of the other and had its own strip of farming land in the vicinity. The high priests and hunters were the principal leaders of a town.

It was after the end of the fifteenth century that the political organization of the Ga towns began to change. Government became more centralized and military companies under captains played a crucial part in administration. Why did this happen? There were three reasons: economic, political and social.

The economic factor is the most important because it resulted in political and social changes in Ga history. Before the Portuguese arrived on the Guinea coast in the late fifteenth century, the southern lands of modern Ghana, Togo and the Ivory Coast were the central termini of important trans-Saharan trade routes. As early as 1400 states began to develop in the forest, because certain peoples were growing wealthy from the trans-Saharan trade and efficient methods of farming root crops. It appears that cloth, salt and fish were brought from the lands east of Benin to the western corner of the Ivory Coast and carried by Mandingo and Dyula traders to settlements around Kumasi. Here kola nuts, gold dust and slaves were collected and taken north to the savanna where they were exchanged for Turkish, European and North African manufactured goods. Prospering from this trade, such sections of the Akan-speaking peoples as the Fante and Akwamu sought access to the coast so as to gain greater control over lucrative trade routes running from the coast to the forest region. It was probably in the late fifteenth century that the Fante and Akwamu reached the coastal plains, meeting the Ga-Adangbe and the Guan. The Fante absorbed some of the weaker Guan principalities. But the southwards expansion of the Akwamu was checked for the time being by the Ga who, eager for more commercial prosperity based on their position at the terminus of a trans-Saharan trade route, and aware of the challenge presented by ambitious neighbours like the Akwamu, began to develop a more centralized system of government. They were thus better prepared for any military offensives against their towns, particularly 'Great' Accra, which was of some strategic commercial importance.

The political and social reasons for the development of more centralized government among the Ga may be considered together. When the Akwamu first encountered the Ga near the Volta they were, according to the Ga, invited by Ga citizens to settle near the famous gold market centre at Abonso. However, this story probably attempts to cover up the fact that the Akwamu people may have settled near Abonso by force of arms. Acting as clients of the Ga, the Akwamu began to dominate the Guan settlements around the mouth of the Volta. Strengthened by their control over the gold trade and the trading routes leading to the forest, the Akwamu succeeded in crushing the Guan between 1625 and 1650. The Akwamu then turned their attention to the Ga and Adangbe; the Ga meanwhile would appear to have adopted some Akwamu and Fante methods of political and military organization. Thus economic self interest, social and political contact with the Akan-speaking Akwamu and Fante, and the military threat of expansionist neighbours probably encouraged the Ga to develop a more centralized and militaristic form of government. How did this new system work?

The influence of Akwamu and Fante
Priests remained in charge of civil matters. But the hunters became 'captains' of new military organizations or companies called

asafo—an Akan word. Farming settlements came together in times of war to defend their town, for each town was really a military confederation of separate villages.

The position of Mantse or father of the town also developed at this time. Following Akan practice, the Mantse was enstooled and given supernatural powers to bring victory in war. The Mantse was not a military leader: he was really a religious symbol of his town's military strength, and was closely guarded in battle by the real warriors—the captains and their *asafo*. In times of peace the Mantse had no political powers of any kind, so he was not really a political ruler or chief, but the religious figure-head of his town.

Thus, the Ga were compelled by the might of their neighbours, the Fante and Akwamu, to copy some of their institutions and methods of government. The military prowess of the Akan-speaking peoples meant that stools and captaincies became important among weaker peoples like the Ga, who adopted the Akan system in order better to defend themselves against expansionist neighbours such as the Akwamu. Military organization among the Ga became more efficient under the captains and companies system, which also carried a certain amount of social prestige. By the early seventeenth century the Ga city-state of Ayase and five other Ga towns were powers to be reckoned with in southern Ghana. The Ga, who controlled the eastern termini of trade routes leading to Accra, were one obstacle to Akwamu expansion; the Adangbe kingdom of Ladoku which lay between Tema and the mouth of the Volta river was another.

By the 1660's, however, the Ga were unfortunate enough to have a tyrannical Mantse at Ayase in the person of Okai Koi. Objecting to Okai Koi's authoritarian ideas, Ga towns quarrelled among themselves. Thus weakened, the Ga were in no position to stand up to the might of Akwamu. And so it was that Akwamu defeated the Ga between 1677 and 1681 in a series of military campaigns. By 1710 the Akwamu empire extended for two hundred miles along the coast and inland.

At this time the Fante, together with the Akwamu, dominated the coast. By 1730 the tables were turned on Akwamu. Defeated by an alliance of the Akyem, Kwahu and Agona states, the Akwamu were forced to retreat beyond the Volta. The Ga and Adangbe

205

city-states regained their former independence, but not for long. By 1750 Asante and Fante had succeeded in dividing the coast between them. Two leading states had emerged from the welter of tiny principalities, independent towns and petty chiefdoms that had existed in the early seventeenth century.

CONCLUSIONS

There were three kinds of change on the coast during this period: the political, the social and the economic. Politically, more centralized forms of government developed in certain areas. Socially, society became more divided up according to whether people were rich or poor, freemen or enslaved. As trade expanded some communities became more wealthy. But because wealth consisted of perishable things like clothes, slaves, wives and houses, economic differences between people did not become rigidly entrenched. Economically, the Atlantic trade became the most important commercial factor on the coast.

Some of these changes were purely indigenous—for example, the shift to sedentary cultivation in Sierra Leone or more effective methods of war-making in that area—but others were due to an external factor, the Atlantic trade. The rise of forest kingdoms which controlled the Guinea coast is an example of such a political development arising out of the magnetic attraction of trade with Europeans.

However, in spite of these changes it is necessary to remember that some peoples went on living in remote valleys or inaccessible swamps as they had done from time immemorial. And so did communities cut off from the mainstream of political conquest, and from the emergence of states in response to the trans-Saharan trade and then to the Atlantic trade in gold, slaves and ivory.

Questions

1 For what reasons did peoples of the interior move into the coastal areas? Illustrate your answer with examples of such migrations.

2 Give an account of the Manes invasion of the Sierra Leonean coast in the sixteenth century. What were some of the effects, so far as we know, of the Manes invasion?

3 Outline the political systems of (a) the Dyola of the lower Casamance river and (b) the Ga of southern Ghana.

4 Consider the ways in which the Ga-Adangbe peoples of southern Ghana were affected by the development of the Atlantic trade and the growing might of Akwamu.

5 What were some of the important changes in life in the coastal zone during this period?

12

The trans-Atlantic slave trade

SLAVERY AND SLAVE TRADING

An essential condition of accurate study of the slave trade is to be on one's guard against use of loose terminology and careless judgement. Slavery is the condition in which one person is the personal property of another. The buying and selling of people who have already become slaves is the slave trade. These two terms are not synonomous.

Slavery as understood by Europeans, and as practised by European settlers in the Americas, was vitally different in concept from that of both the African and the Islamic world. Both in theory and practice, to a European a 'slave' meant a person who was the absolute property of his master. Neither in law nor in custom did the slave have any protection against the whim of his master. The slave could never own property, never marry without his master's consent nor, apart from the chance of abnormal conditions, could he ever earn his own freedom or beget free descendants. He was a tool to be used, and a tool to be discarded when broken. He could be sold away from his family or witness his children being taken away to disappear for ever under an auctioneer's hammer. There was no obligation on the owner to treat his slave with consideration and humanity, and it was not a crime if a free man killed a slave.

In Africa, the legal position of a slave was not much better but his customary situation was significantly different. As a household slave, he was regarded as a member of his master's family and received comparable treatment with the free members of the community. He was a worker, but a worker with rights. He was most unlikely to be sold away from his family or harshly treated unless guilty of serious misconduct. If he proved to have high management ability or military skill, he could rise to a position of eminence in his master's household. In the Niger delta, for example, he could even become head of the household; and elsewhere more than one conquering general or senior administrator started life as a slave. The situation was much the same throughout the Muslim world, which had its religious code of conduct on the treatment of slaves.

By these standards, the slave who crossed the Atlantic was indeed an unfortunate creature. All too often he was destined to be worked intensively on enormous plantations or in underground mines. He would labour long hours for no reward save the lash of the overseer when his effort slackened. There would be no personal contact between him and his master for the enterprises were colossal in scale and the labour force numerous. Any humanity possessed by the owner was thus negated by overseers whose sole purpose in life was to win favour by meeting production targets whatever the cost. If a slave could not stay the pace, work him until he dropped: another could be purchased cheaply enough to replace him. If the business needed additional supplies, sell those slaves who would fetch a good price whether or not they had close family ties on the plantation. This traditional picture is probably emotionally over-drawn but the underlying realities contrast unfavourably with the fate of a slave in West Africa.

THE GROWTH OF THE TRANS-ATLANTIC TRADE

The earliest West African captives taken as slaves to Portugal were destined for domestic slavery in Europe, objects both of utility and curiosity. It became fashionable to have a liveried African man-servant or a lively little African boy as a personal attendant. Such slavery was in tune with African tradition. Furthermore, such a slave trade was incapable of developing into gigantic proportions foreign to African experience because European demand for such human luxuries was limited.

As early as the 1450's, Portuguese merchants were forced to realize that there was no future in slave raiding. They established commercial treaties with local rulers and bought the slaves required for the Portuguese market. At first, slaves were only a small part of a mixed trade in which gold, ivory and pepper were more highly prized and made larger profits. This position was changed by the Spanish settlement of the West Indies.

Spanish settlers were adventurers seeking wealth, not work. At first they used the local West Indians as their labour force but Spanish brutality, overwork and the ravages of European diseases soon decimated the indigenous population. Humanity and common sense dictated that exploitation of the Indians must cease, and at the suggestion of Bartolomé de las Casas, a Christian missionary, it was decided to import West African labour. Thus, in 1510, royal orders were issued for the transport of fifty slaves from Spain to Hispaniola, and the trans-Atlantic slave trade had begun. The export process was speeded up in 1518 by the first delivery of slaves direct from the Guinea coast to the West Indies. By 1530, these early trickles of slaves had become a flood, and by the end of the sixteenth century the main commodity sought by European traders in Africa was slaves. All other items of commerce had become secondary to the lucrative business of supplying the Americas with a cheap labour force.

The bulk of the sixteenth century slave trade was handled by the Portuguese who were granted licences (*asientos*) by the Spanish monarch to supply slaves direct to Spanish colonists. While estimates of the numbers of slaves imported into the Americas during this century vary, one suggested figure is 13,000 per annum.

In the seventeenth century, the annual average rose to 27,000. The demand for labour rose sharply partly because Spanish settlements spread over Central and South America, and partly because other European nations founded their own American colonies. At the same time, control of the slave trade passed into the hands of the Dutch who showed more commercial acumen than had the Portuguese. The state-aided Dutch West India Company used its large capital to enable planters to purchase slaves on credit so that they could buy more slaves than they could immediately afford.

The eighteenth century saw further large expansion in the farming of virgin American soil and every fresh acre brought under the plough produced additional demand for slaves. During this century, the slave trade was the subject not only of intense commercial rivalry among European nations but also of major colonial wars fought on both sides of the Atlantic. The strain of military involvement in Europe and on the high seas proved too much for Holland, which although energetic and ambitious was also small and vulnerable. The field was thus left to the bitter rivalry of the military might of France and the naval power of Britain, and by the end of the century Britain was the undisputed controller of the maritime trade of the world.

The British 'Company of Merchants trading in West Africa' possessed forts on the Gold Coast and allowed any British merchant to use their facilities on payment of a moderate entrance fee, thus reducing competition from interlopers. By 1750, it had taken the lead in the slave trade from the Dutch, and by 1800, British merchants were exporting over half of all the slaves leaving West Africa. It was indeed a thriving trade they controlled. West Indian sugar, the deep South's cotton and maize, Virginian tobacco and Carolina's rice demanded an average annual import of 70,000 slaves throughout the century; and by the end of the century, this average was being far surpassed.

It was ironically fortunate for West Africa that Britain dominated such a large part of the trade in 1800. In 1807, the British government for a mixture of humanitarian, political and economic motives forbade all British merchants to engage in the slave trade. From then on, British governments dealt more and more severely with Britons who ignored this law. Continual pressure was put on other European governments to outlaw the slave trade and increasing naval action was taken to stamp out the major part of the trade. In spite of these checks, the volume of the trade actually increased up to about 1850, and between 1800 and 1865, a further four million slaves landed in the Americas. It was the closure of the United States' slave markets in 1865 rather than attempts to shut off the slave supply that dealt the death-blow to the trans-Atlantic slave trade; and even after this, smaller numbers continued to be exported to Brazil until late in the nineteenth century.

THE ORGANIZATION OF THE SLAVE TRADE

The trans-Atlantic slave trade was big business employing many men and large capital and was highly organized both in Africa and Europe. The commercial demand came from the Americas, the distributive initiative from Europe, the supply from West Africa.

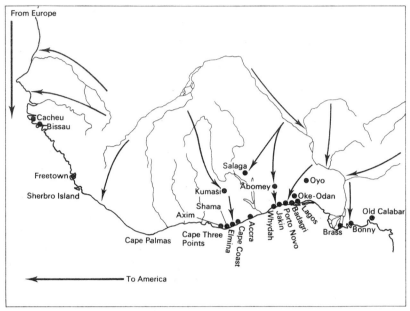

Map XXIII   The Organization of the Slave Trade

External organization
European merchants soon evolved what became known as the 'triangular trade'. European business men equipped ships with the tools of the trade: iron shackles and fetters to chain up the human cargo, feeding bowls and food containers. This equipment would include such items as whips and special chisels designed to knock out front teeth so that slaves who tried to starve to death could be forcibly fed. They then purchased cargoes of European trade goods for sale in West Africa. These included such items as metal bars, knives, enamel bowls, guns, ammunition, spirituous liquors, cloths, clothing and trinkets such as mirrors and cheap, colourful jewelery. With these, they set sail for the Guinea coast where slaves, food supplies and a little gold and ivory were received in exchange.

In West Africa, the European merchants did very profitable business for indigenous traders had no idea of the actual value of these European imports in their countries of origin. Thus, in the 1550's, William Towerson was able to sell a brass basin valued in shillings in England for thirty pounds'-worth of gold. In price-fixing, African dealers were governed purely by anticipated African demand and, although their commercial acumen gradually allowed them to swing the terms of trade more in the African's favour, European merchants always made a handsome return on the wares they sold in Africa.

Ship-masters completed their transactions in West Africa as quickly as possible to avoid loss of life from tropical diseases. They then crowded their slaves on board ship for the journey across the Atlantic, commonly known as the 'middle passage'. Often the number of slaves grossly exceeded the capacity of the ships to accommodate them decently. In such circumstances, slaves might literally be laid on top of each other in the stuffy holds and only be taken up on deck for short exercise periods. With human beings treated less reverently than cattle, this was the worst part of the voyage. In such unhygienic and brutal conditions, disease was likely to occur and to spread with alarming rapidity. Many a slave who left Africa never reached America. Nor were the slave shippers immune from infection themselves, and they knew that if they relaxed their guard over the slaves, these would break free and seize control of the ship. Still the risks were worth it, for the ultimate profit per slave landed in America would be anything from £5 to £36 in contemporary money.

In the Americas, slaves were penned in the acknowledged slave markets to be auctioned to the highest bidder. Prospective purchasers inspected the wares: they prodded slave stomachs, looked at their teeth, peered into their eyes, pinched their muscles and guaged the working capacity of each slave. Then the sale began and lot by lot the slaves passed into the ownership of the highest bidders. The customers—wealthy plantation and mine owners, or dealers trading to more remote markets—settled in local produce to be exported to Europe. Gold, silver, tobacco, rice, ginger, cotton, precious stones and, above all, sugar, rum and molasses were loaded into the holds for export at prices well below their marketable value in Europe. There the merchants took in cash their total profit on the several distinct transactions. The size of

Fig. 10   A band of captives driven into slavery

the profit can be demonstrated by the reported success of the merchants of the city of Liverpool in the years 1783–93. Their total net profit on the purchase and re-sale of about 303,000 slaves was no less than £2,360,000. For such profits, European traders were prepared to take enormous risks.

Beneficiaries from the trade

Although European merchants made enormous profits, they were not the only gainers from the trans-Atlantic slave trade. Without slaves, the planters of America could barely have developed beyond a class of small-scale farmers. Cheap and plentiful labour enabled them to farm enormous acreages from which they derived the great wealth reflected in the munificence of their mansions and the costly comfort of their lives. Some of them were able to live in equal splendour on both sides of the Atlantic. In England, for example, the wealth of planters and merchants enabled them to buy considerable representation in Parliament. The result was that throughout the eighteenth century the 'West India Interest' was so influential in politics that much government policy was shaped by it.

Equally, there were people in West Africa who saw themselves as benefiting from the trade. The export of slaves enabled the powerful to accumulate wealth in the unsatisfactory form of luxury goods hoarded in their compounds. These they could use to purchase local products, reward service and increase their political influence. Coastal traders made profits on the sale of 'trade goods' in the interior: their rulers benefited also from revenue imposed on the trade and from the purchase of guns to defend and expand their frontiers. Powerful rulers of the interior also derived considerable advantage from tolls and taxes imposed on indigenous traders and from the purchase of armaments. Thus, in the nineteenth century, a ruler of Dahomey was to reply to a British invitation to abolish the slave trade in his dominions that a large British subsidy plus the development of palm oil production could not adequately replace his slave trade revenues.

With so many powerful vested interests determined to prolong the slave trade, it is no wonder the nineteenth century movement for its abolition took so long to succeed.

H

Internal organization

European, and later Brazilian, slave traders did not invest their capital in excursions to the Guinea coast in a mere hope of finding slaves to buy. They knew the slaves would be available, and they knew where to buy them. Along the coast, there were a number of major slave ports such as Elmina, Cape Coast, Accra, Whydah, Porto Novo and the city-states of the Niger delta. Their relative importance varied from time to time as a result of internal political changes in the African states, and there were a host of other slaving centres with which European merchants established successful and regular contact. These slaving ports were linked by well-defined routes to the slave markets and capital cities of the interior such as Salaga and Oke-Odan, and Kumasi, Abomey and Oyo. The seasons for delivery at the coast were well known and estimations of market values were closely watched.

Perhaps the most haphazard aspect of the trade was the actual production of slaves themselves. People became slaves by birth as penalty for a crime committed or as recompense for a family debt. Unwary travellers or workers on the outskirts of village farms might be kidnapped. Powerful rulers also received annual quotas of slaves from subject peoples. But by far and away the greatest proportion of slaves sold across the Atlantic were captives in recent wars. Africans of social standing rarely sold members of their domestic slave establishment unless the slave offended seriously against his master.

Slaves captured or bought in the interior were yoked together and marched towards the coast. They might complete the entire journey to the coast as the property of one trader who made arrangements with rulers en route to allow him to pass through their territories in return for payment of tolls and favourable trading terms. Equally, the slaves might change hands a number of times for peoples along the established routes were loth to miss the opportunity of netting valuable middleman profits. Whatever the usual arrangements were in any area, these could be upset by local wars which might close the routes altogether.

Organization at the coast varied from area to area, and generalization as to the predominant form of commercial enterprise in a given area does not exclude the existence there of different forms of trading units. Equally, a broad generalization as to the predominant form of commercial organization in a given area does not necessarily hold true for that area over the entire slave trading era. Broadly, however, the Gold Coast was the preserve of power-ful European joint-stock companies. Backed by enormous capital and able to buy favour with local rulers, they centred their activities on powerful forts. These acted as the homes of their trading agents, the warehouse for their 'trade goods' and prisons to hold stocks of slaves purchased locally. Trading at these forts continued throughout the year, and thus cargoes of slaves could be held in readiness for the arrival of the company's ships.

Along the Slave Coast, there was more scope for smaller com-panies. These were almost invariably compelled by local rulers to set up their trading factories in African towns a few miles behind the coast. Thus the company's agents were decidedly under African jurisdiction and could not use naval armaments to settle trade disputes in their favour. Large enclosures known as barra-coons were constructed to house purchased slaves against the arrival of a company's ships.

Throughout the entire length of the Guinea coast, there were private West African slave merchants who sold slaves to any ship that came along. Their clients were frequently small companies or individual ship-owners who could not afford the expense of setting up their own establishments in West Africa. This trade was far from being as inconsiderable and haphazard as it sounds. Each ship's captain had his own regular trading contacts and provided them with credit facilities to guarantee a supply of slaves on ar-rival. So vigorous and difficult to control was this type of trade that it outlived all other forms of slave trade on the Guinea Coast.

Credit, known as 'Trust', was a major factor in the organization and expansion of the slave trade. It was provided by European merchants in the form of trade goods to be used to purchase slaves prior to the arrival of their ships in the following year. Often a single African trader would be given thousands of pounds worth of goods on credit. The benefit of this to European merchants was that it guaranteed a supply of slaves and greatly decreased the time spent by his ships in African ports with their danger of fatal tropical diseases. The fact that the 'Trust' system obtained all along the coast and that the sums involved were enormous are adequate commentary on the commercial integrity of coastal traders.

Trade took place through the exchange of European goods for

slaves. Very early in the trade, sophisticated techniques were devised of expressing the value of both African and European wares in terms of token units of exchange. On the Slave Coasts, iron 'bars' were one commercial yardstick; in the Niger delta, copper 'bars' were a popular unit. Other units of calculation were brass pans, cowry shells and manillas. Apart from cowry shells and manillas, these tokens were not usually actual currency that changed hands; they were only nominal units for estimating comparative values. Thus you would not actually give nine iron bars for a bale of European goods with which the European would then go to buy slaves. But if you had a slave for sale you would agree that this slave was worth nine 'bars'; then you would bargain with the European as to how many of his wares were worth nine bars. When this was agreed, the goods would be exchanged for the slave. In fact neither of the parties might have owned a single iron bar.

However, even with the aid of universally accepted units of valuation, trade and bargaining were not easy. Real trading prices depended on the current supply of slaves and the demand for particular European imports. European traders found West African fashions could be remarkably fickle, and it was little use having a large cargo of red cloth if yellow happened to be the colour of the year. If such a thing happened, the European would find himself obliged to give larger quantities of his red cloth for a slave than he had done the previous year.

Finally, it is important to emphasize that the actual control of trade at the coast was firmly in African hands. Locally, they held the military power and even where they might be intimidated by a ship's cannon or the arsenal of a fort, they could coerce European merchants by closing the paths inland, thus cutting off the supply of slaves. For if a successful slaving voyage made a large profit, an unsuccessful one made a considerable loss. Thus, apart from acceptable protests of hard bargaining, it was a foolish European who broke the accepted rules of hospitality governing his stay.

These rules were expressed in the terms 'landlord' and 'stranger': coastal chiefs were the landlords, European merchants the strangers. This was an African relationship that obliged the local ruler to settle equitably quarrels between the stranger and local people. He saw to it that African traders did not default on their debts and that his stranger was provided with the necessities of life. In return, the European stranger made traditional payments to his host, was expected not to offend against local custom and had to pay proper respect to the local authorities. In spite of individual crises, this system, based purely on trust, worked remarkably well because it was of mutual benefit to both sides.

One thing coastal rulers resolutely refused to permit: they would not allow Europeans to trade direct with the interior. To have allowed this would have endangered their own control of trade between the coast and its hinterland. Their people would have lost middleman trading profits and their governments might have lost valuable parts of their revenue. Revenues from trade were considerable as can be seen from the taxation imposed on ship's captains entering Whydah. Before they could even start to trade, they had to make traditional gifts to the ruler and important dignitaries. They had to open their trading negotiations with royal officials and to buy the ruler's slaves at fancy prices. Only then could they buy other slaves in the open market, where their purchases were closely scrutinised by government officials to ensure they did not escape payment of duty on every slave bought. Furthermore, if they wanted trade to proceed smoothly, they did not neglect to make generous presents to these officials, nor did they try to by-pass the customary channels for obtaining supplies of fuel, food and water. Indeed, one might be tempted to feel sorry for the slave trader were it not for the fact that he was the man making the lion's share of the profit.

THE RESULTS OF THE SLAVE TRADE

It is difficult to evaluate accurately the effects of the slave trade upon West African history. Once, it was fashionable to regard the trade as the mainspring of West African social, economic and political life for over 200 years. Now, however, it is realized that the main events and institutions of West African history were primarily the product of African minds dealing with African problems in African ways. The slave trade played no more than a secondary role.

Fig. 11   Masters and slaves on a plantation in the Southern USA

The one result upon which everyone is agreed is that the slave trade drained away many of West Africa's people. Although there are no reliable statistics, one sensible estimate is that between fifteen and twenty million slaves actually landed in the Americas. When allowances are made for those who died on the trek to the coast or during the 'middle passage', it is possible that the figure lost to West Africa was as high as forty million. This population loss was the more serious as the slavers only bought the young, the strong and the healthy. If statisticians applied standard birth-rate factors to these figures, imagine what the total figure would be!

Opinions vary as to the seriousness of this population loss.

One view is that had this man-power remained in Africa it could have cultivated virgin land, increased food production and generally stimulated economic growth. A contrary standpoint is that in thickly populated areas such as southern Ghana and Nigeria the slave trade was a blessing in disguise for it prevented surplus population being a drain on existing food resources. This is a monstrous suggestion. A reasonable answer seems to be that in areas thinly populated or inhabited by small, uncohesive groups, the slave trade caused permanent depopulation and economic damage. In the more densely populated areas and centres of power, this tragedy was not so patently obvious and has been further obscured by economic and educational progress in the nineteenth and twentieth centuries. But the tragedy was there: societies depending on man-power can ill afford to lose one youthful pair of hands.

That the slave trade produced human suffering and degradation is well known. Conditions on the march to the coast, on board the slave ships and in American plantations are infamous in fact as well as in fiction. The whole trade showed a gross lack of concern for human suffering and misery.

The existence of the slave traffic also had important effects upon West African trade and industry. It was not so much that local wars created permanent dislocation of economic activity. Indeed, it is remarkable to what extent essential economic activities continued even in actual theatres of war. The more serious problem was that West African markets were flooded with new ranges of goods with considerable consumer appeal. The volume of trade at the coast and within the forest grew out of all recognition. In a comparatively short time, the goods from the slave ships were available in the great marts of the savanna belt. Slowly trade that had formerly gone across the desert was attracted towards the coast and commercial primacy slipped from the north to the south.

Normally an increase in trade is a sign of economic vitality. For West Africa, it was the reverse. Apart from metal, tools and guns, practically all their new imports were consumer goods which did not aid economic development. In exchange, West Africa gave people who could have increased economic productivity and created an expanding demand to stimulate the growth of indigenous agriculture and industry. When industrialized

Britain decided at the end of the eighteenth century that it needed larger markets in West Africa for its manufactured goods, and also larger supplies of West African raw materials, its men of affairs soon set out to stop the export of slaves. But West African industries had not reached the stage of mass production necessary to point this economic moral. With consumer goods so easily obtained for slaves, West Africans had no incentive to develop new industries of their own or cultivate cash crops. Even existing local industries such as cloth-making and iron-working failed to expand through lack of demand for local products. This was surely the most permanently harmful result of the slave trade.

African wars were no mere series of slave raids. All the major wars stemmed from indigenous politics. Some were the product of imperial ambitions seeking political and economic power by war; some were the result of dynastic rivalries or constitutional struggles between rulers and their great chiefs; and others were the product of some serious breach of custom or political etiquette, of independence movements by tributary peoples or of quarrels over local rights and privileges. Thus the primary motives for war in West Africa were certainly not the slave trade.

However, the existence of the slave trade was an important secondary factor in most West African wars during the slave trade era. The immediate profit to be made from the sale of one's captives encouraged the settlement of political disagreements by clash of arms. And many a lesser skirmish was no more than a slave raid upon weaker peoples. Also, as the slave trade made the coastal areas more prosperous, these became more attractive prizes for powerful states in the interior such as Asante, Dahomey and Oyo. At the same time, possession of guns and hope of European military aid tended to make coastal states more determined to resist the will of powerful neighbours inland. Coastal peoples thus molested traders from the interior states, imposed heavy tolls and duties upon them and were not averse to offering gross insults to powerful rulers of the interior. One of the most flagrant examples of this type of behaviour was the attitude of the Fante towards the Asantehene in the nineteenth century. On a more localised scale, the interference of European agents in coastal politics fomented local strife that might otherwise have been averted.

It used to be argued that the slave trade provided the wealth and weapons that facilitated the rise of West African empires. That the empires of the western and central Sudan owed nothing to European trade is patently obvious, and, except for Bornu, firearms played no part in their military success. Also most of the states of the forest achieved military greatness before they even gained access to considerable numbers of guns. Equally, it has been argued that internal slave raiding and quarrels over the distribution of slave booty destroyed these empires. Such claims are grossly exaggerated even though the trade did encourage the growth of commercial individualism.

One of the cries of the humanitarians was that the slave trade produced the moral degradation that encouraged human sacrifice and cannibalism. That there were cannibals in parts of West Africa cannot be denied, yet they were comparatively few and far between. The skulls in the royal shrine at Kumasi and the evidence of large-scale slaughter in Benin when it was conquered by the British have often been quoted as evidence of the human baseness produced by the slave trade. In fact it is nothing of the sort. Human sacrifice was a religious ritual. It provided companions for a dead ruler when he went to join the spirits of his ancestors. On other occasions, it was an act of invocation or appeasement to the gods. In Benin, a maiden was annually split over a paling to invoke the sea god to bring overseas traders; and the colossal carnage British troops witnessed when they entered Benin was the result of the traditional annual customs. The scale of sacrifice may even have been increased by the desire for active spiritual assistance in the face of an imminent British attack. As Christians or Muslims, we can have no sympathy with such religious customs, but let us see them in their proper context.

THE ABOLITION MOVEMENT

The accusations levelled against the slave trade by humanitarians had a worthy objective: the end both of the slave trade and slavery itself. The humanitarians were deeply religious people motivated by the desire to relieve human suffering in Africa and to bring Christianity and Western education to its peoples. By the late eighteenth century, they were an influential group in British affairs and their spokesman in the English parliament was the wealthy, eloquent and powerful William Wilberforce. That his and his successors' efforts were ultimately to be successful in making both slave trading and the ownership of slaves illegal for British subjects was, however, not the result solely of the impact of the undoubted zeal and passion of humanitarians. By the second half of the eighteenth century, the industrial revolution in Britain was well under way. What Britain required was not so much easy profits from distributive trades but new and expanding markets for her mass-produced goods. Her factories also needed expanding supplies of raw materials such as palm oil (for soap and lubrication) and cotton. Therefore industrialists felt that it would be economically better for Britain if West Africans remained at home to produce raw materials and provide potential customers for British goods.

This feeling had strong theoretical backing from the famous economist, Adam Smith, who argued that a free man always works more productively than a slave. Politically, also, the loss of the American colonies meant that Americans rather than Britons would obtain the greatest economic advantage from the continuance of the slave trade. Thus for a variety of motives consecutive British governments put diplomatic pressure on other Europeans to abolish the trade and the British West African Naval Squadron was stationed at Freetown to intercept slaving ships. However, it was not until 1865, after the Southern states had been defeated in the American civil war, that the U.S.A. effectively closed the American market. With that, the trans-Atlantic slave trade was practically dead and the era of 'legitimate' trade and European colonisation was soon to follow.

Questions

1 Explain why the trans-Atlantic trade developed.

2 In what ways did plantation slavery differ from African domestic slavery?

3 Describe the 'triangular trade' and trace its growth.

4 Who profited and who lost from the trans-Atlantic slave trade?

224

5 Describe the organization of the slave trade within West Africa.

6 Estimate the results of the slave trade upon West Africa.

7 'The economic results of the slave trade were its most disastrous impact on West Africa.' Discuss.

8 Suggest some reasons for the rise of the movement to abolish the slave trade and why the trade was so difficult to suppress. (N.B. Full reasons for the difficulties hindering the abolition of the slave trade requires a detailed study of nineteenth century history.)

13

Secret societies and war towns in the western forest

WESTERN FOREST PEOPLES

The lands of the western forest begin in Sierra Leone and end in Liberia.

Little is known about the past of the western forest peoples, partly because the region was not one which attracted the attention of European traders so there is hardly any written information that we know of at present. With one or two exceptions state systems did not exist in the western forest as they did in the forest of Guinea. There, historians have written much on the empires of Asante, Dahomey, Old Oyo and Benin.

Nevertheless, we know enough to say that increasing instability in the western forest gave rise to new forms of social and political organization. Political upheavals in the savanna states, the slave trade and continual invasions by Mande-speaking peoples forced forest dwellers to live in compact fortified settlements. War-making became a vital part of life. Warrior chiefs, armed associations of young men and more sophisticated weapons were all to be found in the independent chiefdoms of the forest.

In this chapter we are going to look at two groups in the western forest—the Mende and Temne of central and southern Sierra Leone. Like so many peoples in this area the Mende and Temne cultivated rice and had powerful secret societies. Local village chiefs paid allegiance to a paramount chief. He, however, had very little real power over the chiefdom unless the secret societies were in agreement with their paramount chief's policies. It seems that one result of the Manes invasion was to increase the authority of the secret societies who now sent companies of youths into battle. For the most part the main secret society for men, the Poro, exerted its power within a chiefdom. But on occasions the Poro operated across chiefdom boundaries, thereby linking territories which were politically independent. Chiefs, on the other hand, could not influence events outside their chiefdom by peaceful means as the Poro could. And so secret societies really had more say in public matters than paramount chiefs.

Migration
During the sixteenth to eighteenth centuries, migration was influenced by three factors: the slave trade, the salt trade and a growing enmity between Muslim and non-Muslim inhabitants of Futa Jallon, which resulted in many peoples moving south into the forest. The new arrivals from Futa clashed with the indigenous inhabitants of the forest.

Some time during the fifteenth century the Temne and their Baga cousins were expelled from Futa Jallon by the Susu. In the early 1500's the Portuguese reported that small groups of Temne were already established on the coast at the mouth of the Scarcies river. The Temne seem to have been attracted to the coast by the salt trade. It was during the early sixteenth century that the Mende were being forced to move south and west from Futa Jallon. This was the first wave of Mende to migrate towards the forest; their reasons for doing so were probably the same as the Temne—unsettled conditions in Futa and the attractions of the lucrative trade in salt. The early Mende settlers were fairly peaceful and lived simply by fishing, hunting and trapping the wild game that then roamed the forest.

Sometime in the sixteenth century there were fierce clashes between the Temne, who lived at that time in the northern areas of Mendeland, and a new group of Mande-speaking invaders. The warrior migrants were possibly of Mandingo stock. Proficient in war, they set themselves up as chiefs over the original Mende inhabitants. While the Mende were absorbing their conquerors, the Temne were building up strong chiefdoms to the west of Mendeland. By the seventeenth century Temne territory extended from the central forest to the Sierra Leonean coast. Temne influence at this time was based on their control over the salt trade and trading routes which ran from the forest to the coast. Becoming ambitious and envious, the Mende may have decided to push south-west. The Mende succeeded in breaking Temne commercial power by carrying out armed forays against them. One result of Mende campaigns in Temneland was that Mende warriors were installed as chiefs over many of the Temne chiefdoms. Nevertheless, no form of centralized government emerged so that, as before, chiefdoms among the Temne and Mende were all independent of one another.

GOVERNMENT BY SECRET SOCIETIES

When communities in the forest facing the Gulf of Guinea expanded, centralized kingdoms and empires sometimes developed. But in the western forest this did not happen. Instead kinship groups, societies and age groups held onto their political functions, while the powers of secret societies increased. Chiefs and societies governed chiefdoms together. Probably the evolution of more centralized forms of government was held back by the difficult terrain, poor communications and a smaller volume of trade in comparison with the Guinea forest.

The principal secret societies in the Mende and Temne chiefdoms of Sierra Leone were the Poro (for men) and the Sande (for women). Among the Vai of Liberia the Poro was known as the Beri and the Sande was called the Bundu secret society. In spite of the different names by which the Mende Poro and Sande societies were known elsewhere, they were practically identical in their organization and functions.

The Mende Poro Society
The name 'Poro' is said to mean the 'laws of the ancestors', thus indicating that the ancestors use their supernatural authority to back up the Poro's power. The Poro never had any formal central organization. Although Poro societies could and did influence the conduct of state affairs both within and between chiefdoms, they operated through independent lodges. Each village in a chiefdom had its own Poro lodge, and the Sande society was run in a similar manner. Boys and girls were initiated into the Poro and Sande societies at about the same time each year. The Poro, for instance, had a sacred spot in the bush where the initiation took place. Boys were taught native law and traditions, singing, dancing, and craft work. They were also hardened by sleeping out in the open and by being put through difficult tests designed to develop physical courage. The initiation

228

school ended with sacrifices to the Poro spirit which was re-presented by a terrifying masked figure; the boys were then regarded as young men fit to enter into battle and to act as junior citizens in the community.

The Poro society, like the Sande for girls, taught boys how to behave as responsible men; it handled the problem of initiat-ing or guiding boys into manhood. But the Poro also had impor-tant functions in the government of a chiefdom. The society was divided into two grades of senior and junior officials. It was the members of the senior 'inner council' who really controlled public affairs; these senior men bought their right to hold senior posi-tions in the Poro. The inner council of the Poro was the para-mount chief's executive body. This council also acted as a legal tribunal which tried delinquents and criminals. In fact such was the legal standing of the Poro that it, and it alone, tried certain cases which involved important citizens. And the Poro could also act as an arbitrator in disputes between chiefdoms by sending a band of its officials masked as 'devils' to pressurise the group which ignored its ruling.

The power of the Poro, like that of less important secret societies, was due to the face that it possessed secret medicines; the Poro was also able to communicate with the dreaded Poro spirit through its shrines. In other words, the Poro had religious secrets known only to its members or initiates. This meant that the public could be frightened easily into doing as the Poro wanted because they were afraid of being punished by the medi-cine and anger of the Poro spirit.

In 1506–10 Valentin Fernandes was able to write that in Sierra Leone 'there are certain houses or churches of idols where women do not enter'. A Portuguese writer, d'Almada, testified in the sixteenth century that there was an 'evil spirit (and) before he appears it is shouted throughout the village, because the evil spirit is coming to visit them'. D'Almada said that this spirit was very powerful, and that nobles went naked through the streets killing anyone unfortunate enough to be caught in the path of the spirit.

The spirit that d'Almada wrote about was, of course, the spirit of the Poro which is represented by a man who wears a terrible mask. So that even four hundred years ago, and probably earlier, the Poro spirit was regarded with great awe and fear. If anyone disobeyed an order issued by the Poro, he was beaten and fined by the society. The senior members would order forty to fifty young Poro men to go out, armed and disguised, to force an offender to obey the Poro's ruling. The Poro also regulated the fishing season, harvest time and the selling value of local products.

The Poro was therefore a most powerful agent of government in the western forest. Among the southern Temne and the Mende, chiefs were usually members of the inner council and the official patrons of the Poro. It seems that a chief could only be really influential if he carried the Poro with him. If the senior members of the Poro lodges in a chiefdom disagreed with their paramount chief's policies, it is unlikely that the ruler's opinion would count for much. The Poro watched over a dying chief and approved a successor to the chieftainship. In spite of its political importance, however, several factors prevented the Poro from becoming all-powerful and from completely subduing chiefs: there was no central organization of all Poro lodges; lineages acted with chiefs to check Poro influence in village and chiefdom affairs; and above all, the people were opposed to any over-concentration of authority in one person or association like the Poro.

In sum, the Poro provided religious sanctions to enforce political decisions taken by chiefs and senior members of the Poro. Religion and public affairs were thus closely inter-related.

MENDE WAR TOWNS

By the eighteenth century continual invasions into the forest of Sierra Leone had transformed settlement patterns. The Manes warriors of an earlier period were succeeded by fighting Mandingo, who became the overlords of more peaceably minded Mende settlers. Each new influx of migrants, whether they were armed or of peaceful intent, caused changes in tribal boundaries. Defensive settlements became the order of the day from the Gambia to Liberia. For the terrors of frequent slave raiding and military incursions by new settlers meant that people everywhere had to defend their villages more efficiently than they had done before this time.

In the Gambia people built defensive villages on valley slopes.

An English captain who visited this part of the western forest in the early seventeenth century described one such village as follows: 'inside the fence', he wrote, 'they have built various rooms which are like little towers. From these they can shoot arrows and throw spears whenever they are attacked. Outside the fence, too, they have a deep trench which is very broad, and outside that again the whole town is encircled by posts and tree-trunks which are set fast in the ground and joined together, so as to make another fence about five foot high. Beyond that again they have another fence'.

However, it was among the Mende of central Sierra Leone that we find the most advanced form of defensive organization in the western forest. These war towns were densely populated. In southern Mendeland up to one thousand people could live in one town alone. The smallest town had about two hundred inhabitants. We saw in an earlier chapter that war towns did not develop overnight.

War towns in the eighteenth century were built on low hills. Archaeological excavations, colonial reports in the nineteenth century and oral traditions tell us that these towns, like the Gambian village described above, were encircled by a number of hardwood stockades which were separated from one another by stake-filled ditches. Any unwary band which attacked the town would die a horrible death impaled on the stakes.

The war town itself was limited to the area within the inner stockades; generally there were three of these stockades. The forest surrounding a town was used to advantage: trees were all felled up to a quarter of a mile away so that it was more difficult for invaders to penetrate to the town's stockades. Because agricultural land within the stockades was very limited, each war town was supported by outlying villages which also acted as defensive out-posts. There could be three to eight of these satellite villages, which were all within a five mile radius of the town. They were important for two reasons: they extended the amount of land for cultivation, and provided food for the inhabitants of the war town during a siege. Satellite villages were often manned by slaves captured in war. In southern Mendeland dense bush concealed secret escape routes, which were prepared in case the town was defeated by enemies. Houses in the war town were built very close together, so that there was a reasonable chance of invaders, who might penetrate the stockades, getting lost in the maze of pathways.

When a town planned to attack another settlement, it sent spies to find out the lie of the land. These men tried to get into the enemy's town by disguising themselves as traders or market people. Their aim was to pick up local gossip about weak spots in the stockades, how pathways in the town were laid out, and where escape routes were located. Raids often took place at night because darkness gave the attackers an advantage over their enemy. Women and children and strong fit young men were usually taken as war captives, but others were killed. Property and food supplies were looted and taken off as booty.

Some war towns formed alliances with one another to increase their fighting strength and defences. When neighbouring towns became allies they would establish small villages on bush land so that eventually the allied towns and their satellite villages formed one large settlement.

Why did war towns develop?
The war towns of the Mende and other western forest peoples were a direct result of the unsettled conditions that came about after invasions by the warlike Manes, Mandingo and other groups. Other political and economic rivalries also produced local wars. People naturally sought to defend their lives and to protect themselves by building fortified settlements. And because many people had to live in a relatively small area of land, generally on top of a little hill or on the side of a valley, irregular rice growing, trapping and fishing gave way to a more settled form of existence. Thus, weaker sections of the Mende were forced by political insecurity to take up rice cultivation in a big way, becoming sedentary agriculturalists.

Once the war towns and a system of settled cultivation were established, warfare was perpetuated. Not only did towns have to go on defending themselves by launching attacks on other settlements which grew too strong; but there were also continual food shortages because too many people lived in too small an area, and the land was over-farmed so that soil erosion became a serious problem. Towns were therefore compelled to fight one another in order to get more food supplies in the form of war booty. In fact, most raids were carried out in the hungry season— the period between the last planting and the new harvest.

Slavery became an integral part of the war town's economy. For war captives were needed to staff the satellite villages and to clear the high forest for rice cultivation. At the same time slaves were used increasingly as a means of buying salt and metal-ware. Slaves were the principal unit of exchange, and acted as 'money' in the western forest until the nineteenth century. A war town which had many slaves, generally war captives, prospered because it had the means of buying weapons, food and other goods.

WAR AND CHIEFS AMONG THE TEMNE

As among the Mende, life among the Temne also changed between the sixteenth and eighteenth centuries. Temne chiefs, like their Mende counterparts, were able to increase their territory by continual war-making. Chiefs used to exchange their enslaved captives for iron weapons; they also used slaves to increase their plantation labour force. Society became more divided up because there were now nobles and chiefs, commoners and slaves. However there was a certain amount of movement between the social divisions of freemen and slaves. Freemen, if they were unlucky enough to be captured, became slaves. And trustworthy slaves who served their masters well in the war town, by proving that they manned the satellite villages responsibly, could rise to positions of leadership in the town.

The Temne were organized into chiefdoms like the Mende. They had defensive villages and war towns, which were surrounded by high mud walls. Apart from the southern Temne, chiefs probably had more political power than Mende rulers; outside southern Temne country secret societies were not quite so powerful as they were in Mendeland. A Temne chief governed with the aid of a principal adviser who was also of royal descent. There were also sub-chiefs from various villages in the chiefdom, who were entitled to proffer their opinion on certain matters. Magistrates were appointed by the chief to try cases in his chiefdom; constables and messengers were chosen by sub-chiefs from among the leading men of their villages.

Unlike paramount chiefs in Mendeland, most Temne chiefs could decide on legal cases as they pleased. Once a chief had been elected from one of the royal families, he could not be deposed.

233

In southern Temneland the chief had weaker powers being more dependent on the Poro society which installed a chief. The Temne chief was semi-sacred, unlike Mende chiefs; for he was surrounded by religious rules and prohibitions which protected his sanctity and his life-giving force that ensured prosperity, the fertility of crops and of women. 'For us', Temne say, 'the chief is priest as well as king. He who has been consecrated and annointed embodies the community . . . therefore he and his country are one.'

A TURBULENT ERA IN THE WESTERN FOREST

In this chapter we have seen that there were many changes in life among the peoples of the western forest. People like the Mende became proficient in war, living in compact and densely populated towns. Slaving ensured that a war town had a plentiful supply of labour to man outposts and to cultivate rice plantations. A town therefore had to go on fighting in order to keep up its supply of war captives.

Secret societies thrived in these unsettled conditions. The Poro in particular became most powerful in government. It taught young men the laws and customs of their people, and supplied armed associations of men for fighting and for punishing offenders against a chiefdom's customs. The Poro appears to have become particularly strong among the Mende and southern Temne where war towns developed on a large scale. For in times of battle it is those who control the men of fighting age, the younger fit adults, who have most to say in deciding public affairs. Elsewhere Temne chiefs retained more power than the Poro; perhaps this was partly because war towns were less developed in these areas, and partly because Temne had a slightly different idea of chiefship. For them a chief was a priest and a political ruler, the embodiment of the community's soul and its law-giver.

Questions

1 What were the principal factors influencing migration in the western forest during the sixteenth to eighteenth centuries?

2 Who were the main peoples of the western forest? Explain why centralized states did not develop here.

3 Give an account of the organization and activities of the Poro secret society.

4 Why can we say that the political and religious aspects of life are combined in secret societies like the Poro?

5 Describe the lay-out of a Mende war town or a fortified settlement in the Gambia. Why did war towns develop? How did they affect economic life?

14

The Akan states of the Guinea Forest: From Bono to Fante and Akwamu

Today, the many Akan peoples form forty-four per cent of Ghana's population; they live in much of southern Ghana and parts of the Ivory Coast and are alike in several ways. Firstly, most Akan speak a number of Twi dialects (Twi is a Kwa language). Secondly, all Akans share common customs, laws and conventions, religious beliefs and political institutions. For example, the different Akan peoples were grouped into centralized kingdoms or states which were governed by sacred kings, court officials and administrators, and state councils. The Akan have the same marriage ceremonies, the same rules which prohibit marriage within the clan one belongs to, and the same forty-day calendar. Thirdly, there is the system of seven or eight matrilineal, and eight or nine patrilineal clans (named, loosely, organized kinship groups) which unite most Akan wherever they live.

THE ORIGINS OF THE AKAN

Where did the Akan come from? At one time, some historians thought that the Akan came from ancient Ghana; others put forward the idea that they originated in the Middle East or Meroë*; and yet others believed that the Akan came to Ghana from east of the river Niger in about the fifteenth century. However, we now know that none of these theories is likely to be correct. Although historians are still arguing about the exact place where the Akan had their ancestral home, it is likely that they emigrated from the western Sudan, moving south to the Guinea forest in little bands over many years: a likely time for this migration is about one

*Meroë was an ancient state in Upper Nile.

236

thousand years ago. When the Akan entered modern Ghana they stayed for some time in the Banda hills and then moved down to their permanent home in the basin of the Pra and Ofin rivers. This area is just south of Kumasi and was a fertile land for the new arrivals to put down their roots.

Afterwards a new wave of migration occurred. In about the thirteenth century some of the settlers in the Pra-Ofin basin moved southwards; they became known as the Fante, one branch of the Akan people. Others went northwards; these settlers became known as the Asante, another branch of the Akan who live around Kumasi. Yet other groups went in a south-east direction and eventually established the state of Akwamu.

Why did the Akan leave Pro-Ofin?
There were two main reasons why different Akan clans gradually moved out from their cradle in the Pra-Ofin basin and sought homes in new lands. In the first place, it is likely that the basin became too populated for comfort, for this area was agriculturally productive in root crops.

The second reason for the dispersal is perhaps the most important—the economic attractions of a share in the gold and kola trade. It is believed that gold prospectors had known about the gold fields around the Pra-Ofin confluence since the early iron age. Kola nuts and gold became important exports to the savanna kingdoms so that the area around the Kwaman forest, from where gold and kola were carried north, became economically attractive.

THE NORTHERN AND SOUTHERN FACTORS IN AKAN HISTORY

No account of the Akan can neglect the part played in their history by what has been called the *'northern' factor*. This term refers to the cultural, political and economic influence of the savanna empires and the states of the Volta basin on the Akan. What concerns us now is the way in which the trans-Saharan trade affected the Akan peoples. By 1400, when some of the clans were still moving out from the confluence of the Pra and Ofin, three main trade routes between the forest and the savanna appear to have been established.

Dyula traders operated from their main base at Begho in the Banda hills. Begho consisted of two sections: Muslims lived in one part and pagans in another. The Dyula, who speak a Mande tongue, took forest products and exchanged them for goods from across the Sahara. These traders also settled in villages and towns in the forest where they could act as middlemen among the Akan. Mande words crop up in Twi dialects, showing that northern traders had some impact upon their Akan hosts.

The effects of this intensive development of northern-directed trade were soon apparent. Commercial prosperity probably did much to encourage the Akan to found many small states. A map of 1629 shows that there were thirty-four separate states in southern Ghana; twenty-eight of these were Akan. The seventeenth century must have been a period of intense political rivalry and war-making in the forest region.

The history of the Akan peoples was not only influenced by northern-directed trade routes and political events in the savanna. After the late fifteenth century another factor entered Akan history. This was the rapid growth of the Atlantic trade, which can be called the 'southern' factor. Slaves of course were exported. But commodities from far distant North Africa, the savanna and the forest were important items for export to Europe, so that the northern trans-Saharan trade linked up with the new trade across the Atlantic Ocean.

The Akan soon realised that whoever controlled trade routes from the coast, where Europeans had their trading stations, would enrich their people greatly. From the sixteenth century onwards ambitious Akan states were to fight for control over trade routes, which led northwards and south to the coast. Customs dues, rents from European castles and stations, and direct access to the source of guns and powder were all attractive to kingdoms eager to dominate their neighbours. In fact, control over the coastal areas became a pre-eminent consideration in the strategy of war and conquest. But it was, paradoxically, inland states which gained most from the Atlantic trade because they had had time to consolidate their political and military organization, based initially on commercial prosperity, before it became necessary to defeat coastal states.

A NORTHERN FOREST STATE: BONO-TEKYIMAN

Historians are still uncertain about the dating of early Bono history. But according to one tradition Bono was founded about 1295, on the northern fringes of the forest about one hundred miles north of modern Kumasi. Conveniently located at the end of the Jenne-Begho trade route, it is said that the first great ruler of Bono, Nana Asaman, founded the capital of Bono-Manso. The very site of Bono-Manso points to the important part played by commercial prosperity in the founding of this state. Although Bono may have been founded in 1295, it is unlikely that this northern city-state really emerged as a powerful force in the forest until the fifteenth century. It was then that the discovery of gold in the Banda hills greatly accelerated the growth of Bono into the state of Bono-Tekyiman.

A great ruler called Nana Kumfi Ameyaw I is said by tradition to have reigned at the time when the gold fields of Banda were opened up. It is not possible to give a firm date for Nana Ameyaw's reign, because the dating of Bono kings is still disputed by historians. However, we know that Nana Ameyaw increased Bono's hold over the lucrative trade route to Jenne, and that he was succeeded by Nana Obunumankoma. This man was a most enlightened ruler who is said by tradition to have ruled for sixty-eight years. Nana Obunumankoma increased Bono power, brought goldsmiths and weavers from the north to the capital, introduced gold dust as currency, established the now famous Asante gold-weights and created the Sanaa or the Ministry of Finance. The Ministry of Finance was a most sophisticated organization which handled price-fixing and commercial matters; its establishment indicated the extent to which Bono-Tekyiman relied on commerce for its prosperity and strength.

Nana Obunumankoma's successors were successful rulers who extended Bono territory, so that by the middle of the sixteenth century Bono-Tekyiman was at the peak of her glory. It was among the best known of the interior kingdoms. Although Bono was later defeated by Asante and reduced to vassaldom in about 1720–25, Bono culture and organization had some influence upon the Asante.

THE SOUTHERN FOREST STATES

The southern Akan states of Twifo, Adansi, Assin and Denkyira were founded by Akan who remained in the Pra-Ofin basin. According to some traditions, Twifo was the first of these nations to emerge as an independent state. We cannot be sure when Twifo was founded but the early fifteenth century is a likely date.

Adansi was another state around the Pra-Ofin basin which became influential at this time. According to one tradition Adansi was founded before 1550; if this is correct, Adansi would have been established after Twifo. However, we know for certain that the Asona clan founded Adansi. According to Bosman, the Dutch historian, Adansi was the dominant state in the Pra-Ofin region in the early years of the seventeenth century.

By 1660 a group of states north of the Pra, which probably included Adansi, Assin and Denkyira, gained control over trade along the coast between Elmina and Cape Coast. These states were called the 'Arcanes' by the Portuguese. The Arcanes appear to be significant in early Akan history, because they were probably the first Akan group to succeed in monopolizing trade between the forest and the coast. This was, of course, a time when the Atlantic trade began to expand considerably. A Dutch agent, Valckenburgh, testified to the commercial influence of the Arcanes by saying that: 'these people then, are those who, already for many years, have annexed the trade along the coast from the castle de Mina as far as Cormantyn (Cape Coast), and are able to thwart their neighbours out of it; so that one trades with no one but them . . . whereby it is wise to be on their better side'.

The first Akan empire: Denkyira (See Map XXVII, page 271)
According to oral tradition, Denkyira, one of the Arcanes states, was founded in the early sixteenth century by an Agona clan family. At first Denkyira was over-shadowed by Adansi. Later on in the second half of the seventeenth century Denkyira conquered Assin, Twifo, Adansi and other early Akan states lying to the north and south-west. In this way Denkyira obtained her objective of gaining a monopoly over the lucrative middleman's trade between the coast and the forest, thus assuring herself a supply of guns. She became an important power of the coastal hinterland.

Denkyira established friendly relations with Dutch, Danish and English traders. In fact these traders were so impressed by the might of Denkyira that in 1694 representatives of European companies arrived at the capital to get on good terms with the king—a strategem to increase trade by siding with the strongest state in the area. And in the reign of Ntim Gyakari (c. 1696–1701), Denkyira gained possession of the rental note for Elmina castle, then in the possession of the Dutch. Elmina was, at that time, the wealthiest market on the Gold Coast.

By 1700 Denkyira had become so powerful that she controlled the entire basins of the Pra, Ofin and Oda rivers. Bosman had this to say about Denkyira's might: 'This country, formerly restricted to a small compass of land and containing but an inconsiderable number of inhabitants, is by their valour so improved in power that they are respected and honoured by their neighbouring nations'. However, like the other early Akan states, Denkyira did not retain her position of supremacy for long. The Asante were enraged when the Denkyirahene demanded of them a larger tax than usual and, in 1701, Asante defeated Denkyira in battle at Feyiase. This dramatic battle marked the decline of Denkyira as a power on the coastal hinterland and the rise of the Asante union.

REASONS FOR THE DECLINE OF THE EARLY AKAN STATES

Having considered early Akan history, it is as well to ask at this point: why did none of these states survive as strong powers for long? It is likely that they suffered from lack of administrative experience, ineffective military organization, and the failure of any truly great leader to emerge.

Before the 1660's guns were not imported in large numbers so that the early Akan states were not able to establish a powerful infantry armed with muskets. And perhaps it is fair to say that none of these states was sufficiently wealthy to maintain constant pressure on hostile neighbours; they collapsed too quickly to establish a strong hold over temporarily conquered populations. But what is just as important, or possibly more so, is that there do not seem to have been any outstanding leaders of men. The personal factors of individual courage, bravery, and wise leadership that make great kings can be crucial in the rise of a state. And so it was presumably not until the eighteenth century that administrative experience, favourable economic conditions, and able leadership coincided to give rise to the Fante union and the Akwamu and Asante empires.

TWO GREAT AKAN STATES: FANTE AND AKWAMU

Moving south towards the coast, the Fante and Akwamu met three different peoples who lived on the coastal plain. They were the Guan and the Ga-Adangbe. According to oral tradition as well as European records, the Fante first came into contact with the Guan principalities to the west, while the Akwamu met the Ga-Adangbe city-states on the eastern coast.

The Fante of Mankessim

Fante oral traditions say that their ancestors lived in Tekyiman, in the northern forest. It was from this area that they migrated towards the coast in five groups led by three old priests. There, they settled at Mankessim which is about six miles distant from the coast. We do not know the precise date of this migration. But Portuguese records reveal that a Fante state was definitely in existence at Mankessim by the end of the fifteenth century. Until the 1650's Fante was really an inland city-state with two villages which functioned as her coastal outlets. (A city-state is a small territory comprising a capital and attached villages.)

Fante clans are said by tradition to have settled at Mankessim in separate quarters, each one of which recognized its own king or Braffo. However, the different quarters also paid allegiance to one of the Braffos as their supreme ruler who was known as the Braffo of Fantyn. The Braffo's position was really one of *primus inter pares*, or first among equals. For the Braffo who ruled in 1653 told the Dutch agent that he had to rule with his principal sub-Braffos and lineage elders, 'without whom he neither could nor might do anything'.

The first phase of Fante expansion:
1660–1690 (See Map XXVII, page 271)
After 1660 the Fante began to expand outwards from Mankessim. Some Fante colonized villages on the coast which grew up to

242

become city-states with their own Braffos; others occupied land inhabited by the indigenous Etsii, or settled in empty areas. As this exodus was the first step in Fante expansion and growing power on the coast, it is relevant to ask why did it take place between 1660 and 1690?

Several considerations must have motivated Fante's attempt to control new territory. Firstly, there was the fact that the population at Mankessim was probably increasing fast, so that there was insufficient land to support everyone. Secondly, as trade with European companies at Cape Coast increased, some Fante groups may have become more ambitious. They sought increased commercial revenues by gaining a hold over trade routes leading to other European trading forts. Finally, we have evidence from Dutch records that there were civil wars between some quarters at Mankessim in January and October of 1653. Weaker lineages may have decided that the way to survival lay in finding a home outside Mankessim.

Each of the new Fante city-states considered itself to be independent, although in theory they recognized the Braffo of Fantyn as their supreme head. It is here that we can see an inherent Fante weakness, which was to be their undoing in the early nineteenth century.

Fante expansion was temporarily halted between 1690 and 1707 by deep-seated divisions between the various city-states that paid allegiance to the Braffo of Fantyn. Most Fante groups occupied an area of about thirty miles square, and were therefore not strong enough on their own to defeat powerful neighbours like Denkyira to the north. Unfortunately each of the Fante states behaved as if they were deadly rivals, continually quarrelling with one another. The Fante were therefore in no position to take on other Akan states.

The second phase of Fante expansion:
the Abora period of 1707–1730
A new factor in Fante history united the previously dissident city-states. This was the emergence of Asante to the north as a real power after she had thrashed mighty Denkyira at Feyiase in 1701. After Denkyira fell, the Fante began to grapple with a problem which was to beset them for the next hundred years and more: how could they maintain some degree of control over their posi-

tion as middlemen in the trade between Europeans and the interior? If Fante failed to grasp this nettle, she would succumb to Asante. For Fante prosperity, and even her survival as an independent people, depended upon several factors: customs revenues, the profits made by Fante middlemen, and direct access to Europeans who supplied guns and powder which the Asante could otherwise use to crush Fante.

The Fante states then set about gaining a hold over trading outlets on the coast like Cape Coast, Elmina and Anomabu. The surest way of accomplishing this laudable aim was to incorporate neighbouring Fante states into a union of all the Fante city-states. And so in the interests of political and economic survival the Fante states rallied together, probably under the leadership of Abora city-state to the north-west, and not under their old capital city of Mankessim. The Fante Union was established in the years just before 1707.

The Fante were also aided in their attempt to reorganize themselves by the fact that they gained a new ally on the eastern borders of Fanteland, Agona, who sought help against the threatening power of Akyem. Also, European traders on the coast were weak and divided among themselves and were therefore unable to put up any real opposition to the new wave of Fante conquest which was now launched from Abora.

Between 1707 and 1730 the Fante extended their sway to all the coastal states between the mouth of the Pra river in the east, and the Ga states in the west. The Fante Union now controlled all this section of the coast and the principal trading stations, except for Elmina.

How was the Fante union governed?
It is unfortunate that as yet we know all too little about the government of the confederation of states called the Fante Union. Nevertheless, the records of Europeans who were then on the coast tell us that Fante had formed a union parliament. The parliament was composed of delegates from the different city-states. The Braffo of Fantyn was at the head of all Fante as their secular ruler. However, as before, the Braffo lacked any meaningful powers: he was just first among equals. The Braffo seems to have shared his position as ruler with the high priest of the Fante people's national god. In European records this priest is known

as Bora Bora Weigya.

The Fante Union suffered from the fact that the associated states had no great leaders who could provide religious symbols to catch the imagination and loyalty of all Fante. The only factor which really held Fante together was a common fear of Asante power. For the first two decades of the eighteenth century the Asante threat was ever menacing. But after the 1720's, it became less apparent and so the Fante Union, feeling comparatively safe, began to fall apart. By 1750, not only had the Union broken up into two parts called eastern and western Fante, but each part also consisted of states which considered themselves more or less sovereign and independent of one another. The Fante had returned to the bickerings and disputes of pre-1707. The only authority they now recognized was the religious authority of the high priest of their national god.

Fante after 1750

This period really belongs to a consideration of Fante-Asante relations. Nevertheless, it is as well to mention that by 1750 Fante was one of the two dominant powers on the coast, together with Asante. In the 1750's the Fante once again became afraid of an Asante invasion; once more the city-states united in the face of the common danger that threatened them. In February 1758 we have a report in European records that 'all the principal people have been assembled for this month past . . . to settle and adjust all differences in their country, to make new laws and appoint a new Braffo'.

In point of fact, Fante only came up against Asante in battle on two occasions: in 1765 when the Fante fought Asante in Abora, and in 1776 when the Fante sent an army to help their allies of the moment against Asante. From 1777 until the end of the century, there was no enmity between the two powers. Internal difficulties in Asante, British support of the Fante, and Fante diplomatic skill ensured that the long awaited Asante invasion did not take place until 1807.

THE SECOND AKAN EMPIRE: AKWAMU (*See Map XXVI, page 269*)

While the Fante states were emerging in the western corner of

245

Ghana, the Akwamu were founding their own state in the regions of the north-east. This state was to become the second Akan empire and a mighty power in the coastal hinterland.

The founding clan of Akwamu, a section of the royal Aduana clan in Twifo forest state, emigrated from Twifo in about the second half of the sixteenth century. Tradition says that in its exodus from Twifo after a disputed succession this breakaway section of the royal clan was led by one Otomfo Asare. Asare founded the present town of Asamankese, which means 'Asare's big state', in the basin of the Birim and Densu rivers. This area is rich in gold and so the Akwamu prospered exceedingly. After the early 1600's, the Akwamu came together and formed a loose union of their peoples. Akwamu then had the military power and, equally important, the commercial strength to launch a programme of territorial conquest. Akwamu expansion took place in three phases: from 1629 to 1650, from 1650 to 1702, and from 1702 to 1710 when the Akwamu empire reached its peak of greatness and glory.

The first phase of expansion: 1629–1650
To begin with the Akwamu contented themselves with strengthening their position in the Birim and Densu regions, enriching their state with the tolls and duties they collected from traders travelling to and from the coast. But in about 1629 Akwamu probably felt strong enough to look outwards. Seeing that Akim to the north-west would be a formidable foe, and that Fante was becoming strong to the south-west, the Akwamu first looked eastwards. Between 1629 and 1650 Akwamu conquered and absorbed the Guan principalities, but she still had to defeat the Ga who barred the way to eastern coastal outlets.

The second phase of expansion: 1650–1702
In this period Akwamu conquered the Ga-Adangbe city-states to the south, the Ladoku kingdoms and the state of Agona. Significantly enough, it was at this time that the first of a number of great Akwamu kings or Akwamuhenes came to sit on the stool.

The first important Akwamuhene was Ansa Sasraku who reigned between 1660 and 1689. Sasraku prepared the ground for his campaign against the Ga and Ladoku by getting onto good terms with European traders. For Akwamu was now eager to establish her dominance on the eastern coast by crushing the Ga at Accra. This was done between 1677 and 1681 in a series of campaigns, which gave Akwamu her coastal outlets and reduced the Ga to the status of tributaries until 1730. Ansa Sasraku's last battle was fought against the Lakoku in 1689, the year of his death.

At the time of Ansa Sasraku's death in 1689, Akwamu was well on the way to embracing much of the Gold Coast. Akwamu territory now extended along the coast from Winneba to the Volta, taking in the important European trading stations in and around Accra. Akwamu also reached out towards the Akwapim hills. The reign of Ansa Sasraku was a landmark in Akwamu history, because it was this great ruler who transformed Akwamu from a small kingdom into an empire made up of several pre- viously independent principalities and kingdoms.

Ansa Sasraku was succeeded by two capable rulers who ruled together from 1689 to 1702. These rulers were called Addo and Basua. It was during their reign that Akwamu took possession of the Danish castle at Christiansborg by a trick; after occupying the fort for one year Akwamu agreed to sell it back to the Danes. Having secured Akwamu's north-western frontier against the Akim, Addo turned his attention to the east and launched an attack which took Akwamu as far as Whydah in modern Dahomey. The successful Dahomey campaign of 1701 to 1702 ended with the accession of a new Akwamuhene.

The third phase of expansion: 1702–1710
The accession of the most capable Akwonno, who ruled between 1702 and 1725, marked the advent of the third phase in Akwamu expansion. Very sensibly Akwonno decided not to over-extend Akwamu on her eastern frontier, but to concentrate on securing her northern boundaries.

Between 1707 and 1710 Akwonno annexed lands north of the Volta, the states of Kwahu and Krepi, and the Fante state of Agona to the south-east where Akwamuland met up with the Akim. In 1710 the great empire of Akwamu had reached its peak. Akwamu stretched for over two hundred miles along the coast, and for a long way inland across the Afram plains as far as southern Togoland.

J

The reasons for the rise of Akwamu
What were the main reasons for the phenomenal rise of this great empire? There were three factors behind the growth of Akwamu city-state into an empire: the political, the economic and the personal factor of individual leadership.

In the first place, the Akwamu were cunning enough to take advantage of the fact that there were no strong states in the region of the Birim and Densu where they had originally founded their city-state. Quickly conquering the Guan principalities, Akwamu was able to grow in commercial strength and military power before she had to take on more formidable neighbours like the Ga and Fante states to the south. If Akwamu had been unlucky enough to have had powerful states nearby, her leaders might have been unable to establish their empire.

Then there is the economic factor. The Akwamu grew rich on the tolls and dues levied on trade routes once controlled by the Guan, Ga and Ladoku. They were then able to buy the arms and weapons which ensured their continuing growth in the late seventeenth and early eighteenth centuries. The Akwamu were much assisted by tentative support from European traders who saw that Akwamu was the new power on the eastern coast. European companies did not therefore try to stem the Akwamu advance by backing the Ga or Fante states: later the British adopted the ploy of divide and rule, backing Fante against Asante.

Finally, we must of course take into account the bravery, shrewd leadership and martial ardour of great Akwamuhenes like Ansa Sasraku and Akwonno. In fact it could be said that the rise of Akwamu was as much due to inspired leadership as to any of the political and economic factors that aided Akwamu in her expansion.

Reasons for the fall of Akwamu in 1730
One may well ask: if the Akwamu empire was so mighty, why did it collapse after the death of Akwonno in 1725? There are two main reasons for this event. The first is that in spite of their administrative achievements, Akwamu's rulers failed to solve the problem of how to integrate vassals into the Akwamu state. The Akwamu empire was the second Akan empire. It was also among the first of the Akan states which had to tackle the difficulties inherent in governing many peoples who had been accustomed to

independence before their defeat. More government officials emerged, but no way was found to secure the loyalty of subjects towards the Akwamuhene. In addition to these administrative failings, Akwamu's rulers were tyrannical in the extreme, taxing their hapless vassals most heavily. Political oppression became more marked during the reign of Akwonno. Suffering and exploited vassals sought to overthrow Akwamu tyranny by the violent method of revolt. It cost Akwamu much in money and men to go on crushing rebellions by discontented subjects.

The second reason for the fall of Akwamu was more immediate and direct. The Akim to the north-west were expanding south in the early eighteenth century towards Akwamu. Akim got together with certain vassals of Akwamu who were eager to throw off the Akwamu yoke. In 1730 the allied armies of Akim, Kwahu and Agona invaded Akwamu and decisively defeated her. The royal clan was chased away over the Volta where modern Akwamu is now situated; and there they stayed never to return.

Thus, discontent with Akwamu's tyrannical and not too efficient government, and Akim strength were two main reasons for the fall of the second great Akan empire.

AKAN KINGDOMS OF THE IVORY COAST

The Anyi kingdom of Sanwi
During the seventeenth and eighteenth centuries some groups of Akan, which later emerged as the Anyi, crossed the Camoé river and settled on the Bandama plains. In about 1750 certain sections of the Anyi left this home on the Bandama plains for Krinjabo in the north where they founded the capital of a new kingdom called Sanwi. Absorbing the indigenous inhabitants, together with their chiefs, four large Anyi clans settled in Sanwi. They all recognized as their king a descendant of the clan which first settled at Krinjabo. The king was a war leader and a sacred figure who sat on the stool of Krinjabo.

Krinjabo was divided into seven quarters, each dominated by a different lineage of aristocratic descent. The chiefs of each quarter sat on an advisory council with other leading chiefs from the provinces of Sanwi; the council met regularly at the palace. Here, nobles and councillors sought audiences with the king; here, the principal officers of state took their decisions on public matters.

Like some other great Akan states, the kingdom of Sanwi was organized on hierarchical lines, with authority centralized in the person of the king. He delegated power to his leading chiefs and, from there, authority was given to junior officials who resided in the provinces. Government was shared by civilian and military leaders. There was, therefore, a balance of power between the army and civilian officials. Both military and civilian principles of organization were united in the Sanwi king: for he was a political ruler and a warrior at the same time.

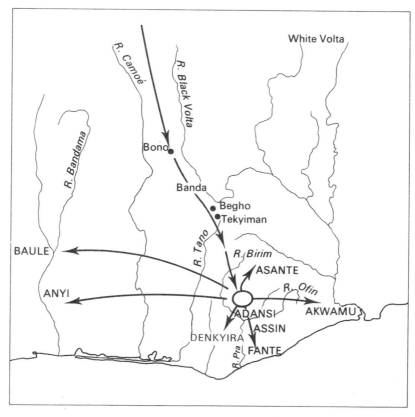

Map XXIV   The Akan Peoples and their Trade Routes

The civil administration centred on three great chiefs from three important clans in Sanwi. One chief came from the capital of Krinjabo; he was the most powerful of the three civil chiefs. Military chiefs, of which there were three important ones, were the descendants of old warrior families who had led the way to Krinjabo. The kingdom was divided into lieutenancies, according to a common Akan practice: there were three lieutenancies.

The king ruled through a permanent council of advisers drawn from the seven quarters of Krinjabo, the three great civil chiefs of Sanwi, the three warrior chiefs from the three lieutenancies and princes of royal blood. The king was responsible for guarding Anyi customs and conventions, for ensuring justice, and for granting rights in land. He also acted as a military overlord. However, the leading chiefs of Sanwi became extremely important in the event of an inter-regnum when they conducted the affairs of state until they had chosen a successor to the stool and installed the king-elect.

The Baulé kingdom

Another Akan kingdom of the Ivory Coast was that of the Baulé. After the death of the Asante king Opoku Ware in 1750, there was a dispute over the sucession—a not uncommon event. One section, later called the Baulé, decided to leave Asante and seek their fortunes in the lands to the west. They are said by tradition to have been led by a courageous woman called Abra Pokou. Tradition has it that on the way these Akan founded little states which conquered the indigenous inhabitants. By the time Queen Abra Pokou had become established around the river Bandama, four principal clans had come together under her rule. These groups are known as the Warébo, the Sâafwé, the Fâfwé and the Nzipri. The Baulé also controlled four groups of vassals.

Queen Pokou died in about 1760 and was buried in her capital town of Warebo. Her niece, in accordance with the principle of matrilineal succession, followed her as queen of the Baulé. It was under this queen that the Baulé took over the gold-bearing lands to the west of the Bandama region. Queen Akwa Bini died in about 1790; after this the Baulé became divided and therefore considerably weaker than before. Nevertheless the Baulé kingdom remained a state of some power in the southern Ivory Coast for the next hundred years or so.

Questions

1 Examine the accounts given of the origins of the Akan. Using examples from the history of the Akan states, explain the reasons for the dispersal of the Akan peoples.

2 What do you understand by (a) the 'northern' factor and (b) the 'southern' factor in Akan history?

3 What factors influenced the development of Bono-Tekyiman? Why did none of the early Akan states remain strong powers for long?

4 'The history of the Fante is one of alternating periods of unity and disunity.' What factors contributed to disunity among the Fante and how did disunity (a) weaken Fante and (b) contribute to its expansion? Give reasons for the periods of unity among the Fante.

5 Trace the rise of Akwamu. Why did it collapse?

6 Write an instructive paragraph on four of the following:
(a) Nana Kumfi Ameyaw I; (b) Assin; (c) Denkyira; (d) clans among the Akan; (e) the Baulé.

7 Give an account of the political organization of the Anyi kingdom of Sanwi.

15

States of the Guinea Forest:
The Akan empire of Asante

For about one hundred and fifty years the empire of Asante was the most important factor in the political and commercial history of modern Ghana, Togo and the Ivory Coast. An empire of unprecedented power on the West African sea board, Asante lasted longer than its two great Akan predecessors—Akwamu and Denkyira—and at her height in 1824 spanned more than two hundred and fifty miles along the Gulf of Guinea. At the least, Asante had established her influence over an area of about 125,000 to 150,000 square miles from the southern coast through the Guinea forest to the far distant northern savanna. Perhaps three to five million people lived in this area.

The capital at Kumasi developed into a large and important city, throbbing with intellectual, artistic and political activity. It was at Kumasi that Asante culture flowered so brilliantly. Here came learned Muslims, chiefs and captains from the forest provinces, envoys and diplomats from many states, Dyula traders from towns to the north-west like Kong and Jenne, and Hausa merchants from the north-eastern centres of Kano and Katsina.

Founded in the later decades of the seventeenth century, Kumasi was described more than a hundred years later, in 1817, by the Englishman, William Bowdich. Greeted by many warriors and soldiers, Bowdich and his fellow traveller marvelled at the magnificent dress of the officials, chiefs and army captains. They found the city of Kumasi most impressive, for 'four of the principal streets are half a mile long and from fifty to a hundred yards wide. . . . There is a senior captain in charge of each of them. Every household burns its rubbish every morning at the back of the street, and the people are as clean and careful about the appearance of their houses as they are about their own appearance'.

Now, how did all this splendour come about?

THE FOUNDING OF ASANTE

It all began sometime in the seventeenth century when the Oyoko clan moved from their cradle in the Pra-Ofin basin towards the north. They settled in the region of modern Kumasi in the Kwaman forest. The Oyoko did not find the land empty for earlier migrants from the Pra and Ofin confluence had made their homes within a thirty mile radius of modern Kumasi, founding a number of petty states and kingdoms. However, Oyoko lineages established five city-states there, one of which was Kumasi. It was that section of the Oyoko people, led by Obiri Yeboa, which is said by oral tradition to have established Kumasi between the 1660's and 1670's. By cunning diplomacy, intermarriage and war. Obiri Yeboa succeeded in establishing Kumasi's influence over some of the other city-states in that region by the end of the seventeenth century.

Reasons for the rise of Asante
There were five main reasons for the rise of the Asante empire from its small beginnings in the city-state of Kumasi. The first was the founding of a number of petty Asante states in the neighbourhood of Kumasi. The second was that Denkyira controlled many of these states. The third was the growth of the Atlantic slave trade. The fourth was the close co-operation that existed between the five Oyoko states. And the fifth reason was the ambition, martial ardour, sagacity and statecraft displayed by the first three great rulers of Asante—Obiri Yeboa, Osei Tutu and Opoku Ware, whose joint reigns lasted from about the 1660's to 1750.

The first factor which contributed to the rise of Asante was that although several petty states had grown up around modern Kumasi, flourishing on trans-Saharan commerce, only the five Oyoko clan states had the decisive advantage of being clansmen who would therefore support one another against other states in the vicinity. The rivalry between states must have been intense, for it was here that two main trade routes from the

Map XXV Asante at the Death of Opoku Ware in 1750

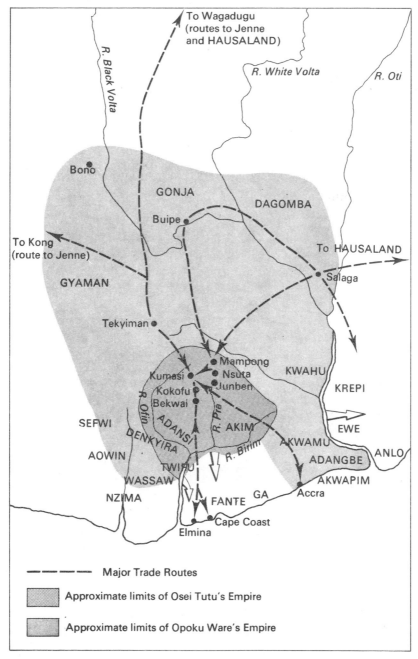

To Wagadugu (routes to Jenne and HAUSALAND)

R. Black Volta

R. White Volta

R. Oti

Bono

GONJA

DAGOMBA

Buipe

To Kong (route to Jenne)

To HAUSALAND

GYAMAN

Salaga

Tekyiman

Mampong

Nsuta

KWAHU

Kumasi

Junben

KREPI

Kokofu

Bekwai

SEFWI

R. Ofin

ADANSI

R. Pra

AKIM

EWE

DENKYIRA

AKWAMU

AOWIN

R. Birim

ANLO

ADANGBE

TWIFU

WASSAW

AKWAPIM

NZIMA

GA

Accra

FANTE

Cape Coast

Elmina

— — — — — Major Trade Routes

Approximate limits of Osei Tutu's Empire

Approximate limits of Opoku Ware's Empire

western Sudan met. The western route from Timbuktu, Jenne and Begho, and the eastern route from Hausaland met in the Kumasi region and radiated southwards to the coast in several directions. The forest here is rich in gold and kola nuts—those mainstays of the trans-Saharan trade—and so some clans like the Oyoko had settled in the Kumasi region with a view to sharing in this lucrative trade. These states were to be the nucleus of the future Asante empire. This fact, which illustrates the importance of the 'northern' factor in Asante history, was of some significance for the future development of Asante power on the basis of commercial prosperity derived from the northern-directed trade.

Another factor which brought the city states of the Kwaman forest together was Denkyira's oppression. Oral traditions and the reports of Europeans confirm that pre-Asante Union states in this region were reduced to the status of Denkyira's tributaries between about 1650 and 1660. Denkyira treated her unfortunate vassals with great harshness, regarding them as slaves. But Denkyira's rulers were not only hated for their oppression. There was also the fact that they prevented these states in the Kwaman forest from reaching down to the coast. Thus, the pre-Asante Union states developed what one observer called a 'common hatred of Denkyira', and were anxious to throw off her heavy yoke, if only they could find the right leader. It was at this moment in time, round about the 1670's, that the Oyoko clan stepped in with their shrewd chief, Obiri Yeboa of Kumasi. He prepared the ground for the establishment of the Asante Union under his successor Osei Tutu.

Yet another reason for Asante's rise to power was the rapid development of the Atlantic trade after the 1660's: this, it will be remembered, is the 'southern' factor in Akan history. The pre-Asante Union states were eager to share in the lucrative profits that could be obtained from the overseas trade in slaves and other goods. However, states which controlled access to European trading forts, like Fante and Akwamu, denied the pre-Asante Union states direct access to coastal forts: they had to buy guns and cloth from Fante or Akwamu traders. And so mutual co-operation and united action was the only way in which they could overcome Akwamu, Denkyira and Fante.

This brings us to the final reason for the emergence of Asante

256

power—the great leadership of the first three kings of the Asante Union beginning with Obiri Yeboa. When Obiri Yeboa led his followers to the place in the Kwaman forest where they created Kumasi, he thought of a most wise and diplomatic thing to do. He admitted the ruling lineages of most of the states in the neighbourhood of Kumasi into the Oyoko clan, after he had ensured their co-operation by peaceful negotiation or by force of arms. Obiri Yeboa thereby enlarged the ranks of the Oyoko clan in Kumasi; he also secured his own position and that of his lineage as future rulers of the Asante Union. Having consolidated his position, Obiri then embarked on a number of campaigns to conquer surrounding states which had so far rejected all offers to join the Oyoko states. Tradition does not accord Obiri any important victories, and he is said to have been killed in battle in about the late 1670's. This man was without any doubt a most talented and shrewd diplomat, able to negotiate his way into a strong position. It was Obiri Yeboa who laid the foundations of the Asante Union which emerged fully under his successor, Osei Tutu.

THE REIGN OF OSEI TUTU: c. 1680–c. 1717

Osei Tutu's reign was the critical event in Asante history. Popularly acclaimed as the founder and first ruler of the Asante Union, this king shows us how important an individual ruler of outstanding abilities can be in the history of his people. Osei Tutu proved to be an even more able diplomat, administrator and warrior than his uncle Obiri Yeboa.

It is not yet certain when Osei Tutu succeeded Obiri Yeboa; the problem is one of getting reliable dates from traditional genealogies of royal rulers. However, it is safe to say that Osei Tutu was installed sometime after the late 1670's when Obiri Yeboa died: it was probably in about 1680. Osei Tutu is definitely known to have been a maternal nephew of Obiri Yeboa; succession to political office among the Akan is generally traced through the mother.

Asante tradition says that Osei Tutu had been staying in Akwamu, after he had first visited Denkyira, to learn about military organization and statecraft. While in Akwamu, Tutu formed a life-long friendship with a priest called Okomfo Anokye who played a vital part in the full establishment of the Asante Union under Osei Tutu. When Osei Tutu returned to Kumasi after Obiri Yeboa's death, it was only natural that he should ask Okomfo Anokye to help, and to go with him when he went home to take over from the regent who had looked after affairs of state when Obiri Yeboa died.

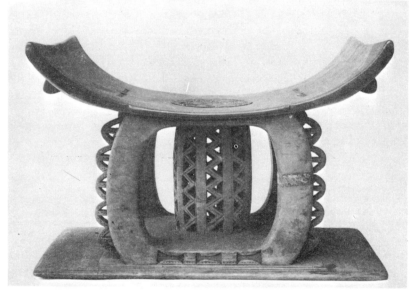

Fig. 12   An Asante stool

Osei Tutu and the Golden Stool of Asante

After Osei Tutu had been acclaimed as ruler, he got together with his friend Okomfo Anokye and assembled at Kumasi all those states friendly to the Oyoko clan. Realizing that they needed something positive and lasting to weld these states together permanently under Kumasi's leadership, Osei Tutu and Anokye found a solution in the revered and sacrosanct Golden Stool. Okomfo Anokye is said by tradition to have brought the Golden Stool down from the sky 'in a black cloud and amidst rumblings'. The priest is then said to have announced to all those assembled that the Stool embodied the soul and unity of the Asante people.

The Golden Stool was never to be lost, the kinship group of Osei Tutu was for ever to be recognized as the head of the Asante Union, and all previous symbols of political authority were to be buried.

Of course, it is a physical impossibility for a stool to drop from the sky. What is more likely is that this story is a way of saying that no Golden Stool (or supreme kingship) had existed before, so that its sudden establishment was as if it had dropped from the sky. The point is that Osei Tutu and Okomfo Anokye had thought of a religious way to express the links between the assembled states. The Stool authorized in religious language the future leadership of Kumasi's paramount chief as the king of the Asante state; and it represented the close national unity of all Asante, incorporating people of different clans into one political unit. People then believed in the ever-immanent presence of the ancestors, who are represented in lineage stools. The common 'kinship' of all Asante was thus represented in the Golden Stool whose occupant was a divinely authorized king, a sacred personage hedged in by taboos and rules designed to maintain his closeness with the royal ancestors and with the gods. Thus were religious ideas used to maintain and validate political relationships between states. In fact, the story about the Golden Stool is a very important example of the way in which rulers used religion to buttress their authority.

The Achievements of Osei Tutu

Assisted by Okomfo Anokye, Osei Tutu contributed to the emergence of the Asante empire in five ways. He completed the formation of the Asante Union under the leadership of his kinship group; devised a constitution for the empire based upon the allegiance of all subordinate chiefs, who swore on the Great Oath to carry out their political obligations to the Asante king; endowed the Union with a capital city, Kumasi; introduced a new form of military organization; and, finally, Osei Tutu continued most successfully to expand the empire's territories.

First, Osei Tutu welded the union of states into a purposeful entity by creating a symbol of their unity, the Golden Stool. A factor which must have predisposed the chiefs to accept the Stool was their common fear of Denkyira, of whom Bosman said: 'Denkyira, elevated by its great riches and power became so

259

arrogant that it looked on all other Negroes with a contemptible eye, esteeming them no more than slaves'.

This done, Osei Tutu and Okomfo Anokye introduced a constitution for the Asante Union which was modelled on existing Akan practices. The head of the Union was the Asantehene, or king of all Asante who was, at the same time, the paramount chief of Kumasi state. The Asantehene ruled with the advice of the Confederacy Council, which consisted of the paramount chiefs (Amanhene) of states in the Union. All heads of states (Omanhene), had to seek the Asantehene's recognition by swearing the oath of allegiance to him. An Omanhene also had to give up the right of declaring war at will upon a member of the Union, and he had to recognize the right of the Asantehene to impose national levies in times of crisis. Each Omanhene was to attend the annual Odwira or 'cleansing' ceremony which, as a rite for the dead, cleanses the nation from defilement and purifies all ancestral shrines as well as those dedicated to national gods. An Omanhene had, finally, to grant his subjects the right of appeal to the high court, which had been set up in Kumasi. In all other spheres the Omanhene enjoyed freedom of action within his own state.

The constitution of Asante is significant for the way in which the individual states and their rulers were—in principle at least—stripped of powers which could result in a rebellion being organized against the Asantehene. Only the Asantehene could declare war and impose extra-ordinary taxes for national purposes. Power had been effectively centralized in the hands of the Asantehene and the Confederacy Council: the member states of the Union had been welded into a nation.

The third way in which Osei Tutu contributed to the establishment of the Asante empire was by making Kumasi, the home of his Oyoko lineage, the undisputed political, commercial and cultural centre of Asanteland. Power lay in Kumasi. This basic fact of life was reflected in the command to all Amanhene to attend the national Odwira festival there.

Fourthly, Osei Tutu and Okomfo Anokye introduced a form of military organization which was to prove very successful. It seems that Asante military organization was borrowed from the Akwamu. However, you will remember that this form of organization was characteristically Akan. For the Anyi kingdom of Sanwi in the Ivory Coast was organized into military divisions called lieutenancies. In Sanwi there were just three such divisions. In Asante there were four—the van, the rear, the right and left wings. Each member state was given a place in one of the wings; and each wing was placed under a commander who was also the king of a state. Military service was compulsory for every able-bodied male. Although Osei Tutu probably borrowed this form of organization from the Akwamu, there is no doubt that it attained a peak of perfection and efficiency under his rule and that of his successors. The army and those military leaders called captains were politically influential. And the organization of the empire on military lines meant that troops could be called up quickly, village defences could be speedily erected, and levies could be paid at once into the national Treasury.

The fifth way in which Osei Tutu consolidated the Asante Union was by waging merciless, brilliant warfare on his enemies. Osei's main aim was to gain control over north-south trade routes. To do this, he had to defeat mighty Denkyira who stood in the way of Asante sharing in profitable revenues from tolls and customs levies.

Osei Tutu's first important compaign was conducted against some neighbouring states like Tafo and Amakom (now part of Kumasi) and Ofinso (fifteen miles north of Kumasi) who still held out against the Asante Union. Then between 1699 and 1701, his immediate problems overcome, Osei Tutu reduced mighty Denkyira and her allies to tributaries. Removing much booty, Asante also got away with a valuable prize—the rental note for the castle at Elmina through which a lot of trade passed. Asante now had a shaky foothold on this section of the coast. Becoming fearful, European traders sent representatives to court Osei Tutu. Indeed, the Dutch dispatched an ambassador to the Asantehene's court at Kumasi as early as 1701.

Next Osei Tutu turned his attention to some allies of Denkyira who still held out against Asante. Akim, considerably weakened by her part in supporting Denkyira in the 1699–1701 campaign, when she is said by tradition to have lost thirty thousand men, was annexed in the early 1700's.

By the first decade of the eighteenth century Osei Tutu was coming up against the administrative problem that had troubled earlier Akan states: how was he to incorporate newly acquired territories into the Union in order to maintain Asante's hold over them? Obiri Yeboa had begun the process of consolidating the Kwaman states under the Oyoko banner. Osei Tutu successfully concluded this process by introducing the Golden Stool and furthering dynastic inter-marriages. Subjects of states like Tafo were incorporated into the Asante union; they were Asante citizens. Thinking of themselves as Asante and not, for instance, as Tafo people, Kumasi's neighbours were more likely to remain permanent friends.

But now the Asantehene was faced with larger states, proud of their independence and more removed from the Kumasi region. Osei Tutu did not apply the policy of full incorporation to states like Denkyira and Akim, perhaps because they were not entirely subjugated and perhaps because they were farther off and conscious of their former independence.

Instead, as we shall see, two systems of government gradually evolved on the basis of this distinction between states belonging to the Asante Union, and states which did not. The metropolitan region of Kumasi, which included the true *amanto* or Union states mostly belonging to the Oyoko clan, was granted a considerable degree of independence from intervention by the Asantehene. The provinces, which included states not incorporated into the Union, were administered directly by the Asantehene and his officials at Kumasi. In this way Asante tried to solve the problem of controlling conquered territories like Denkyira by establishing a centralised administration, which worked through commissioners appointed by the Asantehene to reside in the provinces.

Osei Tutu's Death and the Great Oath
After 1701, Osei Tutu spent the next few years consolidating Asante's hold over her new territories. From time to time the Akim, ever restless, tried to revolt. It was probably during an expedition against one such revolt that Osei Tutu was killed while crossing the river Pra with his men.

Historians are still arguing about the date of Osei Tutu's death: some say he died in 1712, some assert that the right year is 1717, while earlier writers used to put forward the year 1730 for the great warrior's death. The confusion seems to have arisen because there are reports by Europeans that an Asantehene died in 1717. Some historians assume that it was Tutu who was killed in 1712, while another lesser king occupied the Stool until his death in 1717.

This theory, though, is not all that firm. For a record written by a European factor at Accra refers to the Akim-Asante war of 1717. It seems impossible that tradition would give incorrect information about the event that led to the death of such a great king. This was the Akim war, and as it occurred in 1717, we can be pretty sure that Osei Tutu was killed in that year.

Osei Tutu's death gave rise to the most serious oath an Asante can use, the Asantehene's Great Oath. For no one is held in greater veneration than Osei Tutu. The significance of the Great Oath is that it refers to a tragic event in Asante history. To swear the Oath is to incur the anger of the royal ancestors, who resent such references to past tragedies; the penalty for falsely breaking the Great Oath is death, brought about by the royal ancestors. When an Omanhene swears allegiance to the Asantehene he says: 'I speak the Great Oath, that if I do not help you to administer this nation, if ever I am false to you, if you call me by night, if you call me by day, and I do not come, then have I broken the Great Oath . . .' The Asantehene's reply is terrifying: 'If you ever rebel against me, may the gods kill you'.

The death of Osei Tutu was therefore used in a most constructive manner to strengthen the bonds between subordinate states and the central government headed by a semi-divine king, the Asantehene. The original oath of allegiance was sanctified and transformed into a sacred act of obeisance on the part of Amanhene to their king and lord.

A great administrator and diplomat, Osei Tutu was in more ways than one the founder of the Asante nation with his friend Okomfo Anokye. Osei Tutu was most successful in battle. But it is, perhaps, his superb achievements in giving the Union such an impressive national symbol as the Golden Stool, in devising an effective and sophisticated constitution, and in introducing an efficient form of military organization that must rank him among the 'greats' of West African history. Men like Osei Tutu are all too rare in history. Glorious in war, brilliant at thinking out a new constitutional system, and a man with a most commanding personality, his death was a grievous loss to the new Asante nation. Osei Tutu's political and military talents were complemented by the religious knowledge and shrewd powers of his friend Okomfo Anokye. For it was this priest who helped Osei Tutu to establish himself as king of the Asante states, and used the religious beliefs of the people to create a symbol of their unity in the Golden Stool. However, such were the wonderful achievements of Osei Tutu and Okomfo Anokye that the Asante Union survived the ordeal of their king's sad death.

THE REIGN OF OPOKU WARE: *c.* 1720–1750

After a year or two of confusion when contenders for the Golden Stool appear to have fought one another, the grand-nephew of Osei Tutu emerged triumphant as the new Asantehene. This probably took place in about 1720. But Opoku Ware was definitely recognized as Asantehene by 1724 because a Dutch record of that year refers to him as the Asante king.

Opoku Ware reigned for some thirty years, an extremely able ruler and a worthy successor to Osei Tutu and Obiri Yeboa. In fact, Opoku Ware was an even better military leader than his two predecessors. For it was Opoku Ware who used the Asante military machine to expand the Union into an empire. At the same time he consolidated the administrative innovations of Osei Tutu, showing that he was also an astute organiser.

Opoku Ware's reign was principally one of wars, of conquests, and of campaigns against tributary states who dared to challenge Asante's might by rebellion. In the early 1720's he tackled a new threat from Denkyira, Sefwi and Akwapim who had taken advantage of the troubles at Kumasi after Osei Tutu's death to form an alliance. While Opoku Ware was away fighting the Akim, the Sefwi army entered Kumasi and sacked the Union's capital. Sefwi even committed the abomination of killing the Asantehene's own mother as well as other members of the royal family. Outraged, Opoku Ware rushed back and gave the Sefwi the heaviest defeat of their lives. Asante then annexed all Sefwiland.

A new phase opened with Opoku Ware's northward thrust in the years between 1723 and 1724, when he conquered the state of Bono-Tekyiman. During the 1730's Asante had to crush Akim to the south who posed a new threat after she had overthrown Akwamu in 1730. Annexing parts of Akim and Kwahu states, the victorious Asante army thrust south to conquer Akwapim,

Akwamu and the Ga-Adangbe states. In fact, in 1744 a contingent from the Asante army entered Accra. Thus Asante opened up access routes to the coast even to the extent, in 1744, of invading the Dahomean coast as far as Little Popo.

Between 1744 and 1750 the Asante did not extend their conquests in the Guinea forest. Content with routes to the coast through the Ga and Akwamu states, Asante looked north again. During 1744 to 1746, Opoku Ware defeated Gonja and Dagomba in the Volta basin, thus securing some of the key towns on the trans-Saharan trade route. Asante now had overwhelming control of the principal trade routes running between the coastal regions and the southern savanna. Her prosperity from tolls and customs and her military power, which depended upon direct access to supplies of guns, were more than assured. 1750, the year of Opoku Ware's death, saw the Asante empire nearly at its height of territorial expansion and greatness.

The achievements of Opoku Ware
The glorious Opoku Ware, the mightiest warrior king in Asante history, was indeed a worthy successor to the more diplomatic Osei Tutu and Obiri Yeboa. But for his martial ardour the Union might well have been crushed. Opoku Ware's military talents ensured that a union of city-states had emerged by 1750 as a great empire. He was undoubtedly one of the greatest Asante rulers of the eighteenth century. Whereas Osei Tutu was probably gifted at negotiation and territorial expansion by diplomacy as well as force of arms, Opoku Ware seems to have been more gifted with military talents and appears to have concentrated on expansion by military tactics, although he must also have been an assured negotiator. Opoku Ware was recognized as a mighty king by a Gonja historian who said: 'May God curse him, may He take his soul and cast it into the fire. He it was who troubled the people of Gonja; continually and at all times did he trouble them. He seized their possessions. Whatever he wished, so he did, for he was all-powerful in his rule'.

This said, it is as well to point out that Opoku Ware's reign emphasized an important weakness in Asante administration. Unlike Osei Tutu, Opoku Ware did nothing to incorporate newly conquered territories into the Asante Union, which was the nucleus of the empire. Some of the kings of conquered provinces

265

were deposed, but new leaders from the same royal lineages were elected. The institutions and customs of vassal states were left untouched by Asante. All tributaries had to do was to pay tribute, contribute military contingents when called upon to do so, accept one of the Amanhene or Kumasi divisional chiefs as the intermediary between them and the Asantehene, and accept the oath of allegiance to the Asantehene.

Perhaps Opoku Ware failed to devise any effective machinery to govern newly conquered territories because he was too involved in wars, and because his attempts at constitutional reforms at home between 1746 and 1750 appear to have failed. Opoku Ware's lack of success in administrative matters meant that he handed on to his successor a legacy of constitutional problems, which was one reason why the post-1750 period saw many rebellions. Vassal states were treated as second class citizens so they never identified themselves with Kumasi and the Golden Stool; they never thought of themselves as Asante.

THE 'REFORMER' OSEI KWADWO: 1764–1777

When Opoku Ware died, he was succeeded by his uncle, an old man called Kusi Obodum (1750–1764). Then Osei Kwadwo (1764–1777) succeeded to the Golden Stool. The next two Asantehenes were Osei Kwame (1777–1801) and Osei Bonsu (1801–1824). Osei Kwadwo and Osei Bonsu are known in Asante history as the 'great reformers', because they changed the machinery of government in order to weld together Asante's conquered territories, the provinces.

Osei Kwadwo's reign marked a new era in Asante history. Until 1750 Asante had been riding high on a wave of apparently endless conquest. After the 1750's, the second period of Asante history began during which Asantehenes had to do two things: to hold on to and to increase Asante territory, and to push through administrative reforms designed to weld the different states together into one cohesive nation. It was Osei Kwadwo's radical constitutional innovations which gave him the title of 'reformer', and entitles his reign to be called 'the Kwadwoan revolution'.

Asante history after 1750 was influenced by three factors. The first was the entry of the British into coastal politics with their overt support for the troublesome Fante. British agents wanted to weaken Asante by siding with Fante, who would then block Asante from the western areas of the coast. The second factor was the problem posed by the growing division between Kumasi and her conquered provinces: rebellions were an all too frequent event after 1750 as discontented vassals tried to throw off Asante's yoke. The third was the need for administrative reforms which would unite the different states into one empire under Kumasi. To a large extent the success of an Asantehene's rule after 1750 depended upon whether or not he had the ability and administrative genius to solve this latter problem.

THE GOVERNMENT OF THE ASANTE EMPIRE IN THE EIGHTEENTH CENTURY

The empire consisted of two parts, metropolitan and provincial Asante, each of which had its own system of administration.

Metropolitan Asante includes the *amanto* or 'true' Asante states clustered around Kumasi. The principal *amanto* were the five Oyoko states of Kumasi, Nsuta, Juaben, Bekwai and Kokofu; an important non-Okoyo *amanto* state was that of Mampong founded by the Bretuo clan.The solidarity between Kumasi and the *amanto* was expressed in terms of kinship: the Asantehene spoke of the Juabenhene, for example, as his 'brother'.

Bowdich, an Englishman who spent four months in Kumasi in 1817, was the first observer to describe the relationship of the *amanto* to Kumasi. There is every reason to suppose that this was the system of government which had been evolving since the days of Obiri Yeboa. Up to the reign of Osei Kwadwo, *amanto* chiefs were of equal rank; the Asantehene was *primus inter pares* with *amanto* chiefs. Each *amanto* state was largely self-governing with regard to internal affairs and was organized on similar lines to Kumasi. Each chief or Omanhene had his council of hereditary advisers (elders); held his own Odwira ceremony after he had attended the Asantehene's Odwira at Kumasi to confirm his allegiance to the sovereign; maintained his own treasury and raised revenue; ran his own courts from which an appeal could be made to Kumasi; and possessed his own military organization which could be put at the disposal of the Asantehene when necessary.

There were, though, other limitations on an Omanhene's independence of action. On his death a death duty was payable to Kumasi, a chief could be summoned to the court at any time and, in exceptional cases, removed from office by the Asantehene.

How did Kumasi and the *amanto* govern metropolitan Asante? There was a Confederacy Council on which sat important hereditary chiefs from Kumasi and the *amanto*. Apparently the Council had an executive committee or cabinet, whose members included chiefs in charge of military organization in Kumasi and some of the *amanto* chiefs. Among the latter was the Mamponghene, the only chief of a non-Oyoko clan given a leading position in the Council. The Mamponghene's appointment as the commander-in-chief of the armed forces, and his rank as the next most powerful man to the Asantehene, suggests that the Asante were prepared to absorb some non-Oyoko clans into the Union.

During the first half of the eighteenth century membership of the Council was hereditary. But in 1764 Osei Kwadwo began a series of radical reforms, which were followed up by his successors Osei Kwame and Osei Bonsu. Osei Kwadwo embarked on a plan to change hereditary positions into appointive posts. He also created some new stools or chiefships. A key office, for instance, was the new post of Minister of Finance which appears to have been created by Osei Kwadwo. In this way a class of appointive officials developed, men appointed to their post by the Asantehene on the basis of their merit. Obviously such procedures increased administrative efficiency and encouraged individual mobility: some posts were filled by men from outside Kumasi and the *amanto*. Apart from Kumasi, however, offices generally remained hereditary so that elsewhere traditionally powerful families retained their hold over public affairs.

An important result of this revolution in government was that the Asantehene increased his own power at the expense of hereditary chiefs and the *amanto*. By the reign of Osei Bonsu in the early nineteenth century the Asantehene was no longer *primus inter pares* with the *amanto*: he was the supreme sovereign of metropolitan and provincial Asante.

Provincial Asante consisted of all the outer circle of states conquered and annexed by Asante. Until about the 1750's, all these states like Gonja, Denkyira and Akwamu continued to govern themselves in exactly the same way as they had done before. All they had to do was to accept one of the military chiefs of Kumasi as a friend at court, to pay annual tribute and to contribute a contingent to the army when required. The Golden Stool was much less meaningful to the provinces as a symbol of Asante nationhood than it was to the *amanto* states.

Osei Kwadwo wanted to impose metropolitan Asante's authority on the provinces, thereby centralizing the government of the empire. To this end, he tried to change the government of the provinces by stationing regional and district commissioners in these states. Proconsuls were also supposed to reside in the provinces, but sometimes did not do so, neglecting their duties. In 1776 Osei Kwadwo posted three district commissioners to Accra, all of whom were placed under the higher authority of the regional commissioner at Akwapim. Osei Kwadwo's successors continued to find ways of centralizing the government of provincial Asante.

Nevertheless, despite these worthy reforms to increase metropolitan Asante's power, rebellions did occur after 1764. The main reason why Osei Kwadwo's administrative reforms were not entirely successful was that he and his successors left the customs and institutions of the conquered territories untouched. Annexed states therefore remained in spirit, if not in deed, independent units and always looked forward to the day when they would be

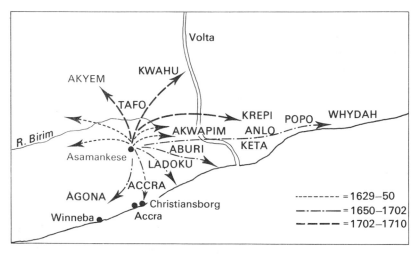

Map XXVI   The expansion of Akwamu

269

free from Asante control, just as in the late seventeenth century the pre-Asante Union states had hated the tyrannical rule of Denkyira. It was the superior military organization of metropolitan Asante, and the courage of her armies, that enabled Asante to crush all these rebellions and to preserve the empire intact. It therefore became more than evident that if the cohesion of metropolitan Asante and the efficiency of the army ever faltered, provinces would withdraw from the empire.

Unfortunately, this is what happened in the nineteenth century. Many, but not all, of the reasons for the eventual disintegration of the empire after 1824 must be attributed to British intervention. That story belongs to the nineteenth century. For the moment, though, we can end our account of the great Asante empire by looking at relations between Asante and Fante during the eighteenth century. For it was here that the British in effect worked through the Fante to weaken the Asante empire, playing upon divisions between provincial and metropolitan Asante.

RELATIONS BETWEEN ASANTE AND FANTE IN THE EIGHTEENTH CENTURY

For the most part, relations between the two powers were cold. Although Fante always expected an invasion of her coastal states during the eighteenth century, it was only on three occasions that Asante actually attacked Fante. These were 1727, 1765 and 1776; but these battles were not conclusive—Fante remained in control of routes between Cape Coast and Assin just south of Kumasi. One of the main reasons for the perpetual enmity between Asante and Fante was that access to the European forts and castles situated around Cape Coast was controlled by Fante.

However, there was no really fierce encounter between Asante and Fante until the wars of 1807 to 1824 when Fante was beaten and incorporated into the Asante empire. In fact 1824, the year of Osei Bonsu's death, marked the maximum territorial extension of Asante: her conquest of Fante was one of the few truly significant conquests since the reign of Opoku Ware ended in 1750. For the most part, there were no important battles

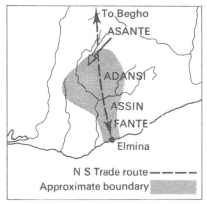

Map XXVII (left) Denkyira at the Height of its Power
(right) Fante Expansion

between Fante and Asante until the second decade of the nineteenth century: there were three reasons for this.

In the first place, during the first half of the eighteenth century
Fante were united under the Fante Union. Asante respected her
power. Secondly, after 1750 Asante kings were, as we have seen,
increasingly preoccupied with constitutional problems, reforms
and campaigns to crush rebellions in the empire. Troubles in
the provinces were duplicated in metropolitan Asante so that,
although Fante became more dis-united after 1750, conditions
were not conducive to further territorial expanion. This was
particularly true of the reigns of Kusi Obodum (1750–1764)
and Osei Kwame (1777–1801).

Kusi Obodum's reign was heralded by civil wars in metropolitan Asante which continued until 1755. The chiefs there were
eager to depose Obodum; their opportunity came in 1764 when
the Asante army was totally defeated by the Akim. So during
Kusi Obodum's reign, the Asante relied on diplomacy to reach
the coast and win back rebellious vassals. The Asantehene was
afraid to leave Kumasi in case he might be de-stooled in his
absence by a *coup d'état.*

For the duration of Osei Kwadwo's reign (1764–1777) conditions remained stable at home. But owing to his failure to squash
rebellions in the ever-troublesome state of Akim and other areas,
the Fante could not be crushed.

Civil wars and political instability marked much of Osei

Fig. 13   A view of Elmina

Kwame's reign (1777–1801). He turned out to be a rather author-itarian but administratively shrewd ruler. He became quite unpopular on account of his attempts to continue the centralizing reforms begun by Osei Kwadwo. He also inclined in favour of Islam and the establishment of Koranic law as the civil code of Asante. *Amanto* chiefs were greatly afraid that such an innovation would deprive them of even more power, concentrating all authority in the hands of the Asantehene who would then become an autocratic ruler like the emperors of Muslim states in the savanna. For these reasons the Queen Mother and some leading chiefs de-stooled Osei Kwame in 1801. Thereupon the Muslim northern states of the empire revolted in favour of returning Osei Kwame to power. Osei Kwame was finally got out of the way in 1803 when he was executed in the reign of Osei Bonsu. So preoccupied were the Asante with their many internal problems, that they did not have the chance to launch any serious campaign against Fante.

The third factor which safeguarded Fante was the attitude of the British. Britain backed Fante whenever she thought that

Asante would attack the coast, and remove all influence from the European traders. As one governor of a trading post said: 'Asante . . . would oblige the garrison to surrender'. However, by 1807 conditions at Kumasi had changed and the long-awaited invasion of the Fante took place. This, though, is another story.

Questions

1 What were the principal reasons for the rise of Asante?

2 To what extent would it be true to describe Osei Tutu as the founder of the Asante state?

3 Write brief notes on each of the following: (a) Okomfo Anokye; (b) the Golden Stool; (c) the Great Oath; (d) the Oyoko clan.

4 Give an account of the achievements of Opoku Ware. How successful was he in continuing the work of Osei Tutu?

5 Why are Osei Kwadwo and Osei Kwame called the 'great reformers'? Explain what is meant by the 'Kwadwoan revolution'.

6 Outline the Asante system of government. What were its strengths and weaknesses?

7 Discuss relations between Fante and Asante in the eighteenth century. What problems faced the Asante in the second half of the eighteenth century?

16

States of the Guinea Forest:
The rise of Dahomey

During the seventeenth and eighteenth centuries a new West African state centred on the Abomey plateau emerged. The state was Dahomey; its rulers the Fon or Agasuvi. The people were a branch of the Aja and the state they founded was a new association of Aja states under Abomey kingship. In the nineteenth century, Dahomey was one of the most famous military powers of West Africa. Its forces instilled fear or admiration into all its neighbours and greatly impressed Europeans at the coast. Its rulers openly championed and practised the slave trade in the face of British efforts to abolish it. Considerable royal revenue and national prosperity accrued from the trade and Dahomey's rulers argued that they could not be expected to abandon it until an equally lucrative form of revenue had been established. They dealt on equal terms with Queen Victoria, ruler of the greatest empire in the world, and sniggered over the size of subsidies that British governments suggested would be adequate compensation for loss of slave trade revenues.

These nineteenth century rulers loved to impress European visitors by massive military reviews which included their redoubtable corps of female warriors. They also outraged some of their guests by large-scale human sacrifices to their gods. Yet such was the calibre and diplomatic skill of these rulers that, in spite of their visitors' antagonism to both the slave trade and the Fon religion, Europeans left the court of Abomey favourably impressed by the quality both of its rulers and of their administrative system.

FOUNDATION OF THE KINGDOM

The small beginnings of this powerful state are recorded in

274

traditions which show that the Fon were an offshoot of the Aja people, whose homeland and primary dispersal centre were at Tado. The story starts with Agassu, son of a Tado princess. In Abomey tradition, Agassu's father was a leopard and it was held that the fierce qualities of a leopard's spirit animated the lives of Dahomey's rulers. However, the Gun of Porto Novo claim that Agassu was fathered by a Yoruba hunter named Adimola. These rival traditions are interesting in that they underline important factors in Abomey's history and group psychology. On the one hand, the Gun are acknowledging Abomey's early tributary relationship to Oyo; on the other, the Fon are stressing the militant independence of their origins.

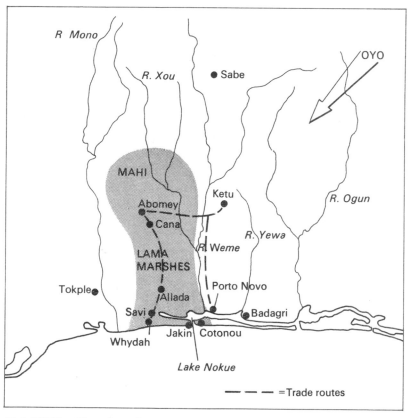

Map XXIX The Rise of Dahomey

As a royal prince, the ambitious Agassu was closely involved in the politics of Tado. On being worsted in a dynastic struggle for control of the state, he led his supporters to seek their fortunes elsewhere and finally founded Allada. Known to European traders as Great Ardra, Allada grew into a substantial state by the beginning of the seventeenth century, notwithstanding its acknowledgement of Oyo's overlordship. Within the first two decades of the seventeenth century, however, there occurred a triangular dynastic contest for the kingship. The two unsuccessful candidates followed the earlier example of Agassu and moved out. One, Agbanlin, moved south to the coast and founded a settlement which later developed into the state of Porto Novo; the other moved onto the Abomey plateau to become the progenitor of the Fon state. His name was Doaklin (or Dogbagri) and he died somewhere between 1620 and 1625. In order not to exaggerate the achievements of these emigrants from Allada, it is necessary to stress that the overlordship of the Aja states was to lie firmly in the hands of Allada's rulers for a further century.

The ultimate future, however, lay with the descendants of Doaklin. Originally, he and his supporters possessed no noteworthy military power and were only allowed to settle peacefully on the Abomey plateau on condition of payment of lavish gifts to the local Ouo chief. Another reason for their peaceful welcome may have been their knowledge of the Aja process of weaving a special fabric from a mixture of bark fibre and cotton. Soon Doaklin's settlement attracted so many kinsmen from Allada that the Ouo chiefs rightly began to see the settlers as a danger to their own authority. The ensuing conflict was resolved during the headship of Doaklin's son and successor, Dako, who held authority from about 1625 to 1650. He established the local supremacy of the Aja clan head over an area about ten miles in diameter. He also founded the important principle of unbroken succession when he appointed Wegbaja heir-apparent during his own lifetime.

THE RULE OF WEGBAJA c. 1650–1680

Although the state Wegbaja ruled was small, his contribution to the rise of Dahomey was considerable. On the military side, he re-organized the Fon war-bands, instituted military training and adopted the tactic of night attacks. He is said to have been the first Fon ruler to own firearms though it is certain that he had insufficient to make a major contribution to his war efforts. Nevertheless, his recognition of the need to treat warfare as a skilled art brought a number of small-scale victories that made him master of the western Abomey plateau, including Kana. The growth of his reputation attracted an invasion from as far afield as Tokple but a successful ambush removed this danger.

More important than his military reforms and successful battles was his contribution to strengthening the position of the Fon monarchy. He won the political support of the peoples of the plateau by lavish hospitality and open-handed generosity, signs not only of political wisdom but also of growing prosperity. On the other hand, he clearly elevated the status of the Fon ruler over his subjects and sub-rulers alike. People under his jurisdiction were forbidden to kill thieves, even those caught redhanded; nor were they allowed to take personal revenge on someone who had harmed them. All such serious cases were reserved for judgement and punishment by the ruler. So insistent was Wegbaja on the upholding of royal authority that he is said to have executed his own son for a breach of one of these new laws.

A further step towards establishing the authority of the ruler was the provision of adequate revenue to support his personal court and power. This was achieved by the institution of a regular poll tax and the introduction of the feudal practice that a dead man's property reverted to the ruler. This was not so much a matter of royal plunder of personal wealth as a device by which the ruler collected a customary amount of death duty and had a powerful claim on the loyalty of those desiring to be confirmed in ownership of their father's possessions. Much of the revenue that Wegbaja collected was directed to the purchase of firearms, the ownership of which was a royal monopoly.

By all these reforms, Wegbaja was providing not only for his immediate needs but was deliberately exalting royal power, rights and precedence beyond the challenge of any group of his subjects. Astutely, he added religious significance to royal exaltation by making changes in burial customs that stressed that he was 'lord of the land'; and it was he who initiated the 'Annual

277

Customs'. These were important religious ceremonies involving sacrifices that underlined the sacred character of his office and established him as undisputed leader of the Fon cults. As we have seen, this was far from being an innovation in the West African state system but it marked out Abomey's ruler as one enjoying the sacred authority and kingly rank so essential to national unity. Thus it is not surprising that Wegbaja was the founding hero of the Fon people, and that some claim it was he who gave Dahomey its name.

Wegbaja's successors
Wegbaja chose Akaba as the son to succeed him. This was a peculiar choice for Akaba had a twin sister; and in Aja custom twins had equal rights. Thus Akaba's sister reigned as co-ruler with him although she exercised no practical power. At Akaba's death, there was the danger that the small kingdom might have to be divided into equal parts between the families of the two co-rulers. This was averted by the political masterpiece of passing the succession to their younger brother, Agaja, who was to become one of the greatest of Dahomey's rulers.

By the time of his accession in about 1708, two important things had happened. First, Akaba had expanded Abomey to its natural frontiers of the river Zou, the Lama marshes and the Mahi mountains, and was able to insist that the rulers within these limits attend his court as tributary rulers. Secondly, the Yoruba of Oyo had twice in less than twenty years ravaged Allada. Thus in order to expand farther Dahomey was obliged to come into conflict with formidable enemies: Allada would be aided by its satellite states such as Whydah at the coast. Even the appearance of success in war with Allada must involve Dahomey with Oyo, then the greatest military power in the forest zone. The risks had to be taken if Dahomey was to improve its political and economic position.

THE REIGN OF AGAJA 1708–1732

Why and how Agaja became ruler of the Fon state is one of history's mysteries. Two conclusions, each compatible with the other, suggest themselves. The first is that the political genius

278

inbred in the Fon constitution was sufficiently flexible to prevent disintegration of the kingdom through slavish adherence to Aja succession custom. The second is that in king-making both ruler and tribal elders regarded fitness for the post as the vital qualification for appointment. Add to these considerations the personality of Agaja himself and at least the logic of his rise to power is clear.

Agaja was a man superbly equipped to govern. A proud man of magnetic personality, he impressed all who met him. Well endowed with the dignity of a ruler, he had also a quick sense of humour to match his courtesy. He was generous to friends and could be magnanimous in victory but he knew how to strike terror into the heart of a foe and let nothing turn him aside from his purpose. In defeat, he never lost his nerve and possessed the valuable ability to revive the morale of his men to the point where they willingly sought to turn defeat to victory. He had a quick grasp of the motivation of men, be they African or European, and a statesmanlike ability to shape them to his major purpose. As a diplomat he was so skilful and devious that even today historians discussing his over-all political objectives do not agree as to whether he set out to monopolize control of the slave trade of the 'Slave Coast' or to stamp out the trade altogether. This is not surprising, for Europeans who visited the coast during his reign give contradictory versions of his intentions. One thing is certain: this far-sighted ruler knew his own mind and kept his closest counsels to himself. By so doing, he attempted to mould events to his major purpose, which was the creation of a Dahomey state freed from the trammels of external suzerainty and from commercial dependence on the political and economic whims of coastal rulers and European slavers.

This vision amounted to a revolution in Aja political thought, an unspeakable violation of established political tradition. For Allada was no mere political suzerain of the Fon: it was the homeland from which they had sprung, their spiritual home. The traditional relationship of Allada to Abomey was one of father and son, and was expressed in those terms. To think of crushing Allada was to contemplate the crime of political patricide. To give practical expression to such an impious thought required daring imagination, impatience at customary restraints, cautious propaganda, meticulous planning and careful consideration of the opportune moment.

K

The events of Agaja's reign furnish ample proof of his technical ability to achieve this 'Dahomeian revolution'. It is also possible to demonstrate that Agaja was capable of such revolutionary thinking long before the opportunity presented itself in 1724. His quick intelligence would have seen that such a 'revolution' was the logical development of the policies of Wegbaja and Akaba. More than that, his reign abounds with examples of his quickness to adopt new ideas that could enhance his authority and improve the efficiency of his state. The manufacture of leather boxes to keep gunpowder dry was learned from Mali traders. He gleaned a knowledge of the European science of fortification from a Frenchman, named Delisle. Another Frenchman, Gallot, provided a ceremonial example for the introduction of distinctive guards of honour as a diplomatic courtesy. From an English captive, Bullfinch Lambe, he learned to load and fire his cannon captured at the coast; and when Lambe retailed to him stories of the wealth of American plantations, he was quick to suggest to the British government that the slave trade should end. The plantations should be established in Dahomey and Britain should provide the technical manpower to make them a success. He even made attempts to become literate in English and Portuguese. No idea of change was barred from the thinking of this shrewd, alert intelligence.

Agaja's military achievements
From very early in his reign, Agaja began to prepare for military expansion. He built up a body of secret agents known as 'Agbadji-gbeto', whose function was to provide political intelligence on conditions and events in near-by states. Also, they had the task of spreading propaganda in Abomey's interest along lines laid down by their royal master. This task was fairly easy as Abomey's special relationship with Aja states to the south provided his ambassadors with an honoured place at royal courts all the way to the coast. As early as 1714, there was a Fon trade commissioner at Whydah. Meanwhile, at home on the plateau, Agaja initiated a military training scheme for boys which drilled them in the movements of the battlefield and the use of guns. They were trained to suffer hardship, to obey orders and to admire courage. When the order to advance southwards was given, there was no force between Abomey and the coast capable of withstanding

them.

This was not entirely a matter of Agaja's foresight. During the early years of his reign, European intrigue was contributing considerably to internal lawlessness and insecurity in the states to the south and was also fomenting bitterness between the local heads of state. The result of this was a general atmosphere of exhausting warfare. These increasing rivalries were sapping the suzerain powers of Allada, already weakened by the Yoruba invasions of 1682–3 and 1698. Also, the strained relations between Allada, Whydah and other princedoms of the Dahomey coast made it impossible for them to present a united front against the common enemy when Agaja finally made his move. This he did in 1724, when a succession dispute in Allada produced a convenient request for his intervention.

Agaja was ready. He over-ran Allada, made it tributary to Abomey, and destroyed the slave ports of Offra and Jakin. At Jakin, he sacked the European factories, took great plunder in men, goods and cannon, and closed the port to the slave trade. In 1727 he fell upon Whydah. Its capital, Sahe, was burned to the ground and over forty Europeans were taken prisoner. The Whydah slave dealers fled for their lives, and Agaja refused to allow them to return home in spite of European pleas that this was necessary for efficient conduct of the slave trade. Nor did Agaja encourage Europeans to leave their bases at Whydah and re-establish themselves at Jakin, now completely under his control. During Agaja's military onslaughts, Europeans had not lifted a finger to help their former coastal allies for they remained hopeful that Agaja would respect their established positions. It was only when Agaja made it clear that he would be no puppet of slave traders that they actively and belatedly worked against him. Soon they were to record the view that there was no prospect of a revival of the Whydah slave trade so long as Agaja was alive.

Agaja's triumph was to bring its own train of dangers and disasters for Dahomey. In overthrowing Allada, he had in effect challenged the suzerainty of Oyo. Even presents sent to the Alafin to deceive him into believing that Oyo's interests were not in jeopardy in the 'Dahomeian revolution' did not blind Oyo to the fact that Abomey was seeking to create a new state system from which Yoruba influence should be excluded. In 1726, Oyo cavalry advanced on Abomey. Confident that his newly captured supply of guns and cannon would mow down the Yoruba horsemen, Agaja stood his ground. But he, like many a historian, laid undue stress on the value of firearms. His defeat was total. Abomey was destroyed, his army decimated, his palace plundered; and he had to accept the ignominy of flight and concealment in the forest around the headwaters of the Mono. So overwhelming was the Oyo victory that its forces withdrew, their mission completed—Agaja's power destroyed.

How wrong they were! The intrepid Agaja emerged from his forest retreat, rallied his people and claimed a tactical victory. His troops were soon in Allada again and were soon to ravage Whydah. He also subdued other princes of the Weme valley. Once again the vanquished appealed to Oyo; and once again Agaja negotiated with the Alafin to avert a collision with Yoruba cavalry. This time, his diplomacy was sufficient to delay an Oyo attack until 1728 by which time he had planned a policy of strategic withdrawal. Prior to the Oyo invasion of 1728, he carefully buried his royal treasure, destroyed food supplies that might sustain the Yoruba invaders and withdrew his forces into a forest hide-out. The Oyo cavalry thus over-ran Abomey without achieving decisive victory and were soon obliged to withdraw through shortage of essential supplies.

Within a month Agaja was master of his capital and former conquests again. But the might of Oyo was not to be so lightly thrust aside. In 1729, the Yoruba invaded once again, this time bringing a body of settlers to establish a town that would maintain Oyo's influence after the bulk of the cavalry withdrew. This time they sought out Agaja in the forest and forced his guerrilla bands into the open. Although their attacks and starvation seriously depleted Agaja's forces, his strategy was proved right when in May shortage of supplies compelled the Oyo cavalry to withdraw. Once again Agaja's forces emerged from the forest; and once again he was obliged to march to the coast to re-establish his authority at Whydah.

Political settlements
Although Agaja was successful once more, he was a wiser man than heretofore. He now realised he could never completely master the combined impact of Oyo cavalry and European intrigue that encouraged coastal rulers to resist him whenever

the Yoruba attacked. Therefore wealthy presents were sent to Oyo as an earnest of Agaja's present and future acceptance of Yoruba overlordship. But the Alafin had no intention of allowing Agaja to buy time. Bands of Yoruba warriors were already lurking in the Dahomey area, and to the north Yoruba diplomats were busy cementing alliances with the Mahi tribes for the destruction of Abomey. Thus in 1730, Agaja faced attacks from both the Yoruba and the Mahi. As an admission that his position at Abomey was militarily untenable and also as a conciliatory gesture to Oyo, he removed his court to Allada. Thus, apart from the change in personnel, the traditional state system with the supremacy of Allada and its own tributary relationship to Oyo was restored. This proved a political basis on which Oyo was prepared to negotiate a settlement with Agaja, and a position from which Agaja would seek a compromise with the European slave traders.

The terms of these settlements can only be guessed at by reference to subsequent events. The scientific guesswork has been done by Dr Akinjogbin and it is likely that further research can do no more than provide further factual evidence in support of his thesis. Therefore, we quote his ideas as facts. By the unwritten treaty of 1730, Agaja was allowed to remain overlord of Allada and Whydah provided that he did not re-establish his capital at Abomey; and provided that he accepted Oyo overlordship. The eastern boundaries of his kingdom were to be lake Nokue, the river So and the river Weme. The Weme principalities were to be independent of Dahomey, and Aja peoples displaced by Agaja's conquests were to be resettled at Ajase Ipo (Porto Novo), which was to be independent of Dahomey. Epe and Badagri also were to be free from attacks by Dahomeian forces. These three ports were to be Oyo's avenues to European trade. Agaja was allowed to maintain imperial forces but had to swear not to use them against Oyo's interests. To ensure Agaja's observance of the treaty, one of his sons was to brought up at the Yoruba court. This son was to succeed Agaja, by which time he would have been trained in his duties as an Oyo vassal. To cement cordial relations between the two families, Ojigi of Oyo and Agaja each married a princess from the rival court.

Agaja realized this was the best he could do towards achieving his ambition; and, indeed, it was a great deal. He now turned to deal with representations from European merchants. Again it is

Akinjogbin who has worked out the probable details of the agreement. Agaja refused to allow the Europeans to dictate the terms
of the political settlement. The Whydah slave traders they had
encouraged to return home were once more chased out. The
Europeans had to abandon their trading factories at Jakin and
move to Whydah where the royal customs headquarters were
established. Agaja was to receive favourable trading considerations and was to have a monopoly of the purchase of firearms.
In return for these large concessions, Agaja would do nothing
to impede the slave trade: both the ports and the slave paths
should be kept open to the traffic. The conclusion of the treaty
was marked by Agaja's distinguishing the English negotiator
with a royal escort to the coast, and with public rejoicing by
both Africans and Europeans in Whydah. Whatever Agaja's
original intent, Dahomey was soon to become the major slave
trading kingdom of the Guinea coast.

Agaja did not long survive this settlement of the political system
in Dahomey. He died in 1732, possibly a disappointed man;
Abomey had failed in its attempt to overthrow Oyo suzerainty of
the Aja peoples and had had to make a compromise with European
slave traders. Such disappointment would only have reflected the
magnitude of his ambitions. He had overthrown the established
state system of his youth, turned the tiny principality of Abomey
into the powerful state of Dahomey and had demonstrated to
Europeans that their role at the coast must remain a purely commercial one. He had avoided destruction by the greatest West
African power of his day and had humiliated such states as
Whydah and Allada which could call on support from Oyo and
military supplies from Europeans. The Dahomeian state, like its
architect, remained restless and ambitious: expansion and escape
from Oyo suzerainty remained the policy of its rulers.

AGAJA'S SUCCESSORS

There is little profit in studying the fragments available on the
individual lives of Agaja's successors down to 1800. Suffice it to
say that his training in the Yoruba court did not divert Agaja's
successor, Tegbesu, from following his father's policy. He restored Abomey as the capital of Dahomey, and until his death in

1774 sought to expand Dahomey's power and escape from vassalage to Oyo. Attacks were made upon the Mahi to the North, the Za Yoruba of the upper Weme, the peoples of the upper Mono and even on Whydah's trading rivals of Porto Novo, Epe and Badagri. Determined efforts were made to give Whydah a monopoly of slave exporting, while at the same time slaves were captured to man royal plantations. Whydah was also developed as an important centre of internal trade along the lagoons. Yet even Tegbesu could not escape acceptance of Oyo supremacy. His early efforts to escape Yoruba dominance brought such severe retribution that from 1748 onwards Dahomey dared not neglect payment of the hated annual tribute to Oyo of '40 men, 40 women, 40 guns, 400 loads of cowries and corals a year.'

Even so, as long as Dahomey was not actively challenging Oyo's authority, there was little interference with her expansion in territory and trade. Even attacks on Jakin, Porto Novo and Badagri were sanctioned to maintain Dahomey's local status so long as loyalty to Oyo was observed. Thus, in the reign of Kpengala, 1774–89, Dahomey co-operated with Oyo in a siege of Badagri and was rewarded by a fifty per cent reduction in tribute for protecting its own interests. Yet, when Kpengala repeated the performance in 1786 without permission, he had to surrender all the plunder to Oyo for this breach of imperial etiquette. Meanwhile, Kpengala had widened the road from Abomey to Whydah to improve military communications and increase efficiency in the slave trade. Yet the tributary relationship was still there: Dahomey could go so far and no farther. Alafins of Oyo did not scruple to remind Dahomeian rulers of this by annoying regulations prohibiting them from wearing royal apparel reserved to the emperors themselves.

Dahomey prospered and waited for a breach in the solidarity of Yoruba power. When this came in the nineteenth century, Dahomey was to win its independence of Oyo and wreak sporadic revenge on southern Yoruba peoples in its efforts to cut Yoruba communications with the coast.

INTERNAL GOVERNMENT

Part of the secret of Dahomey's rapid success was the highly

285

centralized government and efficient bureaucracy established by its early rulers. Wegbaja had laid the foundations when he had elevated the monarchy to semi-divine status and had laid down that all property in the state belonged to the ruler. This enabled Dahomey's kings to keep control of all state business in their own hands at Abomey. They also commanded an almost unique degree of loyalty. Throughout Dahomey's history only two rulers were deposed by palace revolutions, and there were no serious revolutions. Successions to the throne took place with very few crises even though the royal nominee could be set aside by the state council.

The system controlled by the kings of Dahomey was directed towards military efficiency and royal absolutism. Military and civil discipline were strict and there was a clearly defined chain of command. Immediately below the king were two important officials: the Minga and the Meu. The Minga was commander-in-chief of the army, senior civil administrator and also the lord high executioner. The Meu was chief of protocol, senior tax-inspector and official ward of the royal children. Another important official was the Yovogun, who governed Whydah and controlled all dealings with Europeans. In addition, he was head of the secret service that kept vigilant watch on all state officials, sub-rulers and visitors.

The kingdom was divided into six provinces, each controlled by a royal official. All subordinate chiefs and tributary rulers were appointed by local hereditary custom but no appointment was valid until royal approval was formally given. Each province had to submit regular reports to Abomey so that the king was closely in touch with local affairs. These reports had to be made in person by the responsible officials so that few administrators escaped royal perusal for very long. Royal inspectors held regular censuses of the population and reported on agricultural production so that military and fiscal resources could be accurately assessed. Oral records of negotiations and important statistics were kept by women specially appointed for their good memory. Many of these were royal wives known as Kposi. Several accompanied the king at every interview he gave, and royal ministers also had a staff of women recorders.

The entire administrative machine was ruthlessly efficient. Headed by rulers of rare political talent and backed by a people of great military skill and courage it was a dynamic political organism. Furthermore, the dangers that accompanied Dahomey's rise to importance had impressed upon its people the urgency of unity. They expressed this idea in vigorous and emphatic symbolism: the life of the nation was a pot with many holes. Only if all citizens kept their fingers firmly over the holes could the life-giving force, that is the royal power, be prevented from draining away. Nor did it drain away until finally faced by the superior military technology of France.

Questions

1 What factors contributed to the rise of Dahomey?

2 What was the origin of the Fon dynasty? Describe the main stages by which the authority of the monarchy was developed.

3 Assess the contribution of Wegbaja to the rise of Dahomey.

4 Outline the aims and achievements of King Agaja.

5 What were the main obstacles to the rise of Dahomey's power? How were these dealt with by Dahomey's rulers?

6 What do you understand by the 'Dahomeian revolution'? How was this brought about and to what extent was it complete by the end of the eighteenth century?

7 Outline the Dahomeian system of government and show how it contributed to the rise of Dahomey.

8 Write a character sketch of Agaja, showing in what ways he was particularly fitted to rule Dahomey.

17

States of the Guinea Forest:
The empire of Oyo

The Yoruba state of Old Oyo, which intervened so dramatically
and decisively in Dahomeian affairs in the eighteenth century,
was one of the oldest and greatest states to emerge in the forest
zone. Its origins are so shrouded in antiquity that all traditions
relating to its early growth are strongly tinged with legend and
obscurity. Thus we are faced with the frustration of having little
to relate about what we know must have been a long and distinguished history. All that historians have so far been able to piece
together from traditions and the writings of slave traders is no
more than an outline sketch of the rise of Oyo's power. However,
even this sketch enables us to see that Oyo was a formidable
inland state by the end of the fifteenth century and that it reached
the height of its power in the eighteenth.

TRADITIONS OF EARLY RULERS

Oduduwa
The traditional history of Oyo goes back to the founding of Ile
Ife, the primary dispersal centre of the Yoruba people. One
tradition of origin is a mythical creation legend which intimates
that the Yoruba were the original inhabitants of the Ife area. At
the dawn of time, the world was a watery waste. On the orders of
his father—the supreme god, Olorun—Oduduwa climbed down
a chain from the sky. He brought with him a handful of earth, a
cockerel and a palm nut. He scattered the earth upon the water

Map XXIX   The Yoruba Empire of Oyo

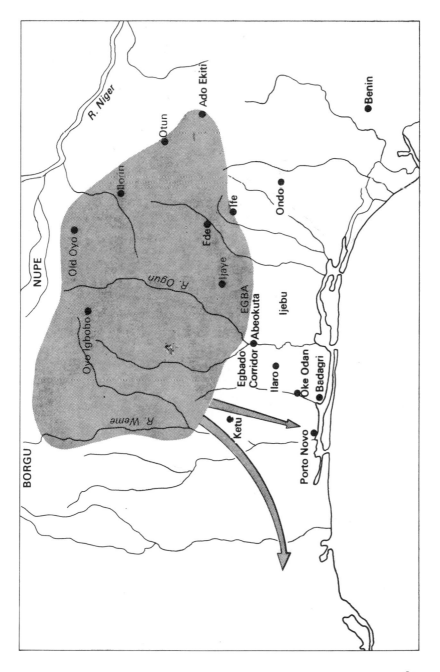

and it formed the land at Ile Ife. The cockerel dug a hole in which Oduduwa planted the palm nut, and up sprang a mighty tree with sixteen branches, each the ruling family of an early Yoruba state. To this day, Oduduwa's chain is preserved among the sacred relics of the Yoruba.

Another tradition indicates that the Yoruba people were produced by inter-marriage between a small band of invaders from the savanna and the indigenous inhabitants of the forest. The story is that Oduduwa was the son of Lamurudu, sometimes described as a ruler from the East, sometimes as a prince of Mecca. When Islam was introduced into his homeland, Oduduwa refused to forsake the religion of his ancestors and he and his supporters were expelled from their native land. After long wanderings, they settled among the forest people and founded the state of Ife.

Oduduwa had seven close descendants. Some traditions say they were his sons; others call them grandsons. These seven young men moved out to found the ruling families of seven new Yoruba states. These are named as the states of Owu, Sabe, Popo, Benin, Ila, Ketu and Oyo. Whether or not there is any historical accuracy in the details of this story, the moral is strong. It represents Yoruba acceptance of a fraternal relationship between the states that were to make up the empire of Oyo and also of their racial affinity with Benin. It is also significant that Oyo was founded by the youngest son, or grandson, and therefore last in time. This idea is consistent with the rise of a new and virile state upsetting existing political relationships.

Oranyan

A combination of traditions of Oyo and Benin then centres our interest on Oranyan, or Oranmiyan as he is called in Benin, the youngest son of Oduduwa. He was unsuccessfully sent to Benin to establish a monarchy that would resolve the internal struggles of this republican village. There, according to one tradition, he married a princess of the former ruling dynasty of Benin and once his infant son was recognized as lawful ruler there, he returned home. Later, he become the second ruler of Ife and made an alliance with his senior brothers for a punitive raid on the people to the north of the Niger who had insulted Oduduwa. During their march northwards, the brothers quarrelled and the army split up. As Oranyan's forces were no longer sufficient to force a crossing of the Niger, he wandered along its southern shores until he came to Bussa. There he was entertained by the local chief who gave him a large snake with a magic charm attached to its throat. He advised Oranyan to follow the snake until it stopped in one place for seven days and then disappeared into the ground. There he should found a city. Oranyan obeyed these instructions and the result was the new city of Oyo.

All of Oranyan's royal treasure and sacred symbols were, however, still at Ife. Either from choice or necessity, he left them there in the charge of Adimu who was to rule at Ife. Henceforth Oyo was to be the political head of the Yoruba, and Ife their religious centre. So sacred was Ife that it was for centuries to remain immune from unfilial attacks by other Yoruba states.

Sango

Before he died, Oranyan established his authority over the environs of Oyo. His successor, Ajaka, was deposed because he was insufficiently warlike and allowed Oyo's sub-chiefs too much independence. The office of Alafin was therefore conferred upon his brother, Sango, a great warrior and terrifying magician. He is said to have breathed fire and smoke from his nostrils and to have attempted to control thunder and lightning. His experiment at calling lightning to earth was disastrously successful for it destroyed his palace and family. Filled with personal remorse and rejected by his angry people, Sango wandered into the bush and hanged himself. He was later deified as the god of thunder and war and became one of the most important Yoruba gods. He is represented in the form of a ram, and throughout subsequent Yoruba history the despatch of the symbols of Sango was sufficient to impose peace on quarrelling Yoruba states. With such a reputation and such future influence, Sango must have made numerous conquests of which we have no details.

Sango's successors

On Sango's death, Ajaka was restored to the throne, a changed man. Ferociously warlike and a cruel tyrant, he is said to have killed over a thousand and sixty rival chiefs. His successor, Kori, troubled by attacks from the Ijesha, sent a mighty hunter called Timi to subdue them. Although the successful Timi proved disloyal and the end result was the rejection of Kori, Timi's expedition

291

founded Ede as a frontier state to control the eastern marches. Thus by Kori's death we have a picture of Oyo in control of the whole metropolitan area.

Alafin Onigbogi's reign saw a temporary halt to Oyo's military successes. An unexpected attack by the Nupe resulted in the destruction of Old Oyo and the flight of its inhabitants into Borgu. Although his successor, Ofinran, was to drive the Nupe from Oyo territory, it was not until the subsequent reign of Egonoju that the Oyo were able to return to Yorubaland. Even then, Old Oyo was uninhabitable and a new capital had to be built at Oyo Igboho. Four Alafins reigned there including Orompoto, whose thousand cavalry horses had foliage tied to their tails to obliterate their tracks in the struggles against the Nupe and the Bariba of Borgu; and Ajiboyede, who held the first Bere festival and was the first Oyo ruler visited by a Muslim missionary. Not until Abipa was there an Alafin with sufficient power and authority to compel his people to return to the supposedly haunted site of Old Oyo and rebuild their original capital. Thus it was that Alafin Obalokun was traditionally able to receive the first European visitor and taste the first European salt in the ancient capital of his ancestors. If these stories are true, this visitor may well have been Portuguese and the time the sixteenth century.

HISTORICAL SUMMARY

Modern historians suggest that Oyo was founded towards the end of the fourteenth century by Yoruba immigrants from Ife. Its early rulers were energetic and warlike, and by a mixture of conquest and diplomatic pressure made themselves masters of metropolitan Oyo during the fifteenth century. Their prosperity and power derived from participation in the trans-Saharan trade. Early in the sixteenth century, Oyo's supremacy was successfully challenged by the emergence of a powerful Nupe state under the leadership of Tsoede. After a short period of recovery and consolidation, Oyo resumed its imperial growth but its direction of advance was primarily towards the south. Historians of Benin tell us that between about 1578 and 1608, Oba Ehengbuda of Benin drove off a major Yoruba attack, and that negotiations at the end of the war established Otun as a frontier town between the two empires.

The seventeenth century

However, the main Oyo advance was not through the dense forest towards the coastline that owed allegiance to Benin. In such terrain, Oyo cavalry could not operate successfully, and there was little commercial incentive to do so as direct trade with Europeans was little developed along the coast from Porto Novo to the Niger delta. Oyo's main interest was in the commercially active coast of modern Dahomey and the prosperous states that lay behind it. Expansion in this direction was facilitated by the natural break in the forest running from Ketu to the southern states of modern Dahomey. Along this route Oyo could deploy its cavalry with deadly effect. Thus by the end of the seventeenth century, Aja and Ewe states had been compelled to pay tribute to Oyo, and Oyo traders were actively participating in trade with Europeans through such ports as Porto Novo and Whydah.

We have already seen that Oyo's policy towards the Aja and Ewe states was to tamper with local affairs as little as possible. The necessary conditions for this freedom from direct Yoruba intervention were exact compliance with obligations to Oyo and free access to coastal markets for its traders. A breach of these conditions was visited with the harshest punishment. Thus Allada was ravaged in 1682–3 and again in 1698. On this latter occasion the Yoruba slaughter at Porto Novo was such that the dead were 'like the grains of corn in the field'. Even the mention of Yoruba cavalry reduced local people to abject terror.

Eighteenth century politics

The eighteenth century saw Oyo at the height of its power and prosperity. Its political emphasis was not so much on expansion as on controlling its existing empire. Throughout the century, Dahomey proved recalcitrant and many expeditions were necessary to restore obedience to Oyo. The true measure of Oyo power is that these expeditions were successfully mounted against Dahomey no matter what internal troubles or external commitments hampered the Yoruba administration.

Yet all was not well in Oyo. In addition to usual internal stresses not worth recording, the third quarter of the century witnessed a

293

constitutional struggle of the utmost magnitude. The underlying issue was whether Alafins or their leading ministers should control national policy. Military success and large accessions of revenue tended to exalt the reputation and personal power of the Alafin. At the same time, freedom from any over-riding national danger enabled politicians to focus their attention on the absolutist tendencies inherent in the exaltation of the Alafin's personal status and wealth. Thus control of royal revenue was a matter of considerable constitutional significance.

Bashorun Gaha The question crystallized around the career of Bashorun Gaha and a fatal political misjudgement by Alafin Labesi. As a newly appointed Alafin in about 1754, Labesi favoured the appointment as Bashorun of Gaha a man of boundless ambition, great energy and ability and utterly devoid of scruples. As a devoted servant of the crown, such a man might well have helped to establish the supremacy of the monarchy. Even if he followed a more independent approach towards the Alafin, there were already two staunch royalists on the Council to balance issues in favour of the Alafin. Within a short time, Gaha had murdered them both and, when Labesi would not accept the new position, he speedily secured the Alafin's rejection. Successive Alafins were made and rejected by Bashorun Gaha's influence as he stamped his personal authority on every major aspect of Oyo policy. That he was fitted to play such a despotic role can be demonstrated by the iron discipline that held the entire empire in obedience to the central government. Less favourable aspects of his fitness to rule were his selfish greed and the excessive favouritism shown to his relatives and friends. Hence the constitutional theory he represented, namely that the head of state should merely provide authority for the acts of his ministers, was to be destroyed by his own nepotism and abuse of power. The constitutional issue that his relationships with Alafins laid bare was to play a major role in the ultimate destruction of central authority.

Alafin Abiodun The immediate cause of his downfall was careless over-confidence. When he secured the appointment of the young Abiodun as Alafin, he was satisfied that the new Alafin would be content to play a secondary political role. The maturing Abiodun probably encouraged Gaha in this belief by ready compliance with his wishes and by remaining aloof from the major issues and politicians of the time. In fact, he secretly built up his own private sources of information and nightly escaped the palace in disguise to plot the downfall of the aging Bashorun. He found an ally in Kakanfo Oyabi and together he they arranged an insurrection to destroy Gaha and every member of his family. The successful plot was executed with the utmost brutality: even unborn children were hacked to pieces to ensure total destruction of Gaha's family.

The result was that in about 1775, Abiodun became ruler in deed as well as name. While the Oyo people approved his successful coup, they were alarmed at the lengths to which he had gone to assert the constitutional authority of his office. Nor can it have been reassuring to his people that Abiodun felt traditional safeguards were insufficient to protect his person and authority. The traditional royal bodyguard formed from the Eso was replaced by four thousand Popo warriors commanded by one of his sons. Also the whole trend of imperial policy during his reign was not merely to restore the traditional authority of the Alafin but to exalt it to heights formerly unknown. Thus the major achievement of his reign, the strengthening of Oyo's hold on the two hundred mile long 'Egbado Corridor', was achieved by methods calculated to strengthen his personal control of Oyo's commercial lifeline.

This strategic stretch of territory running between the rivers Ogun and Weme to the coast, Abiodun successfully colonised with small Yoruba towns each governed by a trusted relative. At Ijanna in the Egbado area, he stationed a royal official responsible to himself to administer the highway and toll stations; and he posted *ilari* (titled slaves, 'scar heads') east of the Ogun to protect his interests there. Thus he, like Bashorun Gaha, was able to control the empire by exercise of personal authority. But the cost was high. This perversion of the established constitution, no less than Gaha's, was to breed an atmosphere of mistrust which both internal adventurers and external enemies could turn to their advantage.

Consequently, Abiodun was the last ruler of a united Yorubaland. The fact that his reign is recorded to have been one of the most peaceful in Oyo's history could mean two different things. Was his reign peaceful because Oyo was so powerful and prosperous; or were internal politics too tense for him to risk unnecessary wars? For Oyo under Abiodun was clearly on the defensive. Sometime between 1775 and 1780, the Egba under the leadership of Lishabi massacred *ilari* stationed in their area and drove off a punitive expedition from Oyo. Equally, Dahomey was becoming increasingly reluctant to pay its tribute. Against this background, Abiodun's activities in the 'Egbado Corridor', and consequent encouragement of trade through Porto Novo and the rapidly developing Badagri, suggest a statesmanlike recognition that it might soon be beyond Oyo's means to inhibit Dahomey's ambitions purely by sporadic expeditions which it might be dangerous to organize.

OYO AT THE HEIGHT OF ITS POWER

The hub of the empire was metropolitan Oyo, the home of Yorubas who spoke the Oyo dialect and who were for practical purposes identifiable with the people of Old Oyo. This area was divided into six large provinces, three to the west of the river Ogun and three to the east. South of metropolitan Oyo, there were other Yoruba states such as those of the Egba and Egbado, whose peoples spoke different Yoruba dialects. These peoples of the forest proper were probably less willing vassals of Oyo and were not so easily controlled as their kinsmen to the north. Thirdly, the sway of Oyo extended over non-Yoruba areas to the south-west: the Aja states of Dahomey and the Ewe of Togo. Imperial policy towards these non-Yoruba states was to allow them almost total local independence provided that they did not seek to escape from their tributary status.

The military might of Oyo and the mobility of its formidable cavalry meant that the imperial court could exert influence on affairs well beyond its ill-defined frontiers. To the south-east of metropolitan Oyo, the Ekiti, Ondo and Yoruba areas formed a kind of buffer between Oyo and Benin frequently raided by Yoruba expeditions to exact tribute and influence local politics. The vague boundary between Oyo and Benin spheres of influence was often lost in the impenetrable no-man's-land of the forest but certainly ran through Otun and Ado. Thus the coast from the Niger delta to just west of Lagos was subject to Benin, and the Oyo empire seems to have made little attempt to push its power to the sea in this area. Nonetheless, such peoples as the Ijebu could ill afford to transgress against the interests of their powerful relations to the north.

Local government

Each metropolitan province was supervised by a provincial governor appointed from Oyo; and each vassal court was headed by a tributary ruler who was the natural head of his own people. Although these tributary rulers were selected and appointed according to purely local custom, they had to be confirmed in office by the central government at Oyo. Thus, Yoruba towns were ruled by their own Obas chosen from the local ruling lineages and their policies had to be confirmed by local councils made up of heads of non-ruling families and local societies. Yet even with the full force of local opinion behind him, it would be a brave Oba who dared offend the imperial government at Oyo.

Both tributary kings and provincial governors had the duty of collecting tribute due to Oyo and for contributing contingents of troops under local generalship to the imperial army in times of major war. Not infrequently, they would be asked to mount campaigns against troublesome neighbours on Oyo's behalf without the backing of the main imperial army. All sub-rulers had to pay homage to the Alafin of Oyo and acknowledgement of the duty of allegiance was renewed annually by compulsory attendance at important religious ceremonies in the capital. The most important of such occasions was the Bere festival which was celebrated to mark public acclamation of successful rule by an Alafin. After a Bere festival, there was supposed to be peace in Yorubaland for three years.

These formal acknowledgements of Oyo's supremacy were not alone considered sufficient safeguard of the interests of the imperial court. Such a vital issue as imperial unity could not be left to chance and assumptions of local fidelity. Oyo was directly represented at each significant sub-court by a royal official known as an *ilari*. His role was to ensure that tribute was properly collected and that the local court did not plot against the imperial interest. Thus, Oyo was continually in touch with political and economic developments throughout the empire, and was able to combine a maximum of local autonomy with strong central direction.

Central government

The Alafin   At the head of the empire was the Alafin of Oyo, the supreme overlord of all his peoples. His duties to sub-states were as considerable as those owed to him by sub-rulers, so that the essential basis of the empire was mutual self-interest. As ruler of Oyo, it was his responsibility to protect tributary states from external attack, particularly from the north. It was his duty, as well as his right, to settle internal quarrels between his sub-rulers and between individual sub-rulers and their peoples. He was thus the supreme judge of the empire; his court, the final court of appeal. He was also the fountain of honours, expected to encourage loyalty and service by the giving of lavish presents and the bestowal of honours and wealth.

The Alafin was carefully selected and commanded enormous respect. No man could be considered for elevation to the imperial throne unless he was directly descended from Oranyan, the founder of Old Oyo. Yet the office did not automatically pass from father to son for there were several distinct lineages of royal descent. In particular, until the early nineteenth century the eldest son of an Alafin was debarred from the succession by a curious custom probably designed to prevent political intrigue against an Alafin by an impatient heir-apparent. During the father's life, an Alafin's first-born son filled the important office of Aremo but at his father's death he too had to die. Nor was he the only one to accompany the deceased Alafin on his journey to the spirit world: all the Alafin's personal officials had to perish with their master. Thus a newly-appointed Alafin had a free hand in selecting his own executives in the spheres of administration, religion and justice and could appoint officers loyal to himself.

The Oyo Mesi   The actual selection of a new Alafin was in the hands of the Oyo Mesi, a supreme council of state, whose seven members were collectively recognised as king-makers. They consulted the Ifa oracle as to which of the candidates was approved by the gods. The new Alafin was then proclaimed as the appointment of the gods. He was consecrated in his office by important religious and political ceremonies during which he was initiated into the mysteries of kingship and control of the sacred cults. Once these rituals had been completed, he was no longer regarded as an ordinary mortal: he was 'Ekeji Orisa', companion of the gods, a semi-divine ruler beyond the reach of ordinary mortals. He was the head of his people in the inseparable spheres of administration, religion and justice. His power, in theory, was unlimited by human agency. Cult priests and government officials were alike appointed by his command; and the usual practice was for the Alafin to appoint eunuchs loyal to himself.

In practice, the Alafin did not have such absolute power. He could ill afford to offend the members of the Oyo Mesi or the Ogboni (earth cult). Although he could not be deposed, the Alafin could be compelled to commit suicide. If both the Oyo Mesi and the Ogboni disapproved of his personal conduct or policies, or if the Oyo peoples suffered serious reverses, they would commission the Bashorun to present the Alafin with an empty calabash or a dish of parrot's eggs. On handing over these meaningful symbols, the Bashorun pronounced a fearful formula: 'The gods reject you, the people reject you, the earth rejects you.' The Alafin was thus informed that his political position had been completely undermined and his removal decided. Custom demanded he take poison.

The Bashorun   The Bashorun, as head of the Oyo Mesi, was a kind of prime minister. Possessed of great power and wealth, he was also in charge of the religious divinations held annually to determine whether or not the Alafin retained the favour of the gods. He was in a position to influence the political decisions of both the Oyo Mesi and the Ogboni, and for a period in the eighteenth century enjoyed far more authority than the Alafin himself. Whereas the Alafin could be virtually divorced from practical politics by strict insistence on religious taboos secluding him from his subjects, the Bashorun was always active in the centres of power.

The Ogboni   Some Yoruba states had their own Ogboni. At the imperial level, this was a very powerful secret society composed of freemen noted for their age, wisdom and importance in religious and political affairs. The Ogboni was concerned with the worship of earth, and as such was responsible for judging any cases involving the spilling of blood. Its leader had unqualified right of direct access to the Alafin on any matter. Even the most important decisions of the Oyo Mesi, especially the rejection of an Alafin, could not be carried into effect without Ogboni

299

approval. Whereas the Oyo Mesi represented the great politicians of the realm, the Ogboni was the voice of popular opinion backed by the authority of religion. Although the members of the Oyo Mesi were ex-officio members of the Ogboni, they were not its senior members even though their informed opinions must have commanded respect.

The Oyo Mesi and Ogboni thus provided important constitutional checks on the personal authority of the Alafin. He was bound to listen to their advice and to ignore their opinions was to invite rejection. The exact degree of real authority exerted by an Alafin depended on his personal popularity, tact, administrative wisdom, political skill and the circumstances surrounding his accession. He could exert great personal influence or he could become a mere tool of his councillors. These constitutional safeguards eventually worked against the interests of strong central government. Except in times of exceptional danger, there was an unfortunate tendency to select a weak Alafin to succeed one of strong character and marked achievements lest a succession of autocratic rulers should transform the constitution into an absolute despotism.

The Eso Another important Oyo-Yoruba institution was the Eso, the society of war-chiefs. These were individually appointed for their military skill and valour in war, and their rank was not hereditary. At the head of the Eso was the Are-Ona-Kakanfo, supreme commander of the imperial army. This official was customarily required to live in a frontier province of great strategic importance in imperial defence. Thus he was well placed to guarantee imperial security against attack and was too far removed from the capital to interfere directly in central politics. On all major campaigns, the Are-Ona-Kakanfo personally commanded in the field. Victory was obligatory; and defeat carried with it the duty of committing suicide. The only escape from this consequence of failure was flight to found a separate state a safe distance away from imperial retribution. Thus did Oyo protect itself against hesitant generalship in the field and 'retire' those generals who clung to military command when their martial vigour was declining.

Factors in the rise of Oyo
Until new external dangers combined with internal tensions to

300

shatter the Oyo empire in the nineteenth century, its constitution was a source of great imperial strength. Its combination of local autonomy with imperial necessity provided an essential element of unity over a vast area in the days of slow communications. The power structure was sufficiently flexible and unobtrusive to enable newly conquered states to be incorporated in the empire with comparative ease and permanence. The political authority of the central government over the Yoruba people was reinforced by the sanctity and religious authority of the Alafin; and the constitution ensured that Alafins could rarely follow policies unacceptable to their Yoruba subjects. Unpopular or unsuccessful Alafins could be removed without great political upheaval, and royal government could be carried on effectively by the Oyo Mesi backed by Ogboni support even if the Alafin had little political ability. Within the army and civil service, there was a high degree of professionalism represented by the Eso and *ilari*. The whole system placed a high premium on success: to be a failure was to perish in the interests of the Yoruba nation. This attitude to responsibility was a harsh one; but it did produce a number of very able Alafins and generals whose individual contributions to the development of Oyo are all too often obscure.

Oyo organization was backed by overwhelming military power, itself the product of good use of environment and resources. Its military striking force owed its effectiveness to its cavalry, its leadership and the valour of its warriors. These martial assets enabled Oyo to conquer and police large areas that brought in enormous revenues in tributes, taxes and tolls to support imperial power and dignity. An estimate of the modern cash value of tribute from Dahomey alone in the eighteenth century is £32,000 per annum. Early military power also brought early commercial control of the southern extension of the trans-Saharan trade, and later of the interior's trade with the coast. This was of infinite economic and political value.

In other words, the organizational skills and martial ardour of Oyo enabled its people to take advantage of geographic, economic and ethnic factors favouring the emergence of imperial power in the Yoruba area. Situated north of the forest, it was established in an area where communications and agriculture were a good deal easier than in the forest proper. Comparatively easy agriculture meant steady population growth and adequate provision of essential supplies with sufficient leisure for ruling classes to develop governmental machinery and devote time to conquest. Conquest was facilitated by easy communications north of the forest, the purchase of horses from the traders of the Sudan belt and by partial freedom from the tsetse fly.

Other vitally important contributions to the growth of Oyo's prosperity and power were the industrial skills of its people. Their early knowledge of iron-working and the existence of iron ore locally meant early possession of efficient tools and weapons; their craftsmanship in weaving and dyeing, in carving and the decorative arts, attracted traders from far and wide. Their economic activities were productive as well as distributive. Thus of all the tiny states lying between the Yoruba forest and the central Sudan, it was Oyo that attracted trade from the north and south. It was Oyo that became the southern emporium of the trans-Saharan trade and dominated the exchange of salt, leather, North African luxuries and horses for kola nuts, ivory, cloth, slaves and other forest products.

Once Oyo had taken the imperial initiative, its continued success owed much to the ethnic unity of the Yoruba-speaking peoples. They shared a common culture: they worshipped the same national gods and Ife was their common spiritual home; for all of them, Oduduwa was the founder of their race; they looked alike, they practised similar customs, they spoke dialects of the same language. While they might quarrel among themselves over political privilege or economic concession, they were conscious of common nationality and a common interest against non-Yoruba people. Their collective success under Oyo leadership was to make the Yoruba tongue a recognized *lingua franca* almost to the shores of the Volta.

REASONS FOR OYO'S COLLAPSE

Disaster was not many years away when Abiodun died, possibly at the hand of his son and successor, Awole. The actual date of his death is not known and estimates vary from 1789 to 1810. What is certain is that the central authority became paralysed by constitutional upheavals, dynastic intrigues, local particularism and

the efforts of adventurers to turn the breakdown of the constitution to their personal advancement. With such a burden of
internal dissension, Oyo could not withstand the advance of the
cavalry of the new Fulani empire to the north nor check Dahomeian raids across the 'Egbado Corridor'. The once mighty
empire collapsed into warring factions, none of which could
succeed in its individual attempts to reunite Yorubaland under its
own authority. Through the short-sighted ambition of Kakanfo
Afonja at Ilorin, the Fulani took Ilorin and razed Old Oyo.
Dahomey became independent and raided at will across Egbado
territory and into the new Egba state of Abeokuta on raids intended
to collect slaves and cut the trade of Badagri and Lagos. The
constant warfare hampered British attempts to develop trade in
tropical produce through Lagos, and disunity prevented the formation of a common front against the British advance when it
came.

By 1896, the fragments of the once proud Yoruba empire were
on the way to being mere provinces of an alien empire. The angry
curse of Alafin Awole at his rejection, sometime in the first twenty
years of the nineteenth century, had been truly prophetic. After
making preparations for suicide, he fired arrows in all directions
and declaimed thus:

'My curse be on you for your disloyalty and your disobedience,
so let your children disobey you. If you send them on an errand,
let them never return to bring you word again. To all the points
I shot my arrows will ye be carried as slaves. My curse will carry
to the sea and beyond the seas, slaves will rule over you, and ye
their masters will become slaves. Broken calabash can be mended
but not a broken dish; so let my words be irrevocable.'

In his anger he clearly saw what the Yorubas were slow to learn:
that Yoruba power had no existence without Yoruba unity and
adherence to acceptable constitutional practices. The loss of an
Alafin was nothing; the breakdown of order was everything.

Questions

1 Write a critical account of the traditional story of Ife and Oyo
   down to the death of Kori.

303

2 Outline the main stages in the growth of the Oyo empire down to the end of the eighteenth century.

3 Write a short paragraph on each of the following: Oduduwa; Sango; Bashorun Gaha; the Are-Ona-Kakanfo.

4 Describe the reasons for the rise of Oyo's power.

5 What serious constitutional struggle occurred in eighteenth century Oyo and what were its effects on the Oyo empire?

6 Describe the Oyo system of government and explain the precise position of the Alafin in the Oyo constitution.

7 What were the main strengths and what the main weaknesses inherent in the Oyo system of government?

8 Describe the achievements of Alafin Abiodun. What was the full significance of his reign?

18

States of the Guinea Forest: Great Benin

Rising out of legends of the past, the empire of Benin achieved its greatest splendour in the fifteenth and sixteenth centuries. The power of Benin, which so impressed European visitors, nevertheless lasted with many ups and downs until the late nineteenth century. A force to be reckoned with for over four hundred years, Benin experienced many variations in her fortunes.

During this long period there were great changes in economic and political conditions in this part of the Guinea forest. The Atlantic trade opened up, missionaries and traders came to Benin, and then in 1897 Great Benin fell to the British government. In spite of changing circumstances during these five centuries, the principal institutions of Benin remained essentially the same. Dynastic continuity contributed to the capital's stability. The present Oba is the thirty-seventh in direct descent from Oranmiyan, the founder of one of the most long-lived dynasties in West Africa.

REASONS FOR THE RISE OF BENIN

Benin is situated just west of the Niger delta where most communities were organized into petty chiefdoms or large villages in which secret and title societies, age-groups and lineage elders managed public affairs. Unlike so many of their neighbours, the people of Benin succeeded in establishing a sophisticated system of centralized government.

Why did Benin evolve a centralized system of government? The answer lies in two sets of factors: the internal and the external. In the first place there are the culture, customs and political

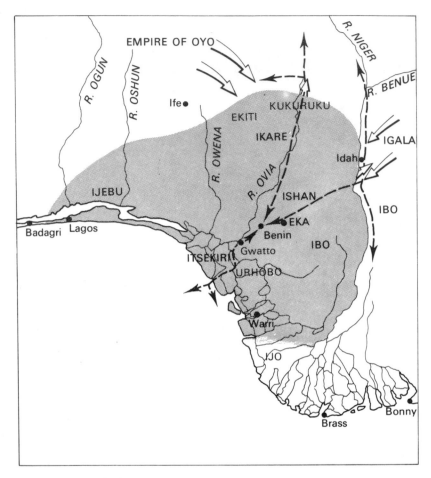

Map XXX   Benin in 1550

inclinations of Benin people. It appears from tradition that Benin
has had kings and some form of centralized government since
earliest times. So from the point of view of internal development,
such political institutions have ever been a part of life in Benin.

In the second place, to take the external factors, we have to
consider three ways in which outside events affected political
conditions at Benin. To begin with, Benin was the southern
terminal of an important trans-Saharan trade route: Binis ex-

ported ivory and pepper to northern markets. Later, after the fifteenth century, ivory, pepper, woman slaves, dyed cotton cloth, jasper stones, leopard skins and blue coral were purchased by European traders. As Binis became more prosperous, more complex methods of government may have been needed than existed elsewhere in the western Niger delta. Furthermore, craft work which always flourishes in such conditions grew to be highly organized and specialized—indicating that as commercial life was well organized so would political institutions be advanced.

The second way in which external conditions influenced the evolution of centralized government at Benin was the impact of her Yoruba neighbours to the west. The Yorubas have always had a centralized form of government. At about the same time as Benin was emerging in the fourteenth century, the Yorubas were founding several kingdoms. Everything that we know about Benin history suggests most strongly that her people were influenced to some extent by Yoruba culture.

The third external condition which affected Benin's history is the fact that her neighbours were poorly organized. To the north, east and south-east lay many small independent chiefdoms or village groups who could not stand up to attacks from an efficiently organized state with an army. And even Yoruba chiefdoms on Benin's western boundaries found that they were no match for the dreaded Bini army. So Benin was able to build up her commercial, political and military institutions without any serious interference or sustained challenges from outside.

THE ORIGINS OF BENIN

The people of Benin who speak Edo, a language of the Kwa family, have lived at their inland settlement for many centuries. We do not know exactly when the Edo arrived there, because it is difficult to get an accurate date from oral traditions. Some place the founding of Benin in about the twelfth century, on the basis of tradition and linguistic research. Other historians are more inclined to settle for a time in the fourteenth century. However this may be, it is quite accurate to say that the Binis were a thriving community with their own kings by the late fourteenth century. We also do not know for certain where the

Edo of Benin came from. Tradition says they came from 'the east'. But it is difficult to ascertain whether this just refers to a later invasion by a warrior élite, or to the direction from whence came the original settlers of Benin.

THE FIRST DYNASTY OF OGISO KINGS

Oral traditions speak of an early dynasty of Bini kings who ruled over Benin or Edo, as the people call their city. Recent research points to the probable existence of an even earlier dynasty, but as with the Ogiso dynasty it is difficult to place any exact date on the period when these kings ruled. Nevertheless, we can safely say that the Ogiso dynasty ruled before the late fourteenth century. They reigned in the legendary past so beloved of folk-lore, when the world was first created, when animals spoke and acted like humans and when the ancestors of the Edo created the first king.

According to tradition, the first Ogiso king was called Obagodo. The last Ogiso ruler, who went by the name of Owodo, was a poor ruler of whom it is said: 'Ogiso never convened a meeting except in times of trouble and crisis'. An untalented man, Owodo also suffered from the fact that although he had many wives he only had one son. Eventually an oracle pronounced that the son should be executed so that the other wives would be able to conceive. Instead, Owodo arranged for the son to be banished; he went and founded the village of Ughoton, which became the port of Gwatto on the bank of the Benin river. Alas, none of Owodo's wives produced any sons and after some years the leading chiefs got together and banished Ogiso Owodo for mis-rule.

There was then an inter-regnum. Two administrators ruled Benin in turn; their names were Evian and Ogiamve and they were intended to be the first rulers of a republican form of government.

THE SECOND DYNASTY OF KINGS: THE COMING OF PRINCE ORANMIYAN

Traditional accounts of Prince Oranmiyan's coming are emphatic that the people of Benin revolted against Evian's attempt to introduce his son as Oba or king of Benin. One well known tradition records that Benin sent ambassadors to Ile-Ife, the ancestral and spiritual home of the Yorubas, asking for a king. Oduduwa, the ancestral hero of Yorubaland, ruled at Ile-Ife in these distant times and is said to have sent a prince called Oranmiyan to the people of Benin to be their king. Oranmiyan was accompanied by a native doctor and priest who presumably provided him with strong magic to quell any dangers on the way.

After some trouble with the ferryman at the Ovia river, Oranmiyan and his courtiers reached the city. There, after more resistance from the administrator, Ogiamve, Oranmiyan took up his abode in the palace which was built for him at Usama. Soon after his arrival Oranmiyan conceived a son by the daughter of a chief from the village of Ego, five miles outside Benin. This boy was called Eweka and became the first king of the second dynasty. After some years, Oranmiyan called a meeting of the chiefs and people at which he renounced his office, remarking that Benin was a 'land of vexation'. Fed up, Prince Oranmiyan returned to Yoruba country where he is said to have founded Old Oyo to the north, becoming the father of the first Alafin of Oyo. Thus, if tradition is correct, Prince Oranmiyan founded two dynasties of kings: those of Old Oyo and of Benin. In this way Benin has been linked by tradition to the people of Yorubaland.

Is the traditional legend of Prince Oranmiyan true?
The traditional account of how the second dynasty of kings was founded has caused much argument among historians. The reason for the dispute is that historians of today do not like to accept traditions uncritically. Their argument over the veracity of the Prince Oranmiyan legend shows us the difficulties that arise when we use oral traditions to re-create the past without being able to refer to documentary or archaeological evidence.

There are two schools of thought about the Oranmiyan legend. One group of historians say that it is true—that Prince Oranmiyan came to rule over Benin at the request of the Binis. Another group, though, asserts that this tradition conceals the fact that Benin was conquered by a Yoruba scion from Ile-Ife. It is really, they say, no more than a convenient fiction to gloss over the hard fact

309

of an unpleasant conquest by strangers.

Where does the truth lie then? We suggest that both schools of thought are right in certain respects. The main point about the Oranmiyan legend is that it links Benin to Yorubaland, emphasizing the influence of Yoruba methods of government on Bini institutions. Indeed tradition distinguishes most firmly between the Ogiso dynasty, which was apparently peculiar to the Edo of Benin, and the second dynasty which shows marked Yoruba influences. The Yoruba system of sacred kingship may have been imposed on Benin by force of arms or by peaceful means: the fact that the Yoruba of Old Oyo have the same legend about Prince Oranmiyan suggests that the story may be quite true. At the same time the Binis were, as the tradition says, receptive to Yoruba culture and gained some prestige from being associated with the ancestral home of Yorubas at Ile-Ife.

Eweka the First

With the accession of Eweka, the son of Oranmiyan, the second dynasty of Bini kings came into its own. Eweka is said by tradition to have had a long and glorious reign. It is Eweka who is attributed with having carried out important innovations in the political institutions of Benin. Eweka created the offices of Councillors of State, or king-makers, called Uzama. There were seven such Councillors whose duty it was to install the Oba-elect according to traditional precedent. These councillors or Uzama passed on their titles to their children.

We cannot be quite certain that it was actually Eweka who created all seven offices, because earlier chiefships existed, including those under the Ogiso dynasty, which may have been transformed into Uzama titles. In other words, it is possible that better known Obas like Eweka have been credited with achievements which might belong to a lesser figure. Tradition generally tends to favour the famous, enlarging on their deeds over the centuries, while forgetting about less attractive or weaker rulers.

Ewedo 'the Idolator'

Ewedo was a grandson of Eweka the First and was apparently a far more successful ruler than Eweka; he was called 'the idolator' on account of his great interest in religion and magic. Ewedo appointed a medicine man as his chief priest. The priest was to

310

supervise rituals and establish earth cult shrines. Ewedo's interest in religion indicates that he may have felt the need for cults and public rituals to strengthen the political power of the Oba. If this is correct, Ewedo reveals himself as a shrewd king who knew how to play upon people's religious beliefs to increase his own power. In fact, 'the idolator' had to struggle hard to establish his right to the Obaship. Ewedo's battle against a faction in the city who opposed him is one of the first examples of succession crises which were to plague Benin. A chief called Ogiamve opposed Ewedo, and so the two armies fought outside the inner walls of Benin. Victorious, Ewedo entered the heart of the city and built his palace there. Until Ewedo's reign Obas had lived at Usama, a place which lies between the inner and outer walls of the city. It is at Usama that a new Oba is installed in a ceremony during which the people celebrate Ewedo's victory over the ambitious chief Ogiamve.

Ewedo is said by tradition to have been a good ruler who created useful laws and built a prison for criminals. He also established more titles and started the custom of chiefs standing in the presence of their Oba: before that, they used to sit down.

A son of Ewedo, Oba Oguola, is credited in some traditional accounts with having built the fine walls which made Benin such a splendid landmark for miles around. Oguola also introduced the famous brass-makers who designed beautiful plaques commemorating the history of Benin in war and in peace. These plaques are an important source of information about the past in Benin. Like other craft workers the brass-smiths were obliged to work solely for the Oba, beautifying the palace and the city.

EWUARE THE GREAT: c. 1440—c. 1473

The mightiest of Bini kings, Ewuare is justly called 'the great'. After his predecessor had been murdered—a not uncommon fate for Obas—the rightful heir was crowned Oba with the title Ewuare, which means 'it is cool' or 'the trouble has ceased'. Ewuare's reign is important not just for his territorial conquests which transformed the kingdom of Benin city into an empire, nor merely for his constitutional reforms. Above all, Ewuare succeed-

L

ed to the Obaship in the nick of time. Before his reign things had been going from bad to worse at Benin: chiefs continually quarrelled, factions fought one another, and all because a number of ineffectual Obas had ruled. A man of great character, Ewuare imposed strong government on Benin and her newly acquired tributaries. He strengthened the Obaship and quelled over-ambitious chiefs who had challenged previous Obas. In other words, Ewuare was a strong ruler who let all know that he was sovereign.

Tradition has this to say of Ewuare the Great: 'Ewuare was a great magician, physician, traveller and warrior. He was also powerful, courageous and sagacious. He fought against and captured two hundred and one towns and villages in Ekiti, Eka, Ikare, Kukuruku, and the Ibo country on this side of the river Niger. He took their petty rulers captive and caused the people to pay tribute to him. He made good roads in Benin city. . . . In fact the town rose to importance and gained the name City during his reign. . . . He made powerful charms, and had them buried at each of the nine gateways to the city, to nullify any evil charms which might be brought by people of other countries to injure his subjects.'

Ewuare was a very great ruler because he was a shrewd politician, a mighty warrior and an able administrator. He was, however, very much a Bini in his ability to use magical practices to support his campaigns and policy-making. Like his ancestor, Ewedo, Ewuare obviously discovered that magical feats and charms paid extensive dividends in building up a political reputation for unassailable power. In this respect, Ewuare strengthened the religious and sacred aspect of the kingship.

The administrative reforms of Ewuare the Great   Having suffered from over-ambitious chiefs who had tried to prevent him from becoming Oba, Ewuare was obviously determined to change the constitution. His reign ushered in the second wave of political reforms. It appears that after Eweka the First had introduced the Uzama or king-makers little had been done to alter the system of administration in Benin. Ewuare's reforms were made doubly urgent by Benin's transformation into an empire: the tributaries would only acquiesce in Benin's rule if there was strong government from the capital.

When Ewuare came to power, Benin was apparently governed by the Oba, the Uzama and the palace chiefs. The palace chiefs were divided into three associations of title holders: the chamberlains, household officials and harem-keepers. Palace chiefs both inherited and achieved their titles by paying fees to their association. What Ewuare found was that the palace chiefs were too powerful, so that it was difficult for an Oba to govern properly.

To strengthen the authority of the Obaship, Ewuare is said by tradition to have introduced another association of chiefs, the town chiefs. Whereas palace chiefs lived in the Oba's compound, town chiefs lived across the street outside the palace. They generally obtained their title on appointment by the Oba: only one title was hereditary. Ewuare appointed four town chiefs to increase his authority against the palace officials; later their number was much enlarged by Ewuare's successors. Town chiefs played an important part in government and the senior town chief, the Iyashere, became the commander-in-chief of the army. They sat with palace chiefs and the Uzama on the State Council, which Ewuare is said to have set up. For the most part, decisions were taken by the Oba in conjunction with senior chiefs. But when important matters cropped up like the proclamation of new laws, the decision to conduct a war, the raising of levies and the like, the State Council was summoned.

RELATIONS WITH THE PORTUGUESE

Oba Ozolua c. 1481–c. 1504
Oba Ozolua was most imperialistic and a great warrior king who extended the boundaries of the empire to the neighbouring kingdoms of Ekiti and Ijebu. However, firearms do not seem to have played a part in Benin's territorial expansion, for the first guns were probably not introduced to Benin until the 1690's. Rather, these successful annexations suggest that Benin had benefited from Ewuare's reforms and that administration in the capital was efficient, for Benin obviously felt strong enough to take on Yoruba chiefdoms to the west.

It was during Oba Ozolua's reign that a Portuguese agent, Afonso d'Aveiro, visited Benin in 1485–86. He established

313

Fig. 14   An ivory mask from Benin

commercial relations between his country and Benin and brought coconuts to the city. D'Aveiro returned to Lisbon with the chief of Ughoton, who acted as the Oba's ambassador. The chief came back to Ughoton to set up a trading factory on behalf of the Portuguese.

Oba Esigie: c. 1504–c. 1550
It is said by tradition that d'Aveiro re-visited Benin during the long reign of Oba Ozolua's successor, Esigie. He advised Oba Esigie to become a Christian, and so Esigie sent the chief of Ughoton to go as his ambassador with d'Aveiro to the king of Portugal. The chief was to request the king to send priests who could teach the Binis about this new religion. In reply the Portuguese king sent the Oba of Benin missionaries and many rich presents, including a copper stool, coral beads and a big umbrella. For some time the traders who had accompanied the missionaries worked at Ughoton. They traded in ivory, pepper, women slaves, Bini cloths, and other commodities in the interest of the king of Portugal.

The missionaries were told to teach Esigie's son the Christian faith and how to read and write. But although some churches were built, Christianity remained a minority religion, confined to the palace of the Oba. However, the missionaries did not only teach. They accompanied Oba Esigie, another great warrior like Ozolua, on his campaign against Idah to the north-east of Benin. This war took place in about 1515–1516, and resulted in Idah paying compensation for her attempted invasion of Benin.

Oba Orhogbua: c. 1550–c. 1578: the last great Oba
During the reign of this educated, Christian and wise king, trade with the Portuguese developed fast. Gwatto became an important port in the western Niger delta and acted as an *entrepôt* for such goods as ivory, palm produce, women slaves, native cloths and pepper which were exchanged for foreign produce. The port was also linked through Benin and Hausaland with the trans-Sahara trade, and so Binis grew rich on the tolls and customs duties which their Oba levied. There is, then, no reason to associate Benin's wealth and growing power with the slave trade. In point of fact it was mainly women slaves who were exported, but the most stable and important exports were ivory and pepper,

315

and later palm oil.

Oba Orhogbua was clearly a strong warrior for he enforced tribute payments from all parts of the empire, and in the mid-1550's conquered all the coastal lands up to Lagos where he left a permanent garrison. Tradition in Lagos says that their first Oba, the Eleko of Eko, was a son of Oba Orhogbua of Benin.

Fig. 15   The city of Benin in the seventeenth century

THE GOVERNMENT OF THE EMPIRE

The empire reached its maximum extension in the mid-sixteenth century when Benin claimed to rule the following territories: parts of Ishan to the north, the Urhobo and Isoko of the lower Niger delta, southern Yoruba country and western Iboland. Indeed, some maps like that of a Dutchman in 1629 depict Benin's frontiers as extending to Bonny in the central delta.

However, there are two reasons why it is unlikely that Benin really dominated the central delta. First, there are no local traditions there which speak of Bini conquest and annexation. Second, even provinces nearer to the capital like Ekiti to the west, or Ishan to the north, went their own way for much of the time. As long as they paid their tribute and acknowledged Benin's overlordship they were left alone. In fact, Benin did not succeed in setting up any really efficient system of provincial government.

316

Provinces were run on the lines of 'indirect rule': overlords who resided at the capital appointed agents to live in their territory or province.

The empire was governed on three levels. The Oba, who became an increasingly secluded and sacred figure during the seventeenth century, was at the top of the hierarchy. On the second level, there were the chiefs who formed the State Council in Benin city. The third level of government consisted of tribute units. A tribute unit corresponded roughly, but not exactly, to a village or petty chiefdom. Each unit was headed by an overlord who represented the interests of his people to the Oba, and told the people what the Oba's wishes were. However, the overlord did not live in his tribute unit but, instead, was represented there by a faithful servant. Overlords received deputations at the capital.

Each overlord was appointed by the Oba. The Queen Mother, the Oba's first son and chiefs in Benin were usually heads of tribute units. The Oba had the right to re-distribute tribute units to prevent any chief from becoming too rich and influential, and to reward any trusty supporters. It was an overlord's duty to transmit appeals from the people in his unit to the Oba's court. He also had to organize the yearly or twice-yearly collection of tribute of yams, palm oil, meat, livestock and other food-stuffs to the Oba.

In principle, this was how the empire was governed. In reality, everything depended on the Oba's ability to mobilize his army to ensure tribute collection from vassal states. There evolved a clear distinction between government of the capital by the Oba and his chiefs and government of the provinces or tribute units where provincial chiefs retained their own institutions and powers.

THE SPLENDOUR OF GREAT BENIN

Benin attained her greatest glory and military achievement in the sixteenth century under Oba Esigie. Such was her progress, political, cultural and artistic, that English visitors testified in the late sixteenth century that Benin had: 'thirty straight streets about one hundred and twenty feet broad', with intersecting streets at right angles to them. They also reported that the Oba could field twenty thousand warriors in one day, and up to one hundred thousand men if necessary. These were the days when Benin exported slaves, leopard skins, pepper and cloth.

In 1702 the Dutchman, David van Nyendael, wrote that: 'the inhabitants of this country, if possessed of any riches, eat and drink very well; that is to say of the best. The common diet of the rich is beef, mutton or chickens and jam (sic) for their bread which after they have boiled, they beat very fine, in order to make cakes of it. . . . The habit (i.e. the dress) of the Negroes here is neat, ornamental and much more magnificent than that of the Negroes of the Gold Coast'.

There were many craft-workers who modelled lovely objects out of wood; there were, too, weavers and metal workers. Others made beautiful gold and ivory jewelry or copper bangles and rings for women. This, then, was a flourishing and most sophisticated culture, where the famous brass-smiths produced works of art to rival those bronzes of Ife in Yorubaland.

REASONS FOR BENIN'S STAGNATION

After the sixteenth century Benin remained an important power in this part of the Guinea forest. But she suffered from succession wars, maladministration of her empire, a line of weak Obas who failed to strengthen the political power of the kingship so that Obas became increasingly secluded religious figures, and growing corruption. It was in the next two centuries that Benin gained what is probably an exaggerated reputation for bloody sacrifices which, even today, are said by the sensitive to darken the city's atmosphere. In a sense, the later period of the empire was one of little change in comparison with the expansionist era of the fifteenth and sixteenth centuries.

Why did Benin stand still, politically and culturally? There were five reasons, which hinge on the changing economic circumstances of Benin and the absence of outstanding rulers. Firstly, Benin slowly became a commercial out-post because the river at Gwatto silted up, so the Itsekiri kingdom of Warri on the Forcados estuary attracted European merchants more; other more suitably placed trading centres also arose in the central and eastern delta. The Oba's revenues from tolls and customs duties therefore declined.

318

Furthermore, power was over-concentrated in the city, while provincial government was too decentralized so that tribute units were all only loosely involved in Bini public affairs. Benin left the institutions of her vassals untouched, and did not bother to find a way of making her subjects universal citizens of Benin as the first Asante kings had done. The extent to which power was concentrated in the hands of a few chiefs and the Oba is shown by the fact that the Oba did not permit his tribute unit heads to reside with their people; also there was no formal machinery of provincial administration as existed, for example, in the late eighteenth century Asante empire. All Obas were extremely afraid that tribute heads would seize the opportunity to organize a rebellion. This suggests poor administration.

Thirdly, there was no sophisticated military organization like Asante had. It is true that there was a standing army and that three associations of chiefs supplied war captains. But there was no proper military division of the empire so that the army was integrated into the political structure; there was, moreover, no proper national militia with specialized contingents supplied by particular divisions.

Again, there was the all-important matter of the succession. The Bini kingship suffered from the fact that the Uzama could not depose or, in theory, elect an Oba. There was, then, no way of getting rid of an unpopular Oba except by organizing a revolt which usually ended in the Oba being murdered. If there had been, as among the Asante, a peaceful way of deposing a bad Oba by de-stoolment there might have been fewer succession crises and civil wars.

Finally, there was no outstanding line of Obas after the reign of Oba Esigie. So the fall in Benin's economic fortunes coincided with a lack of great rulers after the sixteenth century. Individual leadership was crucial in a constitution where much depended upon the abilities of a reigning Oba. A weak Oba meant that the town and palace chiefs stirred up much discontent and trouble by taking over the reins of government.

THE ACHIEVEMENTS OF BENIN

Nevertheless, the later years of Benin, when no real achievements took place, must not blind us to her accomplishments. These were considerable in comparison with those of the petty chiefdoms and village groups in this region of the Guinea forest.

To begin with, Benin was the first African power in Southern Nigeria to maintain regular diplomatic contact with a European state (Portugal) as early as the fifteenth century. The Benin empire was of a fair size, extending at different times to Lagos in the west, and in the east to the shores of the Niger river. Bini culture had some impact upon many of her vassals. For them, it was sometimes a point of much prestige to have a chief of semi-divine nature who could be called Oba. Certain tributaries also adopted Benin's system of chiefly palace associations: various official titles were ranked in order of seniority, and arranged into different 'orders' or associations. Lastly, the Benin bronzes give us plenty of evidence of a complex society as well as of a universally acclaimed artistic achievement.

Questions

1 What were the internal and external factors which, in your opinion, contributed to the evolution of centralized government in Benin?

2 Give an account of the early history of Benin up to the arrival of Prince Oranmiyan. Discuss the conflicting ideas about the truth of the Prince Oranmiyan legend.

3 Compare the achievements and character of Oba Eweka and Oba Ewedo. Why was Ewedo called the 'idolator'?

4 Outline the main events of the reign of Ewuare the Great and describe his principal accomplishments.

5 Consider the relations between the Portuguese and Benin.

6 Examine the way in which the Benin empire was governed.

7 Describe some of the splendours of Benin. Why did the political and economic expansion of Benin halt in the sixteenth century?

19

The city-states of the Niger Delta

The Niger delta stretches for over three hundred miles from the Benin river in the west to the Cross river in the east. It is a low-lying land of innumerable creeks, waterways and mangrove swamps where the inhabitants have always been able to communicate with one another by canoe.

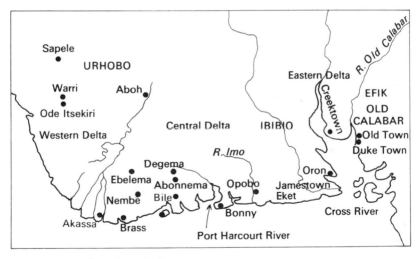

Map XXXI   The Niger Delta

The principal peoples of the delta are the Itsekiri and the coastal-dwelling Sobo in the west, the Ijo in the centre, the coastal Ibibio, and the Efik of Old Calabar who live in the eastern delta. The Ijo, Ibibio and Efik have many similar institutions. But the Itsekiri who founded the kingdom of Warri in the western delta do

321

not really resemble the central and eastern delta peoples. In fact the Itsekiri of Warri have much more in common with the Edo of Benin and their Yoruba neighbours. And so until we come to the section on Warri we will be discussing the history of those Ijo who founded the central delta city-states of Nembe, Kalabari and Bonny, as well as the rise of the Efik state called Old Calabar which lies in the eastern delta.

In the forest zone, empires and kingdoms sometimes developed. But in the delta region no large states emerged. Instead the Ijo and Efik are organized into villages: lineage elders, secret societies—and to a lesser extent age groups—have always formed the major institutions of government.

There are, among all Ijo, some centralized political and judicial institutions. But, although more centralized government developed in certain Ijo city-states which became very important during the hey-day of the Atlantic slave trade, power ultimately resided in lineage and ward ('house') heads rather than in such central organs of government as the village council. Among the Efik the situation is complicated by the important political functions of a secret society called Ekpe which ruled Old Calabar. Wealthy freemen of old families exercised authority by buying their way into Ekpe, so that power resided more in this central organ of government than in lineage or ward heads.

IJO AND EFIK HISTORY

The main theme of the history of the Ijo and Efik peoples during the eighteenth century is really the way in which indigenous forms of political and economic organisation interacted with the Atlantic slave trade. This external factor affected political institutions, trading patterns and relations between different groups each competing for a stake in this lucrative trade with European vessels. The overall political effect of the overseas slave trade was that power and authority became more centralized.

Among the Ijo of Nembe, of Elem Kalabari (capital of Kalabari city-state) and of the Bonny city-states, wealthy men with stronger followings than their rivals came to act as kings. Thus one man represented the city-state in foreign and commercial affairs.

But because a king's power was finally dependent upon the allegiance of other wealthy and influential men in the state, it can be said that in the last analysis power resided in household heads, elders and other men of importance.

In Old Calabar the central organ of government, which was the Ekpe secret society, grew more powerful because an ambitious freeman of means could not achieve real importance unless he became a member. The members of Ekpe, who were drawn from the various villages into which Old Calabar was divided, governed by virtue of their high office in the society.

How and why did these significant developments come about? There are two main reasons. Firstly, states struggled to monopolize the slave trade so as to obtain a greater share of the trading dues ('comey') paid by European ships. It was, then, essential for an ambitious community to produce strong leaders equipped with armed followers. Some kind of force was needed to keep open strategic waterways, which led to the slave-producing hinterland. Therefore, a man of princely birth who had the largest fleet of war and trading canoes, and the strongest following, was likely to emerge as the king of an Ijo city-state. For it was such an individual who could most effectively advance his people's interests.

Secondly, the central and eastern delta states acquired considerable revenue in the form of trading dues paid by European vessels. With the inflow of money (iron or copper bars) and luxury goods, wealth became an essential pre-condition of power. Wealth bought cannons, guns, powder and large fleets of canoes. An Ijo man who toiled hard had a good chance of becoming an influential political figure in his city-state, or a house head. During the eighteenth century Ekpe's position as the central agency of government in Old Calabar was reinforced as freemen of wealth coverted their gains into political power by joining the senior grades of the society.

Why the history of the Delta is important
In an earlier chapter on the coastal areas it was argued that history is not just concerned with great military and political leaders or expansionist empires. A people's past consists of many things—political, cultural, social and economic factors which make up the fabric of their society's heritage. And so in discus-

sing the history of the Niger delta it is important to say why a region which did not produce empires or shattering military conquests is a vital part of West Africa's past.

Clearly, opinions will differ on this matter. To begin with, though, we can note that although delta peoples lived in a similar natural environment, the Itsekiri of Warri have experienced a different history and have evolved different political institutions to the Ijo and Efik. Why has this happened? Here we touch on an important historical principle: history is, among other things, the product of factors which interact over a given period of time. Any variation in the factors produces a shift in the pattern and direction of events, and contributes to the unique element in a people's history.

Thus, political and economic factors have interacted differently among the Itsekiri of Warri and the Ijo of, for example, Kalabari. All too little is known about Itsekiri organization; but it appears that settlements outside the capital at Warri were organized into villages under the authority of a headman or priest—as in most delta communities. Owing to the cultural and political influence of Benin, Warri people recognized a divine king and a panoply of chiefs. Overshadowed by the might of imperial Benin, Warri was blocked from free access to potential supplies of large numbers of slaves. And so political restrictions limited economic development. The Ijo, on the other hand, retained the basic delta pattern of organization into villages under their own heads. Here political conditions actually facilitated full economic development and participation in the overseas slave trade. For the Ijo were not prevented from reaching a populous hinterland, rich in slaves, by powerful kingdoms as were the Itsekiri of Warri.

The history of the Ijo and Efik city-states is important for another reason. It shows how political institutions can adapt to a changed economic situation with comparative rapidity when the material rewards of such changes are experienced immediately. The dynamic events of these states tell us that history can be the story of a fruitful adjustment between political and economic factors.

Lastly, the central and eastern delta is historically significant because it was the first area of West Africa to experience the avaricious demands of an industrializing nation on a large scale. It was here that the nineteenth and twentieth century colonial system of purchasing low-cost raw materials for export to overseas markets was first tried out on a commercially significant scale. This is obviously an important factor when viewed in relation to the history of coastal West Africa in the nineteenth century.

POLITICAL ORGANIZATION

The house system

The term 'house system' in the central and eastern delta means that people are grouped into households and wards. Wards are territorial sub-divisions of a village. The word 'house' is applied both to the household which incorporates the extended family, and to the ward. We should distinguish between two kinds of house system among the Ijo and Efik, because important changes took place in the organization and composition of houses during the eighteenth century. These changes were principally brought about by participation in the overseas slave trade.

Until the eighteenth century villages would appear from oral traditions to have been founded upon the principle of wards or houses being politically equivalent. Government was mainly in the hands of descent group elders. Houses were based on localized descent groups and were very homogenous in their composition, consisting mainly of descent group members, their wives and offspring.

However, during the eighteenth century the Ijo house system changed significantly as commerce in slaves grew apace. By the beginning of the nineteenth century similar, although less marked, adjustments had taken place in the Efik house system at Old Calabar.

What happened was that the traditional way of organizing people into descent groups, which made up the household and the ward, gave way to the 'canoe house' system. Canoe houses were similar to the old house system in that they were based upon the principle that people should be organized into descent groups or houses. But this principle was subject to many modifications, which eroded the descent group ideal that people who were not descended from the founders of the house should not be allowed to hold the political offices of ward (or household) head. In the eighteenth century slaves and low status freemen could rise to the office of canoe house head in Ijo city-states as long as they were wealthy. Canoe houses were much more hetero-geneous in their composition: sometimes slaves and other strangers could outnumber 'true' members of the house—i.e. descent group members. Canoe houses were smaller in size, more compact, and decision-making was more centralized. Above all, canoe houses were founded on the existence and maintenance of a large fleet of war and trading canoes. In fact an Ijo man could not found his own house until he had traded successfully and could afford to purchase the men and materials necessary for building up a fleet. In Old Calabar the equation between com-mercial success as middlemen in the Atlantic slave trade and house-founding was less strict, because farm land was sufficiently plentiful to provide a secondary avenue to wealth and house headship.

Ijo canoe houses were corporate organizations of kinsmen, strangers and slaves assembled for the purpose of successful participation in the overseas slave trade. They were, in fact, trading and military corporations because houses had to keep open strategic waterways that linked the slave-producing hinter-land to coastal ports. To trade, a canoe house needed naval power. New canoe houses were established when a group which possessed a fleet of canoes separated from the parent house. A new house was economically independent but politically subordinate to the mother house; political effectiveness required a house to create alliances, which were cemented by inter-marriage, with other influential houses.

The number of canoes that a house owned was visible proof of its prosperity and strength. As the material rewards for middlemen in the overseas slave trade grew, so did competition between houses and states for a greater share in this lucrative occupation. Trading canoes carried slaves and goods up and down the waterways that linked interior markets with coastal ports; war canoes came into their own as competition increased. In the late seventeenth century the Dutchman, Dapper, wrote that a war canoe in the Bonny area was between fifty to seventy feet long. It had about twenty paddlers on each side, each with his shield and bundle of throwing spears. Such canoes carried about sixty to eighty people, were pointed both fore and aft

Fig. 16 A war canoe on the River Niger

and were six foot wide amidships.

In the late eighteenth century when guns became the usual armoury, canoes were even larger. According to observers, canoes had to carry a minimum of fifty musketeer paddlers; there was a cannon to fore and aft, while a third cannon was often situated on a swivel amidships. These great war cannons were capable of blasting the enemy to smithereens.

Social divisions

The development of the Ijo canoe house system in the eighteenth century was accompanied by another change in life. Before the eighteenth century, there appear to have been three social categories in Ijo city-states: slaves, freeborn and royals. A man's status was therefore determined mainly by his birth—whether he was born a slave, a freeman or a prince. Under this social system only kings and those of royal or chiefly descent could found new houses in Kalabari or Bonny. Accession to the position of household and ward head was determined by age seniority in these city-states and by descent seniority in Old Calabar—the Efik state.

During the eighteenth century, office and leadership in the Ijo states became increasingly competitive. A man acquired wealth by shrewd trading. This wealth bought power in terms of a large fleet of canoes, many dependants, and therefore influence in the direction of house and state affairs.

The new system of ranking people was based on power and wealth: positions were achieved and lost so that Ijo society became extremely competitive and mobile. The principal social categories were princes, chiefs, gentlemen, and 'niggers'. A king was placed at the top of the social hierarchy because he had the resources to command the support of the whole community; a chief was a gentleman who headed a house and commanded the support of all persons in that house; a 'nigger' was a person whom others could command. He might be an impoverished freeman or a slave born into a house. However, if a 'nigger' had ability he could rise to the rank of chief of a house (but not to the rank of king, if he was of slave descent). Only princes were eligible to succeed to the kingship, but they had to be wealthy men equipped with large fleets.

Contrary to some opinions, these two systems of social status co-existed during the eighteenth and nineteenth centuries. A poor freeman could take comfort from his superior birth, which he might compare favourably with that of a rich young trader who was a slave and worked under a master—his house's head. Although birth was still important in Ijo society it was, in reality, power and wealth which counted most in political and commercial affairs. For these were the factors that most affected a man's career.

Similarly, social rank in Old Calabar was increasingly affected by the influence and power that could be wielded by men of wealth. But the principal social categories remained those of nobles, commoners and slaves. Efik living in the eighteenth and nineteenth centuries still attached much importance to descent and birth. In fact wealth could only be converted into such political offices as those of king, ward or lineage head, or senior member of the Ekpe secret society, by men of free birth.

The Ijo canoe house system was flexible in the extreme: powerful and wealthy houses had the most able and talented leaders for, if a house was inadequately governed, it became commercially impoverished and therefore lost political influence in the city-state. A house head, or chief as he was called, had powers of life and death over the persons belonging to his house. But his authority was tempered by the need to maintain a strong following. It was this dependence upon others, plus the dispersal of wealth among a large number of leading men, that resulted in power and authority being distributed among various houses in accordance with the traditional principle of politically equivalent units having an equal share in political matters. And so there was a certain element of structural continuity in Ijo society in spite of the radical changes that occurred during our period.

The city-state
The city-state in the central and eastern delta can be defined as a confederation of houses. The states of Nembe, Kalabari, Bonny and Old Calabar as well as the Itsekiri kingdom of Warri were composed of three territorial units: the capital, colonies of satellite villages, and a trading region in the interior forest belt.

The capital of a city-state in Ijo country was generally built on mangrove swamp. As the water was brackish there was no possibility of farming, so Ijo people had to rely on fishing and trade with the hinterland for their livelihood. The Itsekiri of Warri and the Efik of Old Calabar, however, lived on dry agricultural land in the fresh-water swamp forest; and so farming has always played some part in the local economy of these two city-states.

It might be thought that the divisions of the city-state into capital, villages, and trading empire were a result of the Atlantic slave trade. On the contrary, Ijo traditions tell us that their capital towns were founded in the distant past and that they had close contacts with inland folk, principally the Ibo and Ibibio. Before the hey-day of the overseas slave trade in the eighteenth century, Ijo traded as they do today by selling their fish and salt to up-country sedentary farmers and buying bulk foods like yams, fruits, and meat in exchange. Little villages were established along rivers leading to inland markets in Ibo country.

The overseas slave trade accentuated these territorial divisions; it also increased the number of satellite villages and inland markets. By the mid-eighteenth century the capital which gave its name to the state virtually incorporated neighbouring settlements, which were politically and economically tied to the capital town. More distant villages might claim to be self-governing, but they were economically dependent because they could only trade through a canoe house of the state in whose territory they lay. The delta city-state, which was a naval rather than a military power, was unable to claim political domination over her trading empire. Instead, a city-state protected her traders and merchants by using part of the trading dues (comey) obtained from European ships to pay passage money to villages controlling different sections of the waterways leading inland. Credit was given through canoe house heads to traders in the trading empire, while citizens from the capital sometimes inter-married with people up-country. King Pepple of Bonny, for instance, is said to have had an Ibo wife from Bonny's trading empire.

In the eighteenth century territory occupied by the capital and the economically dependent villages of Nembe was divided into three parts: coastal villages such as Twon; the central area oc-cupied by the capital Nembe and its settlements; and the northern area lying between Nembe and the Niger river, where villages were politically independent but commercially dependent on the city-state. Nembe's trading empire lay northwards towards Aboh. Kalabari had the largest population, and her territory included the area between the Santa Barbara and the New Calabar rivers; her trading empire lay around the Ibo hinterland drained by the New Calabar river. Bonny had the smallest territory and population but her wealth and therefore her power were, by the 1750's, the greatest. Her trading empire lay through Ndokki country on the Imo river, which she controlled. The capital of the Efik state was situated at the junction of the Old Calabar and Cross rivers; her trading empire covered the whole of the Cross river and the hinterland.

Government and the city-state

If oral traditions are correct, Ijo states have always recognized one of their senior ward or house heads as having superior ritual authority over other ward and house heads. Two factors contributed to the development of this titular office into one of some political and commercial power: the overseas slave trade itself, and internal upheavals within city-states.

In each state a man whom Europeans called 'king' acquired sufficient power to become the sole representative of his state in commercial dealings with European merchants. Considerably enriched from acting as chief negotiator with the Europeans, the political office of king developed and successors were provided by the royal lineage. Powerful house heads, often of slave descent, acted as king-makers choosing the new king from princely candidates.

Internally, an era of bitter hostilities and civil wars ended with the emergence of powerful kings by the late seventeenth century when Europeans reported that they could move around freely. But after the mid-eighteenth century a time of war began in Old Calabar where there was civil strife between Old Town and Creek Town; similar civil strife took place in Nembe; and in Elem Kalabari and Bonny two powerful kings emerged. Hostilities between rival houses occurred because ambitious men sought more wealth and political power. Fighting on a serious scale was encouraged by musket imports. As guns are not mentioned in such late seventeenth century documents as James Barbot's report of 1699, but are in late eighteenth century records, it is reasonable to say that guns were imported on a large scale after the 1770's.

Thus, the late eighteenth century saw the emergence of two powerful men in Elem Kalabari and Bonny, Amakiri and Pepple

331

respectively, who established their own houses and developed powerful kingships. In both states the political revolution was such that most of the older houses became extinct, being replaced by houses founded by members of the Amakiri (Kalabari) and Pepple (Bonny) houses.

In Old Calabar the results of civil war were rather different. Two leaders, the kings of Creek and Duke Town, emerged as the principal political representatives of Old Calabar. However, they exercised their authority as the head and deputy head, respectively, of the Ekpe secret society.

Bonny provides us with a well documented example of how a city-state was governed in the late eighteenth century. Bonny was then ruled by a king of the Pepple dynasty who sat with other house heads and notables in a general meeting where they discussed state matters. The king and his general council made laws, acted as arbitrators in quarrels between houses, declared war, executed criminals and negotiated contracts with the European merchants. The king, however, was finally responsible for all contracts and received comey from European vessels. The Pepple king was believed to be partly divine; he had to carry out priestly duties to the most powerful of Bonny's four tutelary deities, the god Simingi. Thus the Pepple king's religious authority validated and buttressed the political and economic power of his office.

No account of government in the delta states would be complete without mentioning secret societies. In Nembe and Kalabari the most important secret society was called Ekine (there was no Ekine society in Bonny). Ekine was divided into sections, each of which produced its own masks and plays. It had some executive functions in that it brought together all important men whose decisions on matters concerning Ekine were then executed by the society's junior members. Ekine was socially and politically significant because its membership cut across house divisions, helping to integrate houses into one political entity—the city state.

Unlike Ekine, Ekpe actually ruled Old Calabar. The two kings were the head and deputy head of Ekpe; senior members were councillors, judges and law-makers of Old Calabar; members of the second grade were the state's executive officers; and the lower grade members who wore disguises acted as the executive's 'police'.

Trade and the city-state

According to Pacheco Pereira in the *Esmeralda De Situ Orbis* (1505–1520), the Ijo inhabitants of the Rio Real area—the region where the city-state of Bonny grew up—were already participating in a complex trading system with the hinterland in the late fifteenth century. Bulk foodstuffs and slaves were brought in canoes by middlemen to coastal settlements. European vessels bought food to feed their sailors, and slaves to transport overseas. Although the trade in slaves became the most lucrative occupation, it is important to remember that salt, fish and agricultural commodities were always commercially significant. In 1820, for instance, the Lander brothers reported that the most important occupations in the central delta after the slave trade were 'making salt, fishing, boiling oil and trading to Eboe (Ibo) country'.

As the slave trade developed so did the trading system become more complex. More traders travelled to such far-off markets as Onitsha, Idah or Lokoja on the Niger. Bonny bought slaves at Idah, for instance, and had a stake in the free open markets of Aboh, which were also popular with Nembe middlemen. Middlemen increased numerically and became more specialized, dealing in particular commodities. By the eighteenth century interior middlemen, generally the Aro of the middle Cross river region, were buying slaves from other inland slave dealers and then selling them to delta middlemen in up-country markets. Trade goods such as cloth, guns, fish and salt went in the opposite direction, from the coast to inland markets. Other delta and Aro middlemen specialized in selling particular types of imported goods such as beads, gunpowder, rum and so on.

By the eighteenth century credit was well organized. One kind of currency was used by Europeans when paying for slaves, while another was used by delta traders when dealing with indigenous buyers. The 'trust trade' was an essential part of the slave trade in the 1700's. The term 'trust trade' means that Europeans advanced credit to reputable middlemen, house heads and kings. The rule was that a white merchant handed over a specified amount of currency, and a certain quantity of goods such as cloth or rum, on credit or trust to indigenous traders. They then sold these to buy slaves at inland markets. The currency used by Europeans consisted of iron or copper rods in Nembe, Kalabari, Bonny and Old Calabar: rods were used to determine the value of all

333

kinds of commodities. A man slave, for example, could be sold for thirty-eight copper bars in early eighteenth century Old Calabar. Inland, another currency in the form of manillas or copper bracelets was also used in determining the price of slaves, raw materials or manufactured goods.

When middlemen had bought slaves at inland markets and carried them to the ship granting them credit, they were paid the value of the slaves less the amount advanced in credit. A certain proportion was also deducted by the ship's master to be paid to the trader's canoe house head: this was comey or trading dues. A prominent Efik trader, Antera Duke, wrote in his diary for 1785 that he received '143 kegs of powder, and 984 coppers (copper bars) besides . . . 3 pieces of Honesty (handkerchiefs)', from a ship's captain, as his payment and dash (commission) after he had sold slaves to the captain.

The following description of the slave trade tells us about the extent of the traffic in human beings. An English captain observed in the late eighteenth century that Bonny was 'the wholesale market for slaves, since not fewer than 20,000 are sold here every year. Of these, 16,000 come from one nation, called the Ibos, so that this single nation has exported, over the past twenty years, not fewer than 320,000 of its people; while members of the same nation sold at New and Old Calabar, in the same period, probably amounted to 50,000 more'.

Why city-states developed in the central and eastern delta
There are several factors that may explain why this particular form of political organization emerged in the central and eastern delta. To begin with, there is the environmental situation. City-states were composed of separate settlements on account of the way in which creeks, rivers and swamps break up the land's surface and restrict the drier areas suitable for house building. Given these topographical conditions, it was perhaps inevitable that dispersed villages should grow up on river banks and estuaries. Owing to the distance between Ijo communities and the principal inland markets, and the virtual impossibility of organizing large military contingents, the trading empire was of necessity politically independent but commercially tied to the city-state. Thus, environmental conditions may have contributed much to those characteristic territorial divisions between the capital, its

satellite villages and the trading empire.

Delta folk were and are predominantly fishermen and traders dependent upon water travel for communication. Horses could not withstand the tsetse fly, while natural obstacles made it exceedingly difficult to assemble large armies dependent upon canoes for transport. So there were many problems facing any people who might have wanted to enlarge their scale of political organization into that of, for example, an expansionist kingdom. The city-state was probably the most suitable political unit under delta conditions.

Secondly, there is the political factor. Ijo and Efik people have always been proudly egalitarian within their system of organization into houses. Even during the height of the slave trade (and then the palm oil trade in the nineteenth century), wealth was distributed between many rich house heads, traders and the like. An Ijo king was probably the richest man in his state if he was an able and shrewd ruler-merchant, and if his house was the most powerful in trade and defence. But his power was always checked by the possibility of rival houses uniting against him. And so traditional principles worked against any evolution of centralized kingdoms with authoritarian monarchies.

Thirdly, there is the economic factor, as significant as any other. Well accustomed to long-distance trading and the role of middlemen, the Ijo of the central delta grafted slave dealing onto their traditional trading system. And so it was easy for a city-state to adjust to the requirements of the overseas slave trade which was at its height in the eighteenth century. Given these commercial pre-conditions, several states were able to compete with one another for a share in the trade: such rivalry between states of roughly equivalent strength prevented one of their number from emerging as the sole political power in the delta. States also experienced changes in their commercial, and therefore their political, fortunes. Kalabari is generally regarded as being the most prosperous city-state of the late fifteenth century, but by the late eighteenth century Bonny had overtaken it.

As we have seen, the overall effects of intensive participation in the overseas slave trade were that the trading system became highly specialized and complex; political institutions shifted in the direction of more centralized authority within an egalitarian framework; canoe houses took over from the traditional house

335

system in the central delta; and social rank, particularly among Ijo, became more dependent on wealth and power than on descent and birth.

ITSEKIRI: THE WESTERN DELTA KINGDOM OF WARRI

The Itsekiri live around the Benin, Forcados and Escravos rivers in the western delta, which is an area of many mangrove swamps. However, the Itsekiri of Warri town, the capital of the kingdom, live on drier agricultural land. This section of the Itsekiri people was much influenced by Benin and Yoruba culture, so that they have less in common with their Ijo neighbours than Itsekiri who live outside Warri in typical delta fishing villages.

So far as we can tell from oral traditions and linguistic evidence, the Itsekiri are probably a mixture of several peoples. The original inhabitants were called *umuale*, but they were soon absorbed by invading groups from the forest. If oral traditions are correct, the hard core of the Itsekiri people of Warri was made up of two parties of immigrants: there is no sound evidence to indicate, as some have stated, that Ijo immigrants contributed significantly to the founding of Warri, or that Warri people are a sub-group of the Ijo. No exact date can be set, but it appears that a party of Ijebu from Yoruba country arrived and settled near the site of modern Warri in the early fifteenth century at the latest. Afterwards, another party of Edo are said to have moved down from Benin in the same century to near Warri; they were led by a Bini prince.

The arrival of Ginuwa
According to Warri and Bini tradition, a prince called Ginuwa left Benin in about 1475 after he had quarrelled with his brother over the succession to the throne of Benin. Ginuwa died at a village on the way, but his son managed to reach a settlement just outside the site of modern Warri. Here, Ginuwa's son was accepted by the settlement head as the new leader of his people: the ruler of Warri is called Olu, or king. The settlement is called Ode-Itsekiri, the land of Itsekiri, after the headman who paid allegiance to Ginuwa's son. In the mid-sixteenth century the

king's palace was removed to the site of modern Warri, which then emerged as the capital of an important kingdom in the delta.

It seems likely, if the reports of early travellers are correct, that Warri was originally subordinate to Benin. Portuguese influence in Warri during the seventeenth and early eighteenth centuries, and a slackening of Benin's hold over the coast at this time, explain the quasi-independent status with which Warri was credited by late eighteenth century travellers. During this period the population of Warri was estimated to be in the region of 3,000 to 15,000 people. Some of the visitors said that Warri was a fine town with broad streets, which were dominated by the Olu's beautiful palace. The palace was like the Oba's building at Benin but smaller.

Warri kings and the Portuguese
It seems that European traders first visited the western delta in the sixteenth or seventeenth century. Pereira in the *Esmeralda De Situ Orbis* makes no mention of a place called Warri, though he does mention a market up the Forcados river which may have been Ode-Itsekiri, the settlement where Ginuwa's son was recognized as chief. However, we do know that Roman Catholic missions sent priests to Warri in the late sixteenth and early seventeenth century, and traders from Portuguese ships may have accompanied them.

In the first decades of the seventeenth century, Mingi, a son of the reigning Olu went to Portugal for ten years to be educated. He returned with his wife, a beautiful Portuguese woman of noble birth, and invited Pope Innocent X to send missionaries to teach the people of Warri about the Catholic faith; they arrived in 1682. It was Mingi's son, Antonio Domingo, who was Olu in the 1680's.

At this time the Itsekiri were reported by Dapper in 1686 to be a Christian people, while several were literate in Portuguese. But the missionaries left by the end of the eighteenth century, tired of the climate and the feeble growth of Catholicism. Evidence of Christian influence—a chapel, a wooden cross and ritual objects in the palace—were visible at the end of the eighteenth century.

One of Warri's greatest kings was a successor of Antonio Domingo's called Olu Erewuja. He reigned from about 1720 to 1800 and saw the peak of Warri's political and commercial

337

expansion. Erewuja used the Portuguese to increase Warri's independence of Benin. He sent representatives to trade on his behalf with Portuguese ships anchored in the Forcados estuary; and encouraged Itsekiri to move down towards the mouth of the Benin river, where they tried to consolidate their hold on strategic commercial outlets. However, observers testify that these settlements were placed under Benin governors: a statement which may indicate that Warri was unable to shake off Benin's control entirely.

Unfortunately, Olu Erewuja was succeeded by a cruel son who became a tyrant. Civil strife racked Warri for much of the nineteenth century until the rise of Nana of Ebrohomi in the 1880's. Much of this internal dissension can be attributed to the way in which the overseas slave trade had enriched chiefly lineages, so that as a body they were able to challenge the wealth and power of the Olu.

IJO: THE CENTRAL DELTA STATE OF NEMBE

In the early 1500's, the Portuguese governor of Elmina castle on the Ghanaian coast, Pacheco Pereira, reported that he had seen Ijo in the Rio Real area. Of them he said 'the Jos (Ijo) are rarely at peace'. Later the English applied the word 'Brass' to the river estuary leading to the capital town of Nembe, and to the coastal port of Twon which was Nembe's principal outlet to the sea. Among the explanations put forward for the name Brass is the theory that the tough competitive people of Twon were called *barasin*, which today means 'let go' or 'leave off'. Another explanation is that the name Brass may come from the brass pans sold in this area for boiling salt.

The origin of Nembe
Nembe was the place where the people of the capital first settled. There are several traditions about the founding of Nembe, which are contradictory in certain respects. The following tradition is that recorded by an historian of the Nembe people, E. J. Alagoa.

According to this tradition, Nembe was first founded by three men called Obolo, Olodia and Onyo; they seem to have come from the region of Benin, Warri or western Ijo country. They became national gods, worshipped as the hero ancestors who met and vanquished the indigenes. At a later period, a new wave of warlike immigrants came to Nembe from either Benin or Warri. It is likely that their leader, Ogidiga, was of the lineage of Ginuwa who founded Ode-Itsekiri, so that this Bini prince may link the people of Nembe to Benin as well as to the Itsekiri of Warri. Afterwards, a third migration occurred in which another band of strangers from the same area is believed to have established the coastal ports of Twon and Akassa.

The dynasty of Kala-Ekule: c. *1450 or* c. *1500*
Nembe is said to have become influential during the reign of a great king called Kala-Ekule, who had contacts with the city-state of Kalabari. E. J. Alagoa estimates that Kala-Ekule's reign took place in about 1450 or 1500. He was succeeded by several kings, the last of whom was called Basua. When Basua died in about 1700 a terrible civil war broke out in Nembe. Two of Basua's sons fought one another for the throne. They were called Mingi and Ogbodo. Neither of them was totally victorious, and so they both set themselves up as kings, each with his general council and an Ekine society lodge.

The dual monarchy from c. *1700*
Mingi became king of Bassambiri, one quarter of Nembe, and Ogbodo later achieved recognition as king of another quarter, Ogolomabiri. Nembe now had a dual monarchy, each king heading a powerful house.

According to tradition, Mingi I was 'very stout, and tall—indeed, gigantic; he could lift and throw a man with one hand, he was repulsive in appearance and stammered in speech; he was also very passionate and very cruel'. The only good thing that the tyrant Mingi appears to have done was that he encouraged Nembe people to cultivate plantations.

Ogbodo, on the other hand, is depicted as being a good and peace-loving man who had a tough time fighting Mingi I. So people who disliked and feared Mingi's oppressive rule joined up with the Ogolomabiri quarter, and the house of King Ogbodo. Although King Ogbodo was rather weak and did not establish a strong dynasty for his successors, the Ogolomabiri quarter is regarded as being senior.

The Bile war: c. 1770–1780

King Mingi I of Bassambiri is believed to have been succeeded by his son Ikata, a wise warrior king. Tradition says that Ikata was merciful in war and generous to captured slaves. He is also accredited with the introduction of war canoes to Nembe at about the time of the famous Bile war.

This war happened when King Ikata sent some traders to contact European merchants off Bonny and Kalabari to the east in about 1770 or 1780. When it was time for Ikata's men to return, King Amakiri of Elem Kalabari gave them an ivory bowl to present to their king. But as the men of Nembe paddled towards the town of Bile, situated near Elem Kalabari, the inhabitants attacked them, killing some and enslaving others. For the moment King Ikata did not try to attack Bile. But after being abused by his sister for his inactivity, Ikata ordered the Nembe war fleet to ambush Bile's war canoes. The Bile fleet was badly beaten, and their king was blinded in one eye by his cousin, Ikata.

This tradition about the Bile war is significant for three reasons. Firstly, it indicates that city-states in the delta had contacts with one another, and that they were sometimes linked by dynastic marriages. The Bile king is said to have been a 'cousin' of the Nembe king, Ikata. Secondly, the war indicates that villages which were conveniently located on strategic waterways could hold a powerful city-state to ransom, and interrupt communications. Finally, city-states may on occasion have realized that alliances could be commercially and politically useful. At about the time of the Bile war, King Amakiri of Elem Kalabari was struggling to strangle the commercial power of the Bonny king, Pepple. So King Amakiri's present to King Ikata of Nembe may have been the opening gesture in an attempt to form an alliance between the two city-states, which could have strengthened Kalabari in her fight against Bonny.

IJO: THE CENTRAL DELTA STATE OF KALABARI

The city-state of Kalabari is separated from Nembe country by the Santa Barbara estuary. The capital, Elem Kalabari, occupied a mere acre or two of drier land and is said by tradition to have been founded in the following way. The Kalabari people emerged out of two groups of settlers: one party hailed from an Ijo settlement on the New Calabar river and was léd by a son of Kalabari. When this party arrived at the place later called Elem Kalabari, they were joined by a group led by Opu-Koro-Ye. Opu-Koro-Ye's party was probably of Andoni Ibibio stock, and not of Efik descent as has sometimes been alleged, because the Efik community was not established until later in the seventeenth century.

The time of Owerri Daba: c. 1550 or c. 1650

Oral traditions are most uncertain about events before the time of Owerri Daba, who is believed to have introduced the slave trade to Kalabari and Bonny. He is also said to have founded important houses in Kalabari, and even one in Bonny. Tradition thus indicates that the Kalabari state was already influential in the sixteenth or seventeenth centuries, and that there was a link with Bonny. Perhaps this contact was the result of civil war in Kalabari: one section of Owerri Daba's house is reputed to have moved to Bonny where they founded their own house.

The time of King Amakiri: c. 1750-early 1800's

Amakiri's reign was one of much strife and warfare. This was the era of the musket which began to be imported after the 1770's; it was also the time when Amakiri had to establish his people's trading routes to their inland markets up the New Calabar river. During Amakiri's time his dynasty emerged as the royal lineage of Elem Kalabari which alone could supply kings.

In the 1750's there was a disastrous fire in the capital—virtually all the houses were gutted—and tradition says that the people summoned Amakiri to come and rule them. Early in his reign King Amakiri had to subdue the Okrika villages, which lay on the east flank of the New Calabar river, because they could shut Kalabari off from her inland markets. Towards the close of the eighteenth century, Amakiri is said to have defeated the city-state of Bonny. However, Bonny traditions deny this, so perhaps the war ended in a deadlock with neither state being totally victorious.

Apparently the closing years of Amakiri's reign were once more

marked by disaster—Okrika attacked and destroyed Elem Kalabari so that the king had to purchase slaves to re-settle the town.
Nevertheless, Amakiri achieved much; and it was in the last years
of his reign that the political institutions, alliances and rivalries
between great houses which existed in the nineteenth century were
fully established.

IJO: THE CENTRAL DELTA STATE OF BONNY

In the late eighteenth century Bonny took over from Kalabari as
the leading slave exporter of the delta. It is generally accepted
that the early settlers of Bonny derived from a section of the
Ndokki people, of Ijo origin, which dwelt on the lower Imo river.
There is no basis in the earliest recorded traditions for asserting,
as some writers have done, that Ibo immigrants played a part in
the initial founding of Bonny.

The time of King Asimini
The original settlers came to Bonny, it is believed, to monopolize
the salt trade. Tradition associates the development of the overseas slave trade at Bonny with Owerri Daba of Kalabari, who
taught its special techniques to the first important ruler of
Bonny—King Asimini. King Asimini, or his successor, opened
up trading relations with Ndokki people on the lower Imo river
by marrying his daughter to a chief there. The son of this marriage,
Kamalu, then emerged as the king of Bonny. This lineage continued until King Warri's reign ended some time in the early or
middle eighteenth century.

The Pepple dynasty: c. 1700 or c. 1750.
A year after King Warri's death a new king, the founder of the
Pepple line, came to the throne of Bonny. This man is said to
have been a distant kinsman of King Kamalu and Bonny tradition
maintains that his name was 'Perukule' (Pepple). James Barbot,
who visited Bonny in 1699, gave presents—'a hat, a fire-lock, and
nine bunches of beads instead of a coat'—to the king of Bonny
and his 'captains' (i.e. house heads) who included one captain
Pepprel. It is possible that this captain Pepprel was a relation
of the Perukule who became king of Bonny.

After Perukule's reign, tradition maintains that a hunchback with webbed fingers and toes ruled over Bonny. As he was child-less he was succeeded by his younger brother Opobo who, according to tradition, reigned from 1792 to about 1830. Opobo was a great king who fought and defeated the Andoni Ibibio who tried to block Bonny from her trade routes along the Imo river; he also defeated Kalabari in a small war. Opobo's long reign was notable because, although he came to the throne on account of the Pepple house's great economic strength, he witnessed the ending of the overseas slave trade in Bonny by a British naval blockade in the early nineteenth century.

A report by one Lt. Holman in 1826 tells us how the Bonny monarchy had developed during the eighteenth century. When the king came to negotiate a contract between his people and the European merchants 'a dinner is prepared, and His Majesty is entertained by the Captain and his officers on board. . . . In order that no point of courtesy may be wanting, it is requisite to send a boat from the ship to meet His Majesty. . . . The king . . . is acknowledged by a salute of seven guns, fired from the ship. . . . His Majesty commonly returns about sunset to the shore when a second salute of seven guns is fired from this ship, and the trade is declared free to all his subjects'.

When Opobo's reign closed, the kingship had grown considerably in power; there was then no general council of house heads, which had existed earlier, to advise the king or take over if he ruled ineffectively. On Opobo's death the weakness of the system which had developed during his long reign became apparent. There was an inter-regnum when no candidate was powerful enough to crush rival claimants.

THE EFIK: THE EASTERN DELTA STATE OF OLD CALABAR

Tradition has it that the Efik-speaking section of the Ibibio people were expelled from their home at Idua near Uruan on the Cross river in about the early seventeenth century. On arriving at the estuary of the Cross river they settled at a place near the present site of Creek Town, and were called 'Efik'. Today this word means 'to press' or 'oppress'.

M

343

After some time there was civil war in Creek Town. And so tradition says that some people went and established Old Town, which had a favourable anchorage that attracted European ships. Envious, other people founded Duke Town after 1748 to prevent Old Town monopolizing the slave trade. Thus, by the 1750's the place that was called Old Calabar by Europeans consisted of, among other settlements, three principal towns: there was Creek Town; Duke Town which at this time regarded itself as part of Creek Town, and acknowledged the authority of Creek Town's king and Ekpe society lodge; and Old Town.

Owing to commercial rivalries between powerful houses which dominated a town, more settlements were founded by dissident groups. However, by the nineteenth century, the number of towns and their respective order of precedence had become more stable. But a town could slip down the power hierarchy, which was based on commercial success, if it had poor rulers who let trade go to a rival settlement.

In the nineteenth century the heart of Old Calabar was recognized as being Duke Town whose ruler, originally called Duke, became known as king. His authority was acknowledged by Old Town and other settlements. Creek Town, on the opposite bank of the estuary, had its own king, but he was not so powerful as the king of Duke Town. The two kings of Duke and Creek Town were the head and deputy head of the Ekpe society, which thereby acted as the central organ of government in Old Calabar.

Government in Old Calabar
Houses in Old Calabar were modelled more on the traditional house system than on the Ijo canoe house system. Wards or a house group were internally self-governing under a ward or house head, and a council of elders. Houses were socially heterogenous by the end of the eighteenth century as they included slaves and strangers, but not to the extent of many Ijo canoe houses. Some of the pressures on the house system were relieved in the early nineteenth century when the slave trade began to end, because many people of slave descent and some poor freemen moved off to farm plantations. These settlers cleared land which then became the property of the wards or houses which they belonged to. Later, in the 1850's, the country farmers organized themselves into an association called the 'Blood Men', which challenged the power

344

of town cliques that monopolized policy-making.

The two kings of Old Calabar, acting in their roles of head and deputy head of Ekpe, enforced laws, adjudicated disputes, led the armed forces and arranged peace treaties with neighbouring peoples. They also recovered debts outstanding to the European merchants, so that the Ekpe society formed the actual government of the Efik state.

Questions

1 Name the principal city-states in the Niger delta. Why did city-states develop?

2 Write brief notes on four of the following: comey; the house system; the canoe house system; city-state; trust trade; a war canoe.

3 Outline the main features of social ranking in the central and eastern delta before and after the eighteenth century.

4 How was a city-state in the central or eastern delta governed?

5 Describe the organization and activities of one secret society in the Niger delta.

6 Give an account of trading relations between the coast and the hinterland in the eighteenth century. In what way did trade then differ from earlier trading relations?

7 Write a short historical account of one of the following city-states: Nembe; Kalabari; Bonny; Old Calabar.

8 Explain the ways in which the western delta kingdom of Warri differed from the city-states of the central and eastern delta.

20

Village peoples of the Guinea Forest: The Ibo and Ibibio

We now turn to the peoples who were the source of so many slaves for delta middlemen—the Ibo and Ibibio of the forest hinterland. Like the delta peoples the Ibo and Ibibio are organized into villages, and many of their institutions are similar to those of peoples in the low-lying swamps. But the inhabitants of the Guinea forest were spared the immediate impact which the overseas slave trade had on delta political organization. There, more centralized government was an important adaptation to internal changes stimulated by external forces. In the forest hinterland, however, the Ibo and Ibibio remained tenaciously attached to their village democracies, resisting any potential innovation which might deprive citizens of their right to share in decision-making. The political system of these communities is an outstanding example of participational democracy: every adult man has an inalienable right to voice his opinion on public affairs at the village assembly.

We know nothing of able leaders among the Ibo; we do not know of any great battles or political crises. The past of any people is often significant for reasons which distinguish that people from its neighbours. And so we consider the Ibo and Ibibio to be important for three reasons.

In the first place the way in which these forest dwellers orgnized their political life provides a fascinating point of comparison with the political organization of centralized states and empires. Secondly, the Ibo in particular had a complex network of trading routes which linked the separate settlements in which they lived. These trade routes and commercial contacts created bonds between settlements which might otherwise have lived in a state of semi-isolation. Thirdly, the remarkable role of the

346

Arochuku group in the political, religious and economic life of the Ibo and Ibibio deserves detailed consideration. It was the Aro people of the middle Cross river who monopolized the slave-carrying trade to the city-states of the central and eastern Niger delta.

THE ORIGIN OF THE IBO AND IBIBIO

The Ibo have no weighty traditions of origin. Nevertheless, oral evidence and settlement patterns suggest that in about A.D. 1300 to 1400 Ibo began to move south and east from the region of Awka and Orlu. Later there seems to have been a second wave of migration to the eastern Isu Ama area around Orlu, and from there parties of migrants went to Aba, the Arochuku ridge, and other places.

The Ibibio believe either that they come from a place called Ibom, or that their ancestor is called Ibom. Early on Ibibio appear to have settled in the lands between Arochuku to the north, Ika to the west and Oron to the south. A second dispersal then took place from a centre around Abak and Uyo when the Ibibio separated into the Anang (western) and Ibibio (eastern) peoples. It is likely that the people who eventually became the Efik of Old Calabar originated in this second wave of migration.

POLITICAL ORGANIZATION

The Ibo and Ibibio were organized in a vast number of relatively small and independent villages. On account of their larger size, Ibo villages were often arranged into a group: that is, they formed a village group. So there were often two levels of political organization in Iboland: that of the village, and that of the village group.

The most characteristic part of Ibo country lies towards the centre around Orlu, Okigwi, Aba and Owerri. Here, among the southern Ibo, several villages were often joined together into a group by a mythical charter of common descent from a found-

347

ing ancestor, whose sons were believed to have established the constituent villages of the group. In other words, territorial divisions were thought of as kinship units. All the lineages in a village were believed to have descended from one ancestor; it is this common descent which justified and validated the existence of the village. Kinship links were sometimes invoked to create special relationships with neighbouring village groups or villages. Owing to their close kinship ties the men of a village had to go outside to find their wives.

In southern Iboland, government was based on village and village group councils. The councils were composed of descent group heads each holding the *ofo* stick (the symbol of their descent group's ancestors), and other wealthy or influential men. One man who held the senior *ofo* of the village or village group was regarded as a titular 'father'. But he had no political powers other than those given to any elder.

The wider community

The village groups were, as we have seen, politically independent. But we need not jump to the conclusion that there were no links between different village groups. On the contrary, Ibo were loosely tied into a wider community than that of the village group and the various links between settlements were important for two reasons. Firstly, they show that the principal objective of government—the maintenance of law and order—can be achieved by other methods than those open to a centralized authority. Secondly, the loose ties between some groups help us to understand why it was that in the absence of centralized government Ibo country was not in a perpetual state of warfare, skirmishes, raids and the like.

One kind of link between villages and village groups arose out of the rule that men were obliged to marry outside their village. (Sometimes, as in the case of Owerri village group or town, men had to marry outside the group). Ibo men looked for wives from other villages in the group, and often from outside their village group. And so villages in a group, as well as neighbouring village groups, were linked by the bonds arising out of marriage alliances.

The second kind of link between Ibo groups arises out of the economic system. Because Ibo country lies inland, the people had to import salt and protein food like fish from the delta. Certain areas in north-eastern Iboland around Abakiliki produced a surplus of yams, which were exported to more populated regions in the vicinity of Awka, Orlu and Okigwi. It is very likely that this system of re-distributing food has been in operation for many centuries. Markets, large and small, sprang up to facilitate the re-distribution of goods. Different Ibo groups specialized in certain craft work, ritual services and the like so that itinerant traders, native doctors and priests covered many miles on their journeys. In this way traders and ritual specialists put village groups in touch with each other and created a wider community than that of the local settlement. Thus, economic organization was well developed before the hey-day of the slave trade in the eighteenth century. In fact local trade routes were used for the slave-carrying trade, which probably developed speedily because there was already an established pattern of trading.

The third link is provided by the network of oracles: some of them were only of local significance, but some were nationally famous. Famous oracles were served by traders acting in the capacity of agents, who brought clients to the oracle from far-off village groups. And so a belief in the efficacy of supernatural judgements and sanctions was used to create an extensive religious community of priests and clients who hailed from different village groups.

ORACLES AMONG THE IBO

Oracles are shrines at which appeals can be made to a god. A priest, who acts as the god's mouthpiece, issues the god's judgement or opinion after offerings are made by clients. Ibo oracles secured the blessings of fertility to barren women and pronounced judgement on disputes.

Four oracles in Iboland became nationally renowned for their 'impartial' verdicts. They were the Agballa oracle at Awka, the Igweke Ala oracle at Umunora, the Amadioha oracle at Ozuzu and—most famous of all—the Ibini Okpabe or 'Long Juju' oracle at Arochuku.

It was believed that the farther away the oracle was from the

349

disputants, the more chance there was of an impartial verdict. However, as G. I. Jones, an authority on the Ibo, Efik and Ijo, has pointed out, the effectiveness and therefore the fame of an oracle lay in its apparent ability to kill by supernatural means those disobeying its verdict. Generally such supernaturally caused deaths took the form of a lingering illness which was put down to disobedience against the oracle.

The other way in which an oracle was effective was when it 'killed' disputants who invoked it falsely: a litigant who invoked an oracle falsely was believed to be the guilty party. Such offenders were said to be killed at once by the oracle, because they were never seen again. People saw trails of blood flowing out of the grove and this was taken to prove that the guilty party was dead. However, old informants told early British district officers that the Ibini Okpabe oracle priests at Arochuku used to sacrifice an animal whose blood was then seen flowing out from the grove. The litigant was hidden for a few days and later sold into slavery. It was in such a manner that 'justice' was done. Nevertheless, it is likely that on the whole litigants were so convinced of a famous oracle's powers that they would tell the truth. And so the final result may have been that innocence and guilt were correctly apportioned.

The Ibini Okpabe oracle at Arochuku
The Aro live on the west bank of the Cross river, near Itu. Tradition says that the Aro village group included people of non-Ibo descent. Aro tradition tells us that an Ibo settler rose up in revolt against his Ibibio landlord. The settler consulted an Ibo doctor friend, who arranged to invite some raiders of the Akpa (a tribe on the east bank of the Cross river) to fight the Ibibio residents. They were successful, but as one of the Akpa warriors was killed the Ibo settler was held responsible and he had to flee. However, the doctor made peace between the Akpa and the Ibo and, after swearing a covenant, they all lived happily ever after.

This myth is told by Aro to explain how it is that of the present nineteen villages in the group, seven claim descent from the Ibo doctor's son, six villages claim to be descended from the Akpa warriors and five derive from the Ibo settler. There are also some Ibibio elements in the village group. Today the senior living descendant of the Ibo doctor holds the title of Eze-Aro or chief of Aro.

Effective political power in the village group was in the hands of the elders who tried to keep the secrets of the oracle from being public knowledge. In this way the oracle helped the Aro to develop a greater sense of political direction and unity than existed elsewhere in Iboland.

The oracle at Arochuku (which means 'the voice of God') became the most famous of all Ibo oracles for several reasons. To begin with, Ibini Okpabe had the most efficient and prosperous network of agents known in Ibo country—the Aro middlemen who monopolized the slave trade and dealt in other valuable commodities. Secondly, whereas other oracles did not administer immediate 'justice', that at Arochuku did. Only one party survived. And so people respected and feared the oracle of the Aro's deity Chuku to the extent that kings of delta city-states brought cases to the oracle. Some historians, repeating the Aro myth, have alleged that the oracle's power lay in its ability to mobilize armed mercenaries from the Abam, Ada and Ohaffia groups near Arochuku. According to G. I. Jones this is not correct: Ibini Okpabe's fame and prestige lay in the deity's ability to apparently administer instant punishment by 'killing' the guilty party. The oracle was feared because people then believed that its supernatural sanctions were indeed a reality, and not because of its alleged power to organize mercenaries to crush the villages of disobedient clients. Armed with apparently effective supernatural powers to kill the guilty, the oracle had no need to mobilize mercenaries.

The third reason for Ibini Okpabe's fame was that the commercial and ritual activities of the Aro had a mutually reinforcing effect. Traders spread the name of the oracle to an increasing number of clients. It is said that, by the late eighteenth century, the Aro had prospered so much from commerce and the fees their middlemen received for providing safe passage to the deity that most people did not need to farm.

THE EXTENT OF THE ARO TRADING SYSTEM

We know all too little about the exact organization of trade in precolonial days. Nevertheless we do know that Iboland seems to

351

have been carved up into spheres of commercial and religious influence. One village group would develop a monopoly of religious or commercial services over a wide but delimited area. Sometimes the same village group increased its dominance by possessing a well known oracle or priest cult, in which case economic influence was reinforced by religious authority. The Aro were the most famous Ibo religious and commercial traders of the hinterland. But there were other village groups too which made a lesser name for themselves.

A village group would specialize in one or two activities, its men travelling widely over a specific territory selling their services. In this way links were created between settlements. Priests from Nri, and blacksmiths from Awka, travelled between northern Ibo country and the river Niger; traders and blacksmiths from Nkwerri journeyed south as far as Ogoni; wood carvers and native doctors from Abiriba near Ibibio country worked in the Cross river area. The Aro trading system stretched as far west as Nri-Awka and penetrated south over much of the central and eastern delta.

It does seem, though, that the Aro trading system penetrated little into other areas outside their sphere of influence. The Aro traded and inter-married with Ọzọ title holders at Awka, for example, but this seems to have been as far as they got in a westerly direction. Perhaps Aro and other groups made informal agreements to divide up their spheres of influence. Or, and perhaps this is more likely, Aro were prevented by sheer distance and problematical communications in the absence of navigable rivers from trading extensively in the Niger area.

Another area where the Aro did not come to monopolize commercial activities was that dominated by the kingdom of Aboh, which is situated where the Niger enters its delta. Aboh had become an important political unit by 1800 because of her strategic position on the Niger: she was able to control access to the more westerly parts of the slave-producing hinterland, and to the coastal ports of Nembe and Kalabari.

Before the slave trade provided the Aro with the chance of dominating the economy of the hinterland, there were rural markets and long-distance trading. Men travelled far to obtain horses and cows from the savanna, and salt and fish from the delta. With the growth of the overseas slave trade such markets as Uburu,

Uzuakoli, Oguta and Bende rose to prominence as slave marts. These markets served as a distribution centre for slaves, which were transported there by a variety of routes. For instance, slaves from northern Ibo country could be taken to Uburu market near Afikpo; from there they would be taken to Uzuakoli, which linked up with Bende to the south-east. At Bende, purveyors would hand slaves over to Aro middlemen, who then sold them to traders from Old Calabar and Bonny. The slaves were of northern origin or of Ibo stock; some Ibo slaves were captured during village raids, and others were sold into slavery to meet pressing indebtedness.

REASONS FOR ARO DOMINANCE IN THE HINTERLAND

How was it that the Aro, lacking centralized government and without a standing army (they just hired raiding parties from the Abam, Ada and Ohaffia), had managed by the nineteenth century to dominate the hinterland both religiously and economically? It is impossible to give a precise answer owing to insufficient factual information. But the following factors appear to be relevant in explaining why the Aro achieved such influence.

The Aro were favourably situated on the Cross river so they had a ready-made communications system. Given a readiness to exploit the demand by coastal city-states for slaves, the Aro could control their immediate section of the Cross river. However, this factor alone does not explain their economic dominance because other peoples on the Cross river also had this geographical advantage.

A second factor of much more significance is that the Aro had cultural and ethnic links with sections of the Ibibio, Ibeku Ibo, the Akpa people of the Cross river, and the Enyong Ibibio. Endowed with a natural talent for salesmanship, possessing an oracle that dealt with judicial and fertility difficulties, and encouraged by the development of the overseas slave trade in the eighteenth century, the Aro exploited these links with other peoples to further their commercial interests. According to G. I. Jones, the Aro used their links with the Ibeku Ibo of the Umuahia area to penetrate south to Ndokki country, where the

353

New Calabar and Imo rivers link the hinterland with the city-states of Bonny and Kalabari. The Ibibio elements in Aro helped her traders to travel in southern Ibibio country, while the Akpa element provided contacts in Obubra and the Cross river area. The Enyong people, who border Arochuku and were a part of the Ibibio group that became the Efik people of Old Calabar, enabled Aro middlemen to trade with this city-state.

Armed with these vital contacts, which provided safe trade routes, the Aro were able to offer slaves for sale to whichever state offered the highest prices. The Aro played off Kalabari traders against merchants from Old Calabar, and even managed to obtain higher prices for slaves in the Nri-Awka markets than other traders. And so during the eighteenth century the Aro obtained a monopoly on supplying slaves by applying their shrewd business sense to exploit their contacts with other peoples.

However, a third factor also contributed to Aro dominance. Acting as commercial intermediaries, they purchased the services of eager warriors from their neighbours—the Ada, Abam and Ohaffia peoples—from time to time. Aro used these warriors to get hold of more slaves, and to defend waterways or nearby trading routes if the need arose.

Fourthly, such activities were bound to have cumulative results. Although the Aro trading system appears to have emerged later than that of, for example, Nri-Awka, Aro people seem to have accumulated wealth quite rapidly. Once middlemen had obtained enough capital from their trading and religious activities, some of them engaged in other enterprises which extended Aro influence yet again. Some Aro settled down at key villages on trading routes. These new settlements became politically independent of Arochuku, but they increased Aro contacts with the local population through inter-marriage. Aro settlers also booked orders from local people who wanted commercial goods or religious services, and passed them on to itinerant traders from Arochuku. Such new settlements as Ujalli or Ndizorgu helped to increase and strengthen the Aro trading network. If a local man needed a loan, an Aro settler would arrange for it to be provided by one of his relatives. The debtor could repay in kind by providing his Aro creditor with an unwanted kinsman to be sold as a slave.

Finally, the Aro's hold over trade between the coast and the

354

hinterland became so strong that they virtually monopolized the supply of guns and shot in the interior. Aro used this highly convenient monopoly to supply raiders from Abam, Ada and Ohaffia with weapons. Warriors from these groups were then better equipped for slave raiding on behalf of the Aro, who paid them for doing this job, and for conducting raids on villages that clients wanted to punish. If a village wanted to humiliate another, representatives would approach an Aro agent. The agent then arranged, for a fee, to purchase a raiding party of Abam or Ohaffia warriors to do the job. Aro agents guided the warriors to the chosen village; when it was sacked, the same agents led the party of raiders back to Abam or Ohaffia country.

These, then, are the factors which could explain the economic and religious influence of Aro in the hinterland by the nineteenth century. But as Aro dominance during this period was much increased as a result of opportunities presented by the slave trade, it seems appropriate to end with a quotation from a book which tells us about the terrible shock and personal disaster experienced by people unfortunate enough to be enslaved.

Olaudah Equiano, an Ibo from near Onitsha, was born in about 1745. He told the story of how he was kidnapped by three strangers in his book, *The Interesting Narrative of the Life of Olaudah Equiano or Gustavus the African*. He wrote: 'My father, besides many slaves, had a numerous family of which seven lived to grow up, including myself and a sister .... One day, when all our people were gone to their works as usual and only I and my dear sister were left to mind the house, two men and a woman got over our walls, and in a moment seized us both, and without giving us time to cry out or make resistance they stopped our mouths and ran off with us into the nearest wood'.

Questions

1 Write short notes on the Ibo and Ibibio traditions of origin. Why do we know so little about the history of the Ibo people?

2 Examine the political organization of villages and village groups among the southern Ibo and explain how Ibo villages

were linked to other village groups.

3 What was the role of oracles in Ibo society and why were they politically important? Discuss the reasons for the pre-eminent position of the Arochuku oracle.

4 Give an account of the Aro trading system. What is the 'Aro myth' and why is it important in Aro history?

5 Examine the factors which you think explain the economic and religious dominance of the Aro in the hinterland by the nineteenth century.

6 Write briefly on each of the following: (a) the organization of trade and markets among the Ibo: (b) democracy among the southern Ibo.

Index

INDEX

and Abomey, 275, 281–3; and
Allada, 276, 278, 281, 283, 284;
and rise of Dahomey empire,
275, 276, 278, 281–5, 288, 293,
296, 301, 303; and relations with
Benin, 289, 290, 292–3, 296, 306,
309–10; local government in, 297;
central government in, 298–300;
factors in the rise of, 300–2;
reasons for collapse of, 302–3;
mentioned, 100; *see also* Old Oyo;
Oyo Igboho
Oyo Igboho, 289, 292
Oyoko clan, 254, 256–8, 260, 262,
268
Oyoko states, 254, 257, 267
Ozolua, Oba, 313–15
Ozuzu, 349

Park, Mungo, 147
Pasha, Judar, 77
Pepel people, region inhabited by,
3, 6, 195; language of, 6;
mentioned, 7
Pepple, King, 330–2, 340
Pepprel, 342
Pereira, Pacheco, 195, 202, 333, 338,
Perukule, King, 342–3
Po, Fernando, 183
Pokou, Queen Abra, 251
Pogas, River, 199
Popo, 269, 290, 295
Port Harcourt, River, 321
Porto Novo, 212, 216, 275, 276,
283, 285, 289, 293, 296
Portugal, and Wolof empire, 22–3;
and Songhai empire, 70; and
battle of El Ksar el Kebir, 77, 170;
and exploration of West Africa,
171, 173–84, 195; and slave trade,
178–80, 185–90, 197, 209–10,
315; and growth of trading empire
in West Africa, 182, 184–7, 196–7,
202; and decline of West African
empire, 187–8; and influence on
West Africa, 189–90; and Benin
empire, 313–15, 320; and Warri
kingdom, 337–8; mentioned, 8,

27, 159, 160, 162, 203, 227, 240,
242
Pra, River, 237, 240, 241, 244, 250,
254, 255, 262
Prester John, 176, 178

Al-Qadir, Abd, 151–2
Qadiriyya sect, 148, 152, 153
Qualli, Fati, 73

Raba, 98, 101
Al-Rahman, Abd, 92
Rano, 86, 89
Rao, 7
Rhobo, 306
Riale, 83
Rimfa, Sarki Muhammad, 91–3, 137,
143
Rio de Oro, 178, 180
Rio Real, 202, 333, 338
Roman Catholic Church, 176, 187,
337
Rumfa, *see* Rimfa, Sarki Muhammad

Sâafwé clan, 251
Sabakura, *see* Sakura, Mansa
Sabe, 275, 290
Al-Sadi, 66, 68, 142
Saghana kingdom, 18
Sagmandir, 51, 67
Sahara Desert, increasing aridity of,
17, 113; major routes across, 18,
164–9; and Soninke empire, 31,
37, 39–43; and Mali empire, 53,
55; and Songhai empire, 66, 70,
81–2; and Hausa states, 87, 91,
93, 106; and Kanuri empires, 123,
125, 126; and Islamization, 133,
134, 139, 140; organization of
trade across, 169–70; decline of
trade across, 170–1; and Asante
empire, 201, 254, 256, 265; and
Akan states, 237–8, 254, 256,
265; and Oyo empire, 292, 301,
302; and Benin empire, 306, 315;
mentioned, 12, 173, 176, 177, 179,
203–4, 206
Es-Saheli, 52

369